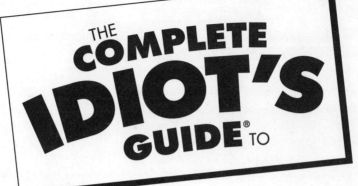

THE COMPLETE **IDIOT'S** GUIDE® TO

Person-to-Person Lending

by Curtis E. Arnold and Beverly Blair Harzog

ALPHA

A member of Penguin Group (USA) Inc.

This book is dedicated to the P2P borrowers and lenders who achieve their financial dreams while helping others.

ALPHA BOOKS

Published by the Penguin Group

Penguin Group (USA) Inc., 375 Hudson Street, New York, New York 10014, USA

Penguin Group (Canada), 90 Eglinton Avenue East, Suite 700, Toronto, Ontario M4P 2Y3, Canada (a division of Pearson Penguin Canada Inc.)

Penguin Books Ltd., 80 Strand, London WC2R 0RL, England

Penguin Ireland, 25 St. Stephen's Green, Dublin 2, Ireland (a division of Penguin Books Ltd.)

Penguin Group (Australia), 250 Camberwell Road, Camberwell, Victoria 3124, Australia (a division of Pearson Australia Group Pty. Ltd.)

Penguin Books India Pvt. Ltd., 11 Community Centre, Panchsheel Park, New Delhi—110 017, India

Penguin Group (NZ), 67 Apollo Drive, Rosedale, North Shore, Auckland 1311, New Zealand (a division of Pearson New Zealand Ltd.)

Penguin Books (South Africa) (Pty.) Ltd., 24 Sturdee Avenue, Rosebank, Johannesburg 2196, South Africa

Penguin Books Ltd., Registered Offices: 80 Strand, London WC2R 0RL, England

International Standard Book Number: 978-1-59257-882-5
Library of Congress Catalog Card Number: 2008937773

11   10   09   8   7   6   5   4   3   2   1

Interpretation of the printing code: The rightmost number of the first series of numbers is the year of the book's printing; the rightmost number of the second series of numbers is the number of the book's printing. For example, a printing code of 09-1 shows that the first printing occurred in 2009.

Printed in the United States of America

Note: This publication contains the opinions and ideas of its authors. It is intended to provide helpful and informative material on the subject matter covered. It is sold with the understanding that the authors and publisher are not engaged in rendering professional services in the book. If the reader requires personal assistance or advice, a competent professional should be consulted.

The authors and publisher specifically disclaim any responsibility for any liability, loss, or risk, personal or otherwise, which is incurred as a consequence, directly or indirectly, of the use and application of any of the contents of this book.

Most Alpha books are available at special quantity discounts for bulk purchases for sales promotions, premiums, fundraising, or educational use. Special books, or book excerpts, can also be created to fit specific needs.

For details, write: Special Markets, Alpha Books, 375 Hudson Street, New York, NY 10014.

Publisher: *Marie Butler-Knight*
Editorial Director: *Mike Sanders*
Senior Managing Editor: *Billy Fields*
Acquisitions Editor: *Tom Stevens*
Development Editor: *Jennifer Bowles*
Production Editor: *Kayla Dugger*

Copy Editor: *Lisanne V. Jensen*
Cartoonist: *Richard King*
Cover Designer: *Kurt Owens*
Book Designer: *Trina Wurst*
Indexer: *Angie Bess*
Layout: *Chad Dressler*
Proofreader: *John Etchison*

Contents at a Glance

Contents

Foreword

Since its introduction to America in early 2006, person-to-person lending has been widely embraced as an innovative way for people to borrow money at lower rates and participate in an attractive asset class that was previously limited to institutions.

People across the country have discovered an alternative way to knock out high-interest credit card debt, start or grow their small businesses, and finance everything from college to green home-improvement projects. Ordinary Americans have become lenders and discovered what it's like to be a bank or microfinance institution, deciding who gets funded and which bottom lines—monetary, social, and/or philanthropic—matter to them in terms of expected returns.

Now that traditional lending sources and Wall Street have been forever changed by the financial crisis of 2008, person-to-person lending transcends the notion of being an "alternative." Person-to-person lending has been thrust into the mainstream as a transparent, durable solution for America's borrowers, investors, and the economy as a whole.

All of this makes entering the world of person-to-person lending incredibly exciting and necessary on many levels. But exciting and necessary mixed with borrowing and investing money can be intimidating, which makes *The Complete Idiot's Guide to Person-to-Person Lending* a vital personal finance companion.

True to form, this *Complete Idiot's Guide* is as rich in its simplicity as it is in its utility and timeliness. Whether you participate as a borrower or lender, this book will arm you with the information and tools you need to quickly and effectively meet your objectives. Regardless of the role you plan to take, you'll realize that understanding person-to-person lending from both a borrower and lender perspective is essential to successfully navigating the variety of available sites and opportunities.

The journey begins with the basic elements of person-to-person lending, including types of loans, social considerations, credit scores, and interest rates. From there, you'll traverse the landscape of reputable sites, from open, auction-style marketplaces for all types of loans to those focused on microcredit, specific loan purposes, or formalizing loans among family and friends.

Equipped with these fundamentals, you're amply prepared to dive into the nuts and bolts of borrowing and lending. Prospective borrowers will gain invaluable insights into how to create an engaging loan listing, what happens after you've been funded, and the importance of budgeting and making on-time payments. Lenders will get in touch with their risk tolerance and learn to develop a strategy for creating a loan portfolio that's in line with their objectives and time horizon.

Perhaps most importantly, readers will come away confident in their ability to participate in person-to-person lending and ready to channel the teachings of *It's a Wonderful Life*, *Wall Street*, or Nobel Peace Prize winner Muhammad Yunus—or maybe even all three. And no matter who your financial heroes may be, in today's world, we may all be inspired to take George Bailey's famous quote to heart, "Now, we can get through this thing all right. We've got to stick together, though. We've got to have faith in each other."

Chris Larsen is CEO and co-founder of Prosper, America's largest people-to-people lending marketplace. Prosper is a continuation of Larsen's commitment to leveraging the Internet to make consumer lending more efficient, transparent, and trustworthy. Prior to Prosper, Larsen co-founded and served as chairman and CEO of E-LOAN. Under his leadership, E-LOAN became the first company to provide consumers with access to their credit scores, and played a critical role in the passage of the strongest consumer financial privacy protection law in the nation. Mr. Larsen holds an M.B.A. degree from Stanford University and a B.S. degree from San Francisco State University, where he was named the 2004 Alumnus of the Year.

Introduction

This book was written for the individual who isn't satisfied with the status quo. Maybe you're in debt and you want a new way to get back on your feet financially. Maybe you want to start a business or fund your college education. Or maybe you're an investor and you'd rather invest in other people than continue to get a low interest rate on your savings account at your bank.

Whether you're considering borrowing money or lending it, you're to be commended for looking for a better way. Despite the title, *The Complete Idiot's Guide to Person-to-Person Lending* never assumes you're an idiot. The approach in this book assumes you're a smart, resourceful individual who is open to new ideas.

In this book, we don't talk down to you. What we provide is practical advice in an easy-to-read format. That way, you can decide for yourself whether becoming a P2P borrower or lender is the right choice for you. You'll learn about the following subjects:

- The emerging P2P lending industry and why it's so popular

- FICO scores and how they relate to P2P lending

- The most popular P2P lending websites and how to choose the best one for your needs

- P2P sites that specialize in student loans so you can get a college education without drowning in debt

- Do's and don'ts for becoming a borrower or a lender on P2P websites

It's all here waiting for you. We have quizzes, charts, and step-by-step guides. Here's what you'll find inside:

Part 1, "The Basics of Person-to-Person Lending," introduces you to this new world. You get the basics of how P2P lending works, but you also come away with an understanding of why it's becoming so popular. You also see what people are getting loans for. We even throw in two chapters on FICO scores and interest rates to help you make the most of your borrowing or investing opportunities.

Part 2, "Prime-Time Players in the P2P Marketplace," gives you the scoop on P2P lenders. You get an introduction to the popular websites and get a feel for how they differ from each other. At the end of this part, you get guidance on how to pick a P2P website from all the available choices.

Part 3, "Borrowing Money," provides you with the information you need to become a successful P2P borrower. You learn how to write loan listings so they get funded by eager lenders. Need a second loan to get your business off the ground? No problem. Here, you learn what the rules are for each website. You also get sound tips on money management that will help you get out of debt once and for all.

Part 4, "Lending Money," starts by answering frequently asked lending questions. Then, you get tips on managing your portfolio, analyzing borrowers' listings, and evaluating your risk tolerance.

Sometimes financial terms can become confusing, so we include a glossary that's easy to flip through when you need to look up something. We also include a helpful resource appendix that includes where you can find all the P2P websites on the Internet.

Note to readers: as you know, the Internet is the virtual Wild, Wild West. In this book, you find information that's currently available—but websites *do* change frequently. Just keep that in mind as you navigate the P2P websites listed in case some changes have occurred since this book's printing.

Also, we give you tips on taxing matters—but bear in mind that these rules frequently change and are often open to interpretation. Check the tax laws and regulations and consult with a tax advisor to make sure you're complying with federal and state laws.

Sidebars

Hey, we know that some of you are pressed for time and prefer to scan pages before reading the chapters. If you're a scanner, you'll enjoy the sidebars, which share some highlights from the text. These boxes explain the jargon, offer good tips, alert you to things to watch out for, and enlighten you with interesting tidbits.

def•i•ni•tion

You get definitions to terms you'll frequently come across in the P2P lending community.

 Good Cents

In this box, you get suggestions and advice that will help you benefit from P2P lending.

In the Red

Sometimes the waters ahead are choppy. This box gives you a heads-up when dealing with some prickly financial issues.

Hidden Treasure

These are interesting, bet-you-didn't-know tidbits that you can talk about at your next cocktail party.

Acknowledgments

We'd both like to thank the folks at Alpha Books for the wonderful job they've done on this book: Tom Stevens, Jennifer Bowles, Kayla Dugger, and Lisanne V. Jensen. And a big thanks to our agent, Marilyn Allen, for her help and unwavering support.

Curtis would like to thank his lovely wife, Nancy, for her encouragement and support in pursuing this project—especially considering that this book was written "right on the heels" of his first book.

He would also like to express his gratitude to the members of the CardRatings.com forum for their interest in person–to-person lending and their dedication to helping other consumers. On a related note, he has been inspired by many consumer educators and would like to recognize a few of them, including Elisabeth Donati, author of *The Ultimate Allowance*; Billy Britt of the Federal Reserve Bank of St. Louis; Dr. Mary Ann Campbell of the University of Central Arkansas; Professor Eddie Ary, CPA, CFP of Ouachita Baptist University; and James Walden of Crown Financial Ministries.

Finally, Curtis is grateful to God for giving him the opportunity to be involved with something so significant that it has the potential to transform the entire lending industry.

Beverly would like to thank her family for their support and for their high tolerance for takeout food when deadlines loomed. She'd like to thank her wonderful husband, Bernd, for his love and for believing in her dreams. And she's grateful to her children, Ashley and Grant, who light up her life every single day. And a special thanks to her parents: to her mother, Mary, for being supportive and always asking how the book was going; and to her late father, John, for showing her that every challenge could be handled.

Trademarks

All terms mentioned in this book that are known to be or are suspected of being trademarks or service marks have been appropriately capitalized. Alpha Books and Penguin Group (USA) Inc. cannot attest to the accuracy of this information. Use of a term in this book should not be regarded as affecting the validity of any trademark or service mark.

Part 1

The Basics of Person-to-Person Lending

Person-to-person (P2P) lending is a simple concept. If you're a borrower, you request a loan. If you're a lender, you choose borrowers who you want to help. One of the reasons P2P is so appealing is that there's no bank involved. It all feels highly personal—although in most cases, you don't know the identity of the person you're borrowing money from or lending to.

In this part, you get an overview of P2P lending, as well as take a fascinating look into what people are getting loans for. To use the concepts behind P2P lending to your benefit, it helps to understand the bigger picture.

Here, borrowers can learn how FICO scores affect their interest rates—and lenders can find out more about interest rates to evaluate borrowers objectively.

"I'm just sayin', if we cut out the middleman we'll both make more dough."

What Are Person-to-Person (P2P) Loans?

In This Chapter

- Why it's difficult to get a loan from a bank
- What P2P lending is all about
- How the concept of credit began
- Why P2P lending is picking up speed
- Borrowing and lending money online

Lately, you've probably been hearing a lot about person-to-person (P2P) lending. Maybe you've read about it in magazine articles, seen ads on television, and heard testimonials from acquaintances. Or maybe you discovered this new industry while researching loans on the Internet.

Whether you want to borrow money or lend money, P2P lending is an option for you to explore. In this chapter, you learn about how the economy has helped to create the P2P lending industry. You also get a glimpse into how the concept of credit got started. Finally, we provide an overview that compares traditional banks and P2P lending.

That's a lot of territory to cover, so get comfortable! Before we get into the finer details, let's take a look at some of the reasons P2P lending is filling a need in our society. And yes, the economy is at the top of the list.

A New Approach to Borrowing and Lending

P2P lending and borrowing is a new twist on an old way to lend and borrow money. You probably already have a couple options for how to borrow money. You can run up balances or get a cash advance on your credit cards. You can go to a bank and get a loan. If you have a house, maybe you have considered getting a second mortgage on it. Or maybe you can go to a friend or a relative to borrow money.

P2P lending is on the rise because it addresses some pressing issues with the current, traditional system of lending and borrowing through banks and financial institutions. It can be difficult, if not impossible, for certain individuals and businesses to get loans from banks or other financial institutions because the current economy has hit a lot of people hard.

In the Red

Have you had one of your credit card limits reduced recently? Due to the economy, some consumers have experienced reductions in their limits on bank-issued cards. This has even happened to consumers with excellent credit, by the way. Sometimes there's no warning. If you depend a lot on your credit cards to get by, be aware that your limit can be reduced.

Even in good times, banks are typically very conservative in their lending standards, and tend to make only those loans that are secured with *tangible assets* (known as collateral). For example, a bank will lend you money for your home because your home is the collateral against that loan. If you do not pay the bank back, they will sell your house and use the proceeds to pay off the loan.

But unless you and your loan fit into one of the acceptable categories (for example, you have excellent credit or tangible assets) at your bank, you can find it hard to borrow money from a bank.

If you own a business, a bank will lend you money against your assets (whatever land, buildings, computers, and equipment the business owns) or in some cases against your receivables (the money you have not collected yet from the customers to whom you sold your products or services). But if you are a small business that does not have those kinds of assets, you can find that getting a business loan from a bank is very difficult, if not impossible.

def•i•ni•tion

A **tangible asset** has a physical form. For instance, equipment, machinery, land, and buildings are all tangible assets. In contrast, assets such as trademarks and patents are considered intangible assets.

If you go to borrow as a business or an individual, you may find that the interest rate that the bank wants to charge you (which depends upon the bank's assessment of how risky your loan is) may be much higher than what you are willing to accept. And if you are a saver, you may find that the interest rate that the bank is willing to pay you on a savings account or a CD is not very "interesting" at all to you.

P2P lending and borrowing is a new way for you to borrow money, or if you have extra cash, a new way for you to lend money and earn interest. So if you're feeling a little squeezed in today's economy, you might be thinking about getting a P2P loan. Or if you're someone who has a little extra cash, maybe you're considering becoming a P2P lender. You may really like the idea of helping someone while possibly still getting a good return on your investment.

Whether you have heard about P2P lending before or this is a brand-new concept to you, you have come to the right place to learn everything you need to know about it.

Are you still comfortable? Great! Stay where you are and dive right in to learn more about this exciting opportunity to become a P2P borrower or lender!

P2P Lending in a Nutshell

P2P lending is an exciting and rapidly emerging industry that connects borrowers and lenders online. The concept is also referred to as peer•to•peer lending, *social lending*, *social finance*, and *microfinance*.

Prosper.com, which started in 2006, is the largest P2P lending site. There are also several other players in this field, including Lending Club, Loanio, Virgin Money, Kiva, Fynanz, GreenNote, and several other new upstarts.

def•i•ni•tion

Social lending refers to the process of a borrower and a lender making a financial agreement without the involvement of an intermediary, such as a bank.

Social finance is a term that was coined by Zopa, a former online P2P lender, to describe financial transactions between individuals. Zopa's U.S. website closed in 2008.

Microfinance generally refers to small loans made to poor and low-income borrowers in developing countries.

Many of the rules and the "platforms," which is the way P2P website lenders deliver their services, differ among sites. We discuss the specifics of each site in detail in Part 2.

Now let's see where the concept of credit first originated.

A Brief History of Loans

In early civilizations, there was no money. Instead, there were cattle, grains, silver, copper, and whatever else a society declared as valuable for trading purposes. It didn't take long for people to realize that bringing along a cow on a shopping trip was inconvenient. And carrying around silver became pretty heavy, too.

It was cattle trading that sparked the concept of interest on a loan. Way back in Sumerian society, you might have loaned some cattle to your neighbor. Cattle were a valuable trading commodity because the lender usually collected interest. A year or two later when the loan was due back, your neighbor would hand over your cattle along with any calves that were born to the herd. The Sumerian word for calves was *interest*. (So there you have the origin for the word "interest.")

The Sumerians kept track of purchases in the city by drawing pictures on wet clay tablets that dried into cumbersome receipts. In fact, it's believed that the art of writing was created to keep track of who owed what to whom.

So imagine lugging a bag of grain to the city to buy food. (Still, it's easier than a cow, right?) You exchange the grain for food, and the merchant draws a picture of what took place. It would have been hard for you to back out of an agreement with a permanent record such as that.

Over time, the Sumerians began to evolve their writing into a type of shorthand. They would bend reeds to create edged lines. This type of wedge-shaped writing is known as *cuneiform*, which is Latin for "writing."

We have come a long way since creditors had to draw "receipts" on clay. But it would still be quite a while before we developed what we have all become attached to: our credit cards.

Charge It!

In 1949, businessman Frank McNamara was having dinner at a New York City restaurant. After his meal, he reached for his wallet to pay. Oops! He had left his wallet in his other suit. Fortunately, his wife was with him, and she had the cash to pay for dinner.

Fast-forward one year. McNamara and a business partner had dinner again in the very same restaurant. When the check arrived, McNamara whipped out a cardboard card called a Diner's Club card to pay for dinner. In *credit card* circles, this event is called the "First Supper."

After McNamara founded the Diner's Club, Americans decided they really liked the concept of "eat now, pay later." The Diner's Club card was technically a *charge card* because the card owner was expected to pay off the debt at the end of the month. But by 1959, both American Express and BankAmericard (now known as VISA) had issued their first credit cards. The concept of "eat now and pay later" had been extended to "buy now and pay *much* later."

def•i•ni•tion

Ever refer to your charge card as a credit card? There's a big difference between the two.

A **charge card** is a card that you don't have to pay interest on. This is because you pay the amount due in full when the bill arrives. This is usually paid on a monthly cycle. Diner's Club and American Express are examples of charge cards. Note that there are usually penalties and fees if you don't pay the full amount when you receive the bill.

A **credit card** is issued by a financial company and gives the card holder the ability to borrow funds. Credit cards most definitely charge interest! Credit cards are designed to be a short-term solution to financing because the interest charges can be high.

In the 1970s, 16 percent of households used credit cards. Today, credit cards are used by more than 73 percent of American households. In defense of some Americans, there are those who only keep their cards for emergencies. Or maybe they charge certain items and pay off the bill at the end of each month.

But unfortunately, there are many who have good intentions but get caught up in overextending their budgets. Thus, credit card debt is high.

Why P2P Loans Are Growing in Popularity

If you think about how much debt consumers have and then think about the current U.S. economy, it's not hard to see why P2P loans are growing.

It's a unique time for the U.S. economy. The mortgage crisis and the credit crunch together have created a double whammy for many folks. The U.S. Monetary Policy Forum recently released a report that estimated total mortgage credit losses will cost $400 billion. About half will be borne by financial institutions, and the rest of the tab will be picked up by investors and taxpayers.

P2P lending has started to cross over into mortgages as family members and friends lend and borrow money from each other. Sites such as Virgin Money and LoanBack are now available to facilitate these kinds of mortgage loans.

In the Red

As of 2007, 50 million households had mortgages. If home prices drop another 15 percent, it would put 21 percent of these mortgages, or $2.6 trillion, into negative equity.

When you dive into the P2P sites, you'll notice many people have turned to P2P lending to get home equity loans from relatives. Because the mortgage dilemma has made it more difficult to get *home equity loans*, many experts predict that other P2P lenders will venture into lending money for mortgages to borrowers they've never met. This may seem like a far-fetched idea to you, but as the conventional path to a mortgage becomes increasingly blocked, people will turn to a new source, like P2P lending.

During the 1992 election, a presidential advisor coined the phrase, "It's the economy, stupid." Those words weren't intended to imply that Americans were stupid. They meant, "Well, isn't it obvious why we're hurting?"

def•i•ni•tion

Equity is the difference between what you owe on your home and what your home is worth. For example, if your home has an appraised value of $300,000 and you owe $200,000 on your mortgage, your equity is worth $100,000. Getting a **home equity loan** turns that difference into cash that you can use for other expenses. It's also called a second mortgage.

You're reading this book so you can learn about the P2P industry. This shows that you're savvy and you know what the basic problem is: the economy is not doing well, and that makes it difficult to get a loan from a bank. Given the state of the economy, it might have seemed obvious that people would seek new ways of making ends meet. What probably wasn't obvious, though, was the *way* they'd do it.

Who Needs a Real Bank?

This chapter opened with a discussion about banks. To be clear, brick-and-mortar banks are still good to have around. For one thing, the Federal Deposit Insurance Corporation (FDIC) insures your money in banks. You put your money in the bank, and then the bank lends your money to someone else.

Your Bank Deposits Are FDIC-Insured

Banks are required to retain 3 to 10 percent of deposits. And generally, depositors are protected up to $100,000. So if you deposit $500, your bank might retain $50 as reserve money. The bank then loans the rest—$450—to a customer who wants to borrow the money.

It is nice to know that you can get that money when you need it, isn't it? Nothing in life is risk-free, of course, but this is a situation where your money is pretty darn safe while it's in the bank.

It has been a long time since people lost their savings during the Great Depression. You're probably too young to have lived through that, but you may have seen that famous "run on the bank" scene in *It's a Wonderful Life*. It's the scene where George Bailey and his new wife,

> ### Hidden Treasure
>
> The economic bailout of 2008 temporarily increased the FDIC-insured amount from $100,000 to $250,000. This new limit is effective from October 3, 2008, to December 31, 2009.
>
> After December 31, 2009, the FDIC-insured limit is expected to go back to $100,000.

Mary, are about to leave for their honeymoon. It's pouring rain and they see everyone running toward the bank. Scary image, isn't it? Not to worry. Our current system usually protects us against that specific scenario.

A Comparison Between Banks and P2P Lending

Our current banking system charges us high interest rates. There is room, though, in our society for both traditional banks and P2P lending.

You've probably never given this much thought, so let's take a look at the similarities and differences between banks and P2P lending. And hey, if you're hearing about P2P lending for the first time, then this section is especially for you!

Here's a quick roundup to show you the differences between bank lending and P2P lending:

- P2P lending is all done online. You don't have to worry about making it to the bank before it closes.

- When you loan money to someone on a P2P lending website, in most cases your money is not insured. If it stays in the bank in an account, it's FDIC-insured.

- There's a social component involved with P2P lending. You're loaning money to, or borrowing from, a real live person instead of an institution.

- Interest rates on bank loans aren't usually negotiable. But whether you're borrowing money or lending it, interest rates are usually negotiable on P2P lending sites.

> **Good Cents** _____
>
> It's true that you'll pay a high interest rate on your P2P loan if you have poor credit. But because you'd probably have trouble getting a loan from a bank, it's an option to explore. If you make your payments on a P2P loan on time and consistently, you have an opportunity to rebuild your credit. It takes time, but it can be a good start for you if you're in good enough financial shape to make the payments.

Let's look at how bank lending and P2P lending are similar. With both types of lending, the following statements are true:

- If you have less-than-good credit, you'll pay higher interest rates.

- Your money is paying for someone else's loan.

- ◆ They both "create" money in the economy by funding loans.

- ◆ Trust is involved. When lending money, you never know whether it will be repaid.

We mentioned high interest rates at banks. As a lender, P2P lending gives you an opportunity to help someone who may have been rejected by a bank or someone who's temporarily down on his or her luck. So, although you give up FDIC security on your money that stays in a savings account, you gain a lot in the "feel good" department. And in some cases, you get a pretty good profit on your investment, too.

Are banks competing with P2P lending? Not exactly, but the emergence of the P2P lending industry has made banks take notice. Banks see that consumers have an option to take financial matters into their own hands.

There's another aspect of P2P lending that's just getting started which might make banks think even harder about P2P lending—the secondary lending market. Lending Club was the first P2P site to offer a secondary lending market. To enter this market, P2P lending sites must register with the Securities and Exchange Commission (SEC) and enter a *quiet period*. We'll get into this concept in more detail in Chapter 10 when we talk about Lending Club.

Basically, the secondary lending market allows lenders to trade their loans to other lenders using a trading platform that's accessible on a P2P lender's website. After the approval process is completed, the P2P lending site can come out of the quiet period and resume business activities, which would then include offering a secondary lending market.

def•i•ni•tion

A **quiet period** is the extent of time between when a company files a registration statement with the SEC and when the SEC declares that the registration statement is effective.

Hidden Treasure

An October 2008 report from Gartner, Inc., a consulting firm in Stamford, Connecticut, reviewed the impact of the secondary lending market on banks. Gartner recommended that banks monitor the secondary lending market for both opportunities and threats. Gartner reasons that the secondary lending market offers P2P lenders more liquidity (making it possible to convert an investment into cash much sooner than expected), which makes it even more attractive to individuals. The future relationship between banks and P2P lending should be interesting to follow.

If you're a borrower, P2P loans give you a second chance to get the money you need if you've tried at a bank (or several) and been rejected. And if you have a poor track record with credit, getting and successfully repaying a P2P loan can help you improve your credit record.

The rise of the P2P lending market has come at a good time for both lenders and borrowers. This book will help both of you take advantage of the opportunity.

The Least You Need to Know

- ◆ Even during excellent economic times, it is hard to get loans or earn decent interest on a savings account.

- ◆ People have been using credit for a very long time.

- ◆ The state of the economy has spurred P2P loans.

- ◆ It's predicted that people will turn to P2P lending for home equity loans as it becomes increasingly difficult to get these loans from banks.

- ◆ There are both similarities and differences between banks and P2P lending.

- ◆ P2P lending can often be mutually beneficial for borrowers and lenders.

2

Types of P2P Loans

In This Chapter

- ◆ Interesting things people do with P2P personal loans
- ◆ Using a P2P loan to start a new business
- ◆ How P2P loans are used to keep small businesses going
- ◆ How P2P loans help entrepreneurs in developing countries
- ◆ Using P2P loans to fund college expenses

Now that you know what the P2P lending fuss is all about, you're probably curious to find out what all these people are getting money for.

And some of the reasons, you'd expect. For example, a family of four needs $9,000 to pay off credit card debt, or a catering business needs $2,500 to repair its delivery truck. But other reasons may surprise you. A pregnant woman needs $2,000 to hire a midwife for a home birth, or an expanding reptile breeding business needs $3,000 to purchase a stud iguana.

No, we're not making these up (okay, we made up the part about the stud iguana). But the point is that P2P loans open a new economic avenue for funding that simply wasn't an option before.

In this chapter, we look at the types of P2P personal loans. Then, we cover business and student loans. Just for fun, we toss in a few examples of listings from P2P websites so you can start getting an idea of how all the websites look. But don't worry about deciphering the terms on each listing. We cover the details about terms used in the listings in Part 2.

Personal Loans

So what's the most common reason given for a P2P personal loan? The desire to get out of credit card debt. With interest rates so high, it's not surprising that P2P lending is filling this need.

Javelin Strategy & Research, a quantitative research company that focuses on the financial services industry, says that people seek P2P loans for one of these three reasons:

- Want a better interest rate: 36 percent

- Want to avoid credit cards: 33 percent

- Don't qualify for a bank or credit union loan: 27 percent

The research also predicted that the demand for using P2P lending to pay off credit card debt will increase from $38 billion in 2007 to $159 billion in 2012. The good news for borrowers is that the study also showed that the motivations of lenders were about equally split between wanting to help others get out of debt and wanting a higher return than what banks offer.

Credit Card Debt

Who says you can't borrow your way out of debt? If a borrower has the self discipline to pay off a consolidated loan debt, this approach can save the borrower money.

Hidden Treasure
Did you know that 58 percent of consumers are likely to carry a balance on at least one credit card in the next six months? And 44 percent of these consumers say they're likely to use a P2P lending site to pay off their balances.

Let's say you've ended up with $7,000 of debt on five different credit cards. Wouldn't it be helpful (and cheaper) to consolidate your debt into one loan?

In the world of P2P lending, you can ask for a *fixed interest rate* loan for $7,000. You'd then take the $7,000 P2P loan and pay off all five of your credit cards (most cards have a *variable interest rate*, according to CardRatings.com). Now you're responsible for paying off one consolidated loan at, hopefully, a lower *annual percentage rate* (*APR*) with a lower monthly payment.

Because most credit cards have a variable interest rate, your rate (and your APR) fluctuates with an interest rate index that it is tied to, such as the prime rate. The prime rate is the lowest interest rate that banks charge their best customers. The prime rate is also the most common index used for variable-rate credit cards.

When the prime rate changes, your rate changes. The amount of the change depends on your card-holder agreement. Many of the card agreements allow for rate changes that match the changes in the prime rate. For instance, if the prime rate increases by .30 percent, then your credit card interest rate increases by .30 percent.

Let's face it, going to a bank and asking for help so you can lower your *interest rate*—and thus the amount you owe to said bank—isn't likely to go very far. Javelin predicts that because of this, the demand for P2P lending services to pay off credit card debt will continue to grow.

def•i•ni•tion

An **interest rate** is the amount charged per year on a loan. A **fixed interest rate** remains the same throughout the term of the loan. Mortgages often have fixed interest rates. A **variable interest rate** moves up and down in tandem with the movement of an interest rate index. The **annual percentage rate (APR)** is the amount charged per year on a loan *plus* the fees and costs paid to acquire the loan.

Visit any P2P website and you'll see tons of requests for debt consolidation loans. These are frequently accompanied by photos of adorable pets, attractive people, and small children.

But hey—these photos often work!

PERSONAL LOAN

PAYING OFF A HIGH-RATE 401(K) LOAN AND
PAYING OFF CREDIT CARDS
$14,000 @ 13.81%

FUNDING: 26% funded
BIDS: 49 Bids

CREDIT PROFILE

A credit grade	25% DTI

DEBT CONSOLIDATION LOAN

PAYING OFF A CREDIT CARD AND ESTABLISHING A
BETTER CREDIT SCORE
$15,000 @ 35%

FUNDING: 40% funded
BIDS: 68 Bids

CREDIT PROFILE

C credit grade	28% DTI

DEBT CONSOLIDATION LOAN

PAYING OFF CREDIT CARDS
$25,000 @ 18.69%

FUNDING: 5% funded
BIDS: 8 Bids

CREDIT PROFILE

A credit grade	21% DTI

DEBT CONSOLIDATION LOAN

A GROWING FAMILY WANTS TO BECOME DEBT-FREE
$6,000 @ 20.08%

FUNDING: 16% funded
BIDS: 12 Bids

CREDIT PROFILE

B credit grade	33% DTI

Home Improvement

According to the Mortgage Bankers Association, almost 4 percent of prime mortgages are past due or even in foreclosure. This is not a good time to convince your bank to invest in your home. Chances are that by the time this book is published, that number will be worse.

But you know your neighborhood and your family's needs, so if you think it's a good way to boost your home's value, then a P2P *unsecured loan* is an option. Borrowers have gotten P2P loans for kitchen or bathroom remodeling, new furniture, new HVAC units, home repairs … you name it.

Note that P2P loans are unsecured. With *secured loans*, you need to put up property, stock, or other assets as collateral.

def•i•ni•tion

When someone borrows money that is not secured by collateral, such as a house or stocks, it's called an **unsecured loan**. On the other hand, a **secured loan** involves pledging property to cover the debt. This way, the lender has security in case the borrower defaults on the loan.

All Things Automotive

Ready to unload your Suburban for a more fuel-efficient car? Or maybe you need to get your business's delivery van repaired. Borrowers are looking for a variety of loans when it comes to transportation.

Here are just a few automotive-related examples of what borrowers want money for:

 ◆ Expensive vehicle repairs
 ◆ Motorcycles

- Pickup trucks

- New or used cars (because interest rates at a bank are higher for used cars than for new cars, some venture into P2P loans to get better rates)

Entertainment

Sometimes you just need to relax. You'll see listings where people are *really* in need of a vacation. For example, one listing showed a burned-out borrower who had not been on a vacation in 30 years and wanted to go to Europe to visit his homeland. But many others are just trying to pay for a simple vacation at the beach with their families or friends.

You'll also see loan requests for new boats, vacation homes, and so on. There's nothing wrong with this. These are all reasonable requests on a P2P site—as long as the lenders and borrower are confident about the borrower's ability to pay back the loan, that is.

A Little Help from Your Family and Friends

Most of us would agree that when it comes to family and friends, lending or borrowing money is not a good idea. But what if you use an outside intermediary that focuses on loans between family and friends, such as Virgin Money, to set up a payment schedule for a loan you give to your cousin?

We're not saying that there still couldn't be problems. But at least going the P2P route gives you a chance to help a family member or friend while keeping the arrangement as businesslike as possible. Documentation of a loan goes a long way toward keeping things civil.

Here Comes the Bride

Love may be a many splendored thing, but it can be downright expensive, too. It shouldn't surprise anyone that P2P lending has become a popular way to fund a couple's path toward wedded bliss.

Here are just a few items that engaged couples might need funding for:

- The engagement and wedding rings

- The reception

- The trousseau

- The rehearsal dinner

- The honeymoon

- The flowers and music

- Travel expenses for out-of-town guests

- The perfect (most likely expensive!) wedding gown

- Renting the tuxedos

Medical Bills

Even if you have health insurance, a health-care crisis can really set you back when you're struggling to get a handle on out-of-pocket expenses. And for the 46 million Americans who don't have health insurance, a health crisis can turn into a financial crisis.

Imagine that you needed a $48,000 hip replacement surgery but you had either a huge deductible or a limited amount of insurance (or zero insurance). Many people in this situation turn to P2P loans.

Good Cents _____

Don't be afraid to think outside the box if you need funds. We've seen loan requests for surgery for a Yorkie, for getting out of an abusive marriage, for pet adoption expenses, for financial assistance to start over after a divorce, for infertility treatments, for funding self-published books, for financing an online therapy business, and for opening a dog salon and spa.

Moving Expenses

Imagine that you want to move so you can live closer to your grandparents. Or maybe you've lost your job and are moving to a different city to take a new job. It's great if your company is paying your moving expenses, but moving can be expensive when you're on your own and are paying for every cent of the relocation.

This is just a partial list of what someone who is relocating might need funds for:

 ◆ Moving van expenses (with gas prices unstable, this part of moving will only get more expensive)

 ◆ Help with packing

 ◆ Real estate closing costs

 ◆ Turning on utilities at a new place

Military Deployment

When a spouse is deployed, lots of financial issues can result for the spouse who is left behind. Sometimes a borrower will ask for a loan to cover travel expenses to meet with a deployed spouse who is stationed in another city. For lenders, this is a great opportunity to help those who are serving our country.

Mortgages

Someone who wants to take family togetherness to a new level can borrow money from or loan money to a relative in order to buy a house. At Virgin Money, this is called a Family Mortgage—and it's a great way for Aunt Sophie to help a niece or nephew buy a home (especially now, when getting a mortgage at a decent rate can be difficult, if not impossible, for some).

We cover this topic in more detail when we review Virgin Money in Chapter 9, but here's a quick look at the benefits of using a site such as this one when lending money between friends or family:

 ◆ Legal documentation for the loan is provided.

 ◆ An official payment schedule is set up.

 ◆ Bank accounts are set up for automatic money transfers.

 ◆ Year-end tax statements are sent.

 ◆ Making it legal may help alleviate some of the emotional issues that can occur when loans are made within a family (or between friends).

Remember that keeping the loan businesslike won't always eliminate the emotional issues that can crop up, but it certainly helps. And having another entity that functions as the *intermediary* is a win-win situation for both the borrower and the lender. As a result, P2P lending results in the *disintermediation* of banks.

def•i•ni•tion

The P2P website becomes the **intermediary** for the financial transaction instead of the bank. This means that the P2P website is the middleman that facilitates the transaction between a borrower and a lender. Sometimes you'll see this phenomenon referred to as the **disintermediation,** or displacement, of banks.

Business Loans

Maybe you've always wanted to start a business, and now you have a great idea that's guaranteed to set the world on fire! You meet with your bank, but unfortunately, the loan officer doesn't share your vision. Or maybe you do get approved for a loan, but the interest rate is so high that you're not comfortable moving forward.

Start a New Business

After credit card debt, starting a business is the next most cited reason for delving into a P2P loan. Small business owners have a tough time getting funding from banks or venture capitalists, so P2P loans give them a chance to do the following:

- Get investment capital for startups.

- Get funding for product inventions.

- Hire employees to grow their businesses.

- Hire an advertising agency or marketing consultant.

Here's an example of a listing for a startup business:

BUSINESS LOAN	
 START A PERSONAL SHOPPING/WARDROBING BUSINESS $11,000 @ 12.54% FUNDING: 35% funded BIDS: 40 Bids	
CREDIT PROFILE	
AA credit grade	29% DTI

BUSINESS LOAN

OPEN A PUBLIC RELATIONS AGENCY
$9,000 @ 11.85%

FUNDING: 70% funded
BIDS: 26 Bids

CREDIT PROFILE

A credit grade	32% DTI

Fund an Existing Business

For those who are already running a business, changes or improvements are often necessary to stay competitive. Business owners might need to:

♦ Expand a current business (for example, recently on Kiva.org there was a butcher shop owner in Tanzania who needed $2,875 to open a second shop)

♦ Use a loan to increase inventory

♦ Buy new equipment or upgrade a computer system

♦ Hire employees

♦ Pay for advertising expenses

Business Loans in Developing Countries

On Kiva, lenders can help entrepreneurs in developing countries. And due to the lower costs of living, the amounts that the borrowers are looking for are relatively small. A loan of $25 can make a huge difference to one of these entrepreneurs.

Here's an example of a featured entrepreneur on Kiva who needed inventory for her store:

Ms. Reyes

LOCATION:	Dominican Republic
ACTIVITY:	General Store
LOAN REQUEST:	$900.00
REPAYMENT TERM:	3 months
LOAN USE:	Merchandise to sell

You will see many listings similar to this on Kiva's website. In Chapter 8, we spend more time talking about Kiva and its unusual P2P lending platform.

Student Loans

Many people think that getting into college is the hard part. But unless you're on a full scholarship or are lucky enough to be an heir or heiress, coming up with money every semester is the really hard part. P2P lenders love to get involved when it comes to educational goals; this really gives lenders a chance to feel like they're making a difference in someone else's life.

Anyone who worked his or her way through college can appreciate how difficult it is to pay for an education. It's darn tough to work all day and then stay up half the night studying for that microbiology test. A borrower can get the funds he or she needs and maybe just work part-time (and then maybe even get some sleep).

Here are a few more reasons why people request student loans:

♦ To pay for their kids' education. Tuition costs are tough on parents, and these costs come at a time when they're trying to save for their own retirement.

♦ To go back for a graduate degree. A lot of adults in their 30s, 40s, 50s, and beyond are going back for graduate degrees. Some of these people are sweetening their resumés in their current fields, but some are also changing careers.

♦ To pay off other student loans. Some students may be stuck with high-interest-rate student loans that will take the rest of their otherwise carefree 20s (and sometimes beyond!) to pay off. This is one of those times when borrowing money at a lower rate to pay off a higher-interest-rate loan makes sense.

Sites such as Fynanz.com and GreenNote.com specialize in student loans. You'll learn about these "specialty" P2P lending websites in Chapter 11. You'll also find options at Virgin Money and at mainstream sites such as Prosper and Lending Club.

The Least You Need to Know

♦ People ask for and get P2P personal loans for a wide variety of reasons.

♦ People are attracted to P2P loans because they can get lower interest rates and lower monthly payments.

- ◆ Getting rid of credit card debt is the number-one reason why people turn to P2P loans.

- ◆ The demand for using P2P loans to get out of credit card debt is expected to go from $38 billion in 2007 to $159 billion in 2012.

- ◆ P2P loans are often used to either start a new business or expand an existing one.

- ◆ P2P loans can be used to pay for current college expenses along with older student loans.

3

The Social Science Behind Social Lending

In This Chapter

- ◆ Why social lending appeals to both borrowers and lenders
- ◆ How peer pressure affects success in social lending, particularly in Prosper groups
- ◆ How the popularity of social networking has made us comfortable with online lending
- ◆ Do's and don'ts for borrowers, lenders, and those involved in Prosper groups

Recent research by Rice University's Jones Graduate School of Management found that online P2P lending sites are more attractive to people than banks. The study "The Democratization of Personal Consumer Loans?" analyzed a database of 5,370 P2P loans from Prosper.

The research brought some important points to light:

- ◆ Borrowers are attracted to P2P lending because they can get better interest rates on loans. Lenders like it because they can get better returns than from a bank.

♦ Lenders are unlikely to be influenced by the gender or race of the borrower. Like Facebook, P2P sites often let borrowers post photos, and these photos help emphasize the social part of social lending.

Of course, some borrowers don't use photos of themselves. Instead, a borrower might post a photo of the car that he or she plans to buy with the loan or a picture of his or her adorable 3-year-old twins. That's okay, too.

♦ Lenders make decisions in a rational manner. They review a borrower's credit rating and read over his or her income and expense statements before making a decision.

When it comes to putting their own money on the line, Americans prove to be very objective. They want a good return on their money, and they look at an individual's situation regardless of sex or race.

The result? Both borrowers and lenders feel that they're getting a fair shake.

The Attraction of Social Lending

The Social Futures Observatory, a British research firm that focuses on academic topics and then applies them to real-life settings, did a study on why people are attracted to P2P lending. Interestingly, a lot of reasons were shared by both borrowers and lenders.

Declining Trust in Financial Institutions

Both borrowers and lenders like the *transparency* of the transactions. In a time when we've witnessed the Enron and WorldCom disasters, the public trust of large institutions is at low levels. And many have lost their faith in Wall Street, given the recent credit crunch and mortgage woes.

A lot of people lost their retirement investments, along with their faith in large institutions. There's something about the way that P2P lending sites do business that strikes a positive chord with folks.

Here are some reasons why:

♦ When you borrow money on a P2P site, you know you're getting a loan from a person who saw your situation and decided to help. On most sites, you see lenders competing with each other to loan you money! It's hard not to feel good about that.

♦ When you're a P2P lender, you choose the person to whom you want to loan money. You read the stories and decide who you think deserves a break. Lenders want to get a good return—there's no question about that—but most of them also have altruistic motives.

This situation is a bit risky, after all. But you can see the borrower's financial data and also learn some personal details. There's definitely a trust element involved with P2P lending.

♦ There's a community feel to P2P lending. There's a "we're all in this together" sentiment that you don't get when you walk into a bank.

def•i•ni•tion

Transparency means that information about the product, services, or financial data is readily available. In the case of P2P lending, people like knowing all the facts involved in the financial transactions.

All's Fair

Borrowers and lenders both say they feel they're getting a fair shake. Borrowers usually like the interest rates, because a better rate usually translates to lower monthly payments (in addition to savings on interest charges). A lower payment gives the borrower a chance to save money for emergencies or even to save a little for retirement. Having a little money tucked away that you can access in an emergency is especially important if you need to rebuild your credit. And if you're in credit rebuilding mode, the last thing you need is another late payment incident showing up on your credit report.

Here are more reasons why they feel that way:

♦ When a loan officer at a bank reviews a borrower's credit and sees the numbers (the client's credit score), the officer makes a decision based on the facts. The borrower may have compelling reasons why he or she fell behind in some payments and may even have proof that he or she is making enough money now to meet loan payments. Loan officers are human, and they may sympathize with a borrower's plight—but in the end, there are bank guidelines to follow.

If a borrower has a low credit score, no matter what the reason, he or she is probably not getting that loan from the bank. P2P lending gives both the borrower and the lender a chance at a fair rate and a fair return.

- For many borrowers, P2P lending is a second chance. On a P2P lending site, a borrower can tell his or her story and get a chance at a loan. He or she still may not get the loan, but the person has another *chance* to get it.

- Lenders have the opportunity to come out ahead. A better rate for the borrower is often a better return for the lender than what he or she can get from a CD or from a money market account.

Nothing Like Feeling Self-Empowered

Borrowers and lenders like being directly involved in the financial transaction.

If you're the borrower:

- You love the fact that you're not a faceless account number. On a P2P lending site, you're a "real" person to lenders.

- You decide what your loan listing says. You have a chance to explain the numbers if that's an issue for you.

- Borrowing money this way feels like you have more control over your destiny. You decide the loan amount (and, in some cases, the interest rate).

- You're an active participant rather than a hopeful observer. If you're on a website that auctions loan requests to drive down the interest rate, then you really feel like you're involved. You're not in the driver's seat exactly, but at least you're riding along in the front seat.

If you're the lender:

- You like knowing exactly where your money is going. For example, you offer $50 to help a borrower named Tim who lives in Michigan and needs money to buy a new HVAC system. You decide to fund part of his loan. You feel great knowing that you're helping keep his family warm during those cold Michigan winters.

- You get to be the one to analyze the borrower's financial situation. Instead of your deposit in a bank being loaned out the way the bank sees fit, you're in charge.

- On some sites, you can even ask a borrower such as Tim questions about his credit history or current income and expenses.

Social Lending Feels Good

Altruism is alive and well among Americans. Make no mistake, we're a capitalist society—but helping others is still a prominent goal for many.

On most P2P sites, financial gain *is* still the goal—which is true for both borrowers and lenders—but knowing that a loan is helping someone with a serious need can really feel great for the lender. And for the borrower, it's nice to know that someone read his or her story and was moved enough to want to help—even if it's for profit.

You may know about the "helper's high" that people get from volunteering. Well, this is the same kind of feeling. Call it a "social lending high" that lenders get!

Good Cents

The helper's high that people get from volunteering is explained in *The Healing Power of Doing Good*, by Allan Luks and Peggy Payne. It's a feeling of exhilaration and energy followed by a feeling of serenity. The helper's high has been compared to the feeling one gets after intense exercise, when the brain is flooded with endorphins. So becoming a lender may even be good for your health!

High Comfort Level with High Tech

Being comfortable with the computer is no longer the domain of the young. Online banking is the norm, and millions of people visit Facebook, MySpace, LinkedIn, and Second Life. And for the really high-tech enthusiast, now there's *Twitter* (and "tweeting"). By the time this book is published, there's no telling what else will have been invented in the name of social networking. Telepathically transmitting our thoughts to each other via cell phones, perhaps? Let's hope not!

The point, ironically, is that these virtual communities are making people feel connected. What we call social networking and social lending entails no face-to-face contact. We have evolved as a society to the point where online communities feel comfortable.

Ten years ago, the idea of lending or borrowing money from an online site would have given you the jitters. But now, you probably find yourself saying "Google it!" when your 10-year-old asks you a question. You may even have your own Facebook page. Maybe you even Twitter.

def•i•ni•tion

Twitter is free, and it's one of the newest social networking tools. It lets users send text-based updates, or tweets, via cell phones to people who have signed up to "follow" them. Your friends can get your updates on their phones, on your Twitter webpage, on your blog, or on Facebook.

Like we said, teenagers aren't the only ones online. Here's a snapshot of who is surfing the Internet these days, according to a May 2008 survey by the Pew Internet & American Life Project:

- Adult women: 73 percent

- Adult men: 73 percent

- Age 18–29: 90 percent

- Age 30–49: 85 percent

- Age 50–64: 70 percent

- Age 65 plus: 35 percent

There's a decrease once users hit age 65, but this demographic includes a lot of people who came of age after the Internet hit the scene. But still, according to a 2007 survey done by Pew, when all users are grouped together, 92 percent send and read e-mails, and 81 percent cruise the Internet looking for information about services in which they're interested.

Social Networking Meets E-Commerce

Think about Facebook and LinkedIn for a moment. Facebook has always focused on the social part of networking, whereas LinkedIn is more of a professional network. Facebook is actually developing a business component as well, however—at least for older users.

The overlap between social networking sites and e-commerce actually started a long time ago. It has just been very gradual—so gradual that we have hardly noticed the shift.

Hidden Treasure

The P2P Lending Club got its start on Facebook. The "Lending Club" Facebook group was designed to match up "friends" who needed to borrow money with other "friends" who were willing to loan money.

P2P lending sites combine both social and e-commerce aspects. It's as if eBay, Facebook, and LinkedIn were all mingled together. There's a community of borrowers and lenders, but the goal is all business (similar to eBay). Most of the P2P sites have blogs or forums where borrowers and lenders come together and ask questions. This environment helps create the community feel.

Peer Pressure

This community feeling actually keeps people on their toes. Borrowers want to succeed and pay back their loans. Lenders want to help borrowers. It's people helping other people—no faceless banks involved.

But with this environment comes a little peer pressure. (No, not the kind you had to endure in middle school when you had to choose between the popular kids and the nerds.) This kind of pressure is what you feel when you don't want to let someone down. It's more like making a promise to a friend and then keeping your word.

If you get involved in a borrowing or a lending group, this peer pressure is especially effective. We talk more about groups in Chapter 16, but in general, groups have a credit rating that they've earned as a group. Anyone in the group who defaults on a loan lowers the group's credit rating.

Try explaining why you missed a payment to other angry group members. In other words, groups are good at keeping everyone in line for the good of the entire group. The group concept probably seems a little foreign to you at this point, but don't worry. You'll learn more about it in Part 3, when you learn more details about being a borrower.

Proper P2P Lending Etiquette

What's P2P lending etiquette, you may ask? Maybe you're familiar with Virginia Shea's book, *Netiquette*. Published in 1994, *Netiquette* was pretty cutting edge at the time. The Internet was the virtual Wild, Wild West. It was so wild, in fact, that we didn't even know that we needed lessons on how to be nice. As it turns out, we *do* need to be reminded of things such as, "Remember the humanity of others" and "Respect others' privacy online."

If you've visited any discussion forums recently, you've probably witnessed some not-so-nice behavior. There's something about sitting in a room alone while typing on your computer that can bring out a person's belligerent side. It's easy to be a bully when there's no one standing in front of you who just might smack you in the face for your rudeness.

Well, borrowing and lending money online brings with it a new set of potential hot-button issues. If you thought people could get testy over a movie review, then think about how offended they could get over money matters.

To save you from the bad judgment of others (or from yourself, for that matter), here are some handy guidelines for playing nice on P2P lending sites.

Borrowers Behaving Badly

You're no doubt a wonderful, nice person, but it never hurts to take a brief refresher course on Internet courtesy. The problem with the Internet is that there are no non-verbal cues that let us know how the other person is reacting.

We all tend to process these nonverbal cues on a subconscious level. If you make a statement to someone and they respond with an angry look, you know you need to rephrase your statement. Likewise, if someone you're speaking with appreciates your comment, you'll notice a smile or something similar that lets you know the conversation is moving along swimmingly. But on the Internet, sometimes you just have to bend over backward to get your point across without offending anyone.

Here are some mistakes that users frequently make on P2P lending websites:

- Not telling the truth. This is a no-brainer, right? If you're taking the time to read this book, you're probably an honest citizen. You're taking the time to learn about P2P loans so that you can make an informed decision about how (and *whether*) you should proceed.

  So this warning isn't really for you, our dear reader. But just in case this topic ever comes up at a cocktail party, you can let people know that lying on a credit application is a federal crime.

- Stalking a lender. Stalking may seem like too strong a word when you're sending an e-mail that says, "Bid on my loan! Please!" But this approach does feel like stalking to a lender.

  Don't do it. This is like sending spam—really desperate spam. And this doesn't engender confidence in your abilities to repay a loan. Prosper says lenders report that this is a real turnoff.

- Avoid hyperbole. Don't say in your listing, "I'm the best risk you'll ever take!" or "I've never been late on a credit payment in my whole entire life! Just ask my mom!"

No one is likely to believe you, for one thing. Be straightforward and honest, and leave off the exclamation points. In football, there's a saying about how you're supposed to act when you score a touchdown. *Act like you've been there before.* Don't act like this is the first time you've ever tried to get a loan. Be dignified in your appeal, and let your listing do the talking in a calm, rational manner.

In the Red

Most P2P lending sites will ask you to leave if you violate their codes of ethics. Always read the site's policy and/or etiquette statements and follow them.

Lenders Behaving Badly

Borrowers aren't the only ones who need to be tactful. Remember, borrowers have put their finances out there for the world to see—and in most cases, borrowers are in some kind of financial jam. So be respectful and nonjudgmental in your online interactions with borrowers on P2P lending websites.

Here are some common mistakes that lenders need to avoid:

- Stalking a defaulted borrower. Okay, there's that "stalking" word again. But hey, this situation goes both ways. You knew that P2P lending was inherently risky when you got on board. If the ship starts sinking, it's not your place to start harassing the borrower. Your P2P website will handle defaulters. Grab the nearest life jacket and hope for the best.

  This is the reason why we talk about diversification in Chapter 19. Spreading out your risk is important so that you don't overreact when one of your boats springs a leak. If you have an entire fleet, losing one isn't so bad.

◆ Asking borrowers inappropriate questions. On some sites, you'll have a chance to ask borrowers questions.

Here are some examples of appropriate questions:

"Are you a homeowner?"

"Your debt-to-income ratio is a little high. Do you plan to cut back on expenses in order to make the loan payments?"

Here are some examples of inappropriate questions:

"How did you get yourself into so much debt?"

"What's your age/sex/religion/ethnicity?"

◆ Deciding to become a loan collector. This isn't *The Sopranos*. You can't attempt collections on your own. There are state and federal laws that must be followed.

Groups Behaving Badly

You'll learn about joining P2P lending groups in Chapter 16. For now, all you need to know is that some P2P lending sites allow borrowers and lenders to form groups. Groups of borrowers or lenders are very popular on Prosper.

You might have a group of lenders that loan money to borrowers, or you might have a group comprised of borrowers who have good credit ratings. Then again, you might find a group that welcomes both borrowers and lenders. These groups have a few things in common: membership is based on a common interest or goal, the groups are managed by a group leader, and groups are often looking for new members.

Here are a few mistakes to avoid if you end up in one of these groups:

◆ Violating the privacy of other group members. Don't praise or criticize your group leader in your listing. Don't mention the names of other group members, either. In most cases, you made an agreement when you joined the group to keep identities private.

◆ Stalking borrowers or lenders to get them in your group. (There's that "stalking" word again.) Don't send e-mails to borrowers or lenders extolling the virtues of the "1957 Chevy P2P Lending Group."

As it turns out, not that much has changed since Shea's *Netiquette* book was published. Internet manners never go out of style, and in this case, they can even help you get a loan or make money.

The Least You Need to Know

- People are attracted to social lending because it makes them feel valued as human beings.

- Borrowers and lenders believe they're treated fairly with P2P lending.

- We're comfortable with the concept of online lending because we have grown so accustomed to technology.

- Both borrowers and lenders should treat each other with respect when interacting on P2P lending sites.

- P2P groups should always respect the privacy of other group members.

Chapter 4

Keeping an Eye on the Industry

In This Chapter

- ◆ Federal regulations for P2P lending
- ◆ A variety of federal credit protection laws
- ◆ P2P lending regulations and usury laws that vary state to state
- ◆ How WebBank works with P2P lending sites
- ◆ Legislation on the horizon that might affect bank loans

As consumers, most of us aren't aware of just how many laws are protecting us. There are lots of regulations that prevent credit discrimination. The P2P lending industry is subject to these regulations just as your credit card company is. Here's a crash course in everything you need to know about who's watching over the P2P industry—and who's looking out for you, too.

Federal Regulations

There are many federal regulations that protect consumers. In fact, you'll probably be surprised at the extent of the laws designed to ensure fairness. Following are some of the federal regulations with which P2P websites must comply.

The Consumer Credit Protection Act (CCPA)

The Consumer Credit Protection Act (CCPA) protects employees from being discharged in the event that their wages are garnished. The CCPA also limits the weekly amount that can be garnished. For example, if a borrower defaulted on a P2P loan and collection procedures progressed to the stage of wage garnishment, the borrower's employer can't fire the borrower (the employee).

For more information about the CCPA, visit www.dol.gov/compliance/laws/comp-ccpa.htm.

The Truth in Lending Act

The Truth in Lending Act is designed to ensure that lenders provide all pertinent loan information to consumers before they enter into lending contracts. Each consumer should be able to make a decision, compare choices, and take the best option.

P2P lending websites have to comply with this regulation. You should be able to get lending information from each P2P website and then be able to make an informed decision about where to get your loan.

For more information about this act, visit www.fdic.gov/regulations/laws/rules/6500-200.html.

The Equal Credit Opportunity Act (ECOA)

The Equal Credit Opportunity Act (ECOA) protects consumers from credit discrimination due to sex, race, marital status, national origin, religion, age, or because they receive government assistance of any kind. This act gives everyone an equal chance to obtain credit. If you're trying to get a loan on a P2P website, this law protects you from discrimination by potential lenders.

For more information about the ECOA, visit www.ftc.gov/bcp/conline/pubs/credit/ecoa.shtm.

The Fair Credit Reporting Act (FCRA)

The Fair Credit Reporting Act (FCRA) regulates the dissemination, collection, and use of consumer credit information. When you request a loan on a P2P website, you are asked to submit your credit report. The FCRA protects your privacy.

For more information about the FCRA, visit www.ftc.gov/os/statutes/fcradoc.pdf.

> **Hidden Treasure**
>
> The FCRA also covers disposal of information obtained by credit agencies. In 2007, a mortgage company agreed to pay a $50,000 civil penalty for disposing of consumer credit information in an unsecured dumpster.

The Fair Credit Billing Act (FCBA) and the Electronic Fund Transfer Act (EFTA)

The Fair Credit Billing Act (FCBA) and the Electronic Fund Transfer Act (EFTA) were enacted to establish procedures for correcting any mistakes that end up on credit billing and electronic fund transfer account statements (for example, charges or electronic fund transfers that show the wrong dates or amounts). This is important since most P2P lending websites use electronic fund transfer. Lenders can transfer funds to an account to be used for lending, and borrowers can have loan payments automatically debited from their accounts.

For more information about these acts, visit www.ftc.gov/bcp/edu/pubs/consumer/credit/cre16.shtm (FCBA) and www.fdic.gov/regulations/laws/rules/6500-1350.html (EFTA).

The Fair Debt Collection Practices Act (FDCPA)

The Fair Debt Collection Practices Act (FDCPA) protects consumers from being treated unfairly by debt collectors. Under this act, debt collectors can't be abusive, unfair, or deceptive. Hopefully, this won't happen to you. But if you're late with payments or appear unable to repay the loan, this regulation ensures that you have a right to be treated with respect.

For more information about the FDCPA, visit www.ftc.gov/bcp/edu/pubs/consumer/credit/cre27.pdf.

> **Good Cents** _____
>
> Debt collectors may contact consumers only between the hours of 8 A.M. and 9 P.M., and they must identify themselves on the phone. If a consumer does not want to take these calls, he or she can ask the caller to cease contact. If the consumer requests this in writing, the collectors can't contact the consumer again by phone.

The Electronic Signatures in Global and National Commerce Act (ESIGN)

The Electronic Signatures in Global and National Commerce Act (ESIGN) is the federal law that offers the guidelines for *e-commerce*. Every state has laws regarding electronic signatures. ESIGN ensures that a contract signed electronically is just as good as a signature on paper. This law also gives consumers the right to insist on a paper signature instead of an electronic one. You can also request a paper signature on P2P websites, but the electronic option is much more convenient.

def•i•ni•tion _____

Electronic commerce, known as **e-commerce,** is the buying and selling of goods or services over the Internet. It's also sometimes referred to as e-business.

For more information about ESIGN, visit www.ftc.gov/os/2001/06/esign7.htm.

The Federal Trade Commission (FTC)

The Federal Trade Commission (FTC) has a list of consumer categories on its website in the credit and loans section. You can get more information ranging from buying automobiles to mortgages.

For instance, if you select "Automobiles" from the menu, you can get details about buying, financing, leasing, and renting cars. You can also get facts about maintenance issues. This website also provides advice on other topics such as credit, divorce, choosing credit counselors, and steps to take before filing for bankruptcy.

For more information about the FTC, visit www.ftc.gov/bcp/menus/consumer/credit/loans.shtm.

The Federal Reserve

Check out the Federal Reserve's website to find information on consumer protection laws at http://federalreserveconsumerhelp.gov/?District=0. In addition to learning more about consumer protection laws, you can also obtain advice related to many credit-related topics. Here are some examples of the topics discussed on this site:

◆ Consumer credit

◆ Credit reports

◆ Home mortgages

◆ Foreclosures

◆ Small business

◆ Electronic banking

◆ Deposit insurance

There's also information on this site about how to file a complaint against a bank. In the current economic climate, some banks are having a difficult time staying afloat, so it's a good idea to know where to turn if you have serious issues with your bank.

Knowing What Your Rights Are

Whew! You didn't know you were that protected, did you? It's good to know what your rights are. If you suspect discrimination or an invasion of privacy, it's important to know about the laws that protect you. When you're informed about your rights, you're more empowered to protect yourself.

Lenders should also take note of these laws. P2P websites, for example, have strict rules against contacting a borrower who is late with a loan payment (remember in Chapter 3 when we used discussed stalking?). The reason is because the laws that were just reviewed protect the borrower's privacy and lay out procedures that must be followed. Respect these laws because when you're on the other side and you're the borrower, the laws protect you, too.

State Laws

State laws vary widely, so to get information specific to your state, see your state government's webpage, contact your state's attorney general's office, or check with your own attorney.

Here's a rundown of the types of regulations and laws your state might have:

- The Uniform Consumer Credit Code

- Usury or rate ceiling laws

- Consumer loan acts

- Mortgage lending acts

- Mortgage banker and broker acts

- Secondary mortgage acts

- Retail installment sales acts

- Seller and lender credit card acts

- Home solicitation sales acts

- Home improvement contracts acts

- Rental purchase agreement acts

State Usury Laws

There are different types of state laws that may make interest rates a little difficult to decipher. State *usury laws* limit the amount of interest rates on loans between individuals. That rate cap is called the *usury limit*. Usury laws and limits differ by state, and in many cases there are multiple exceptions to the rule. Sometimes you need to consult with an attorney to sort through the legal exceptions to see what the rate actually is.

Most states also have a *legal rate*, which applies to loans that don't specify the date when the loan must be repaid. If you entered into an agreement to borrow $5,000 but didn't specify when the loan was due, the state's legal rate for interest would apply. So the individual who loaned you the $5,000 could charge interest at whatever the legal rate is for your state. And then there's the *judgment rate*, which is the rate that a judge would apply in a court of law.

def•i•ni•tion

State **usury laws** cap interest rates at certain levels. That rate is called the **usury limit.** Most states also have a **legal rate,** which covers contractual obligations without a specific term. The **judgment rate** is the rate that judgments bear.

Most P2P lending sites cover this issue. But instead of relying on someone else's information, it's good to be informed about your own state's usury laws when you're the borrower. If you're the lender, it's good to know what the interest rate limits are in the state where you're considering giving a loan.

One state's usury laws are so complex that we already suggest you get an attorney. That's you, North Carolina! And as of late 2008, Indiana has usury legislation pending.

When you take a look at the following chart on usury rates, you might scream, "My credit card company is charging me too much!" Unfortunately, banks are not subject to usury laws. Those who are licensed (for example, banks and pawnbrokers) can charge higher interest rates.

> **Hidden Treasure**
>
> In 1980, the federal government passed a law exempting national banks from state usury laws. There was high inflation at the time, so the government decided that banks could set their rates at a certain number of points higher than the Federal Reserve discount rate.

Usury rates tend to change quite a bit, so use the following interest rate chart as a guideline only, and follow up with the state's website or with an attorney as needed.

State	Legal Rate	General Usury Limit	Judgment Rate
Alabama	6 percent	8 percent	12 percent
Alaska	10.5 percent	Current Federal Reserve rate plus 5 percent	
Arizona	10 percent		
Arkansas	6 percent	17 percent	10 percent per annum (or the lawful agreed-upon rate, whichever is larger)
California	10 percent		
Colorado	8 percent	45 percent; maximum rate to consumers is 12 percent per annum	
Connecticut	8 percent	12 percent	

continues

continued

State	Legal Rate	General Usury Limit	Judgment Rate
Delaware	5 percent higher than Federal Reserve rate		
District of Columbia	6 percent	Greater than 24 percent	
Florida	12 percent	18 percent (loans below $500,000)	
Georgia	7 percent	16 percent (loans below $3,000); 5 percent (loans more than $3,000)	
Hawaii	10 percent	12 percent	
Idaho	12 percent		5 percent higher than U.S. Treasuries Securities rate
Illinois	5 percent	9 percent	9 percent
Indiana	10 percent	None; pending legislation	10 percent
Iowa	10 percent	12 percent	
Kansas	10 percent	15 percent	4 percent higher than federal discount rate (18 percent maximum on first $1,000; 14.45 percent maximum if higher than $1,000)

State	Legal Rate	General Usury Limit	Judgment Rate
Kentucky	8 percent	Federal Reserve rate plus 4 percent or 19 percent, whichever is less; no limit on loans more than $15,000	12 percent compounded yearly
Louisiana	One point higher than average prime rate but no less than 7 percent and no greater than 14 percent	12 percent	
Maine	6 percent		15 percent if under $30,000; average discount rate for T-bills plus 4 percent if over $30,000
Maryland	6 percent	24 percent (many exceptions)	10 percent
Massachusetts	6 percent	20 percent	12 percent (18 percent if defense finds suit frivolous)
Michigan	5 percent	7 percent	5-year T-note rate plus 1 percent
Minnesota	6 percent	8 percent	"Secondary market yield" for 1-year T-bills

continues

continued

State	Legal Rate	General Usury Limit	Judgment Rate
Mississippi	9 percent	More than 10 percent or more than 5 percent higher than the Fed's rate	9 percent
Missouri	9 percent		9 percent
Montana	10 percent	6 percent more than New York City banks' prime rates	10 percent per annum
Nebraska	6 percent	16 percent	1 percent higher than a T-bill auction price (bond yield equivalent)
Nevada	12 percent		
New Hampshire	10 percent		
New Jersey	6 percent	30 percent (many exceptions)	
New Mexico	15 percent		Fixed by the court
New York	9 percent	16 percent	
North Carolina	8 percent	8 percent; complex exceptions, so consult with a lawyer	
North Dakota	6 percent	5.5 percent higher than the 6-month T-bill rate	
Oklahoma	6 percent	May not exceed 10 percent unless lender is licensed to make consumer loans	T-bill rate plus 4 percent

State	Legal Rate	General Usury Limit	Judgment Rate
Oregon	9 percent	12 percent (if less than $50,000)	9 percent
Pennsylvania	6 percent	6 percent (if less than $50,000—many exceptions)	
Puerto Rico	6 percent		
Rhode Island	12 percent	21 percent (or T-bill rate plus 9 percent)	
South Carolina	8.75 percent		14 percent
South Dakota	15 percent		12 percent
Tennessee	10 percent	24 percent (or 4 points higher than average prime loan rate, whichever is less)	10 percent
Texas	6 percent		18 percent or rate in the contract, whichever is lower
Utah	10 percent		12 percent
Vermont	12 percent	12 percent	12 percent
Virginia	8 percent		8 percent
Washington	12 percent	12 percent or 4 points higher than average T-bill rate for past 26 weeks	12 percent or contract rate, whichever is higher
West Virginia	6 percent	Maximum "contract" rate is 8 percent (some exceptions based on market rates)	

continues

continued

State	Legal Rate	General Usury Limit	Judgment Rate
Wisconsin	5 percent		12 percent (except for mortgage foreclosures, where the rate is a contract rate)
Wyoming	10 percent		10 percent (or a contract rate, if lower)

Source: Lectric Law Library, "State Interest Rates and Usury Limits," www.lectlaw.com/files/ban02.htm.

What's WebBank?

Lots of P2P lending sites use WebBank to handle their financial transactions. WebBank is headquartered in Salt Lake City, so it operates under the state laws of Utah. The bank is FDIC-insured and operates under federal law for licensing issues. WebBank offers credit cards, lines of credit, and installment loans. In addition, WebBank can also take deposits because it is FDIC-insured.

Through WebBank's industrial bank charter, it can also provide niche financing, such as P2P lending. WebBank is partnered with both Prosper and Lending Club. Prosper, for instance, makes loans through WebBank.

Future Legislation

In December 2007, former President Bush announced an agreement with mortgage servicers to freeze interest rates on a certain set of subprime mortgage borrowers. Subprime borrowers are those who typically have lower credit ratings.

The freeze applied to homeowners who obtained adjustable-rate mortgages between January 1, 2005, and July 31, 2007. It was designed to help those who faced such a steep increase in interest that they'd no longer be able to afford to keep their homes.

It's unclear how all this will affect future changes to the P2P loan industry—but expect more congressional involvement if the housing industry or the economy worsens.

The Least You Need to Know

- Be aware of federal regulations that protect you, such as the CCPA, the ECOA, and the Truth in Lending Act.

- Be aware of your state's usury laws, and know that they can change.

- Many of the P2P lending websites handle financial transactions through WebBank.

- The mortgage crisis may result in future legislation that further affects borrowers' abilities to get loans from banks.

Keeping Score

In This Chapter

- What's in a FICO score
- How each component of the FICO score is weighed
- How to obtain FICO scores free of charge
- Fixing mistakes on your credit report
- Some ways to bump up your credit score

Before you take a journey through the P2P lending world, you need a really good grip on FICO scores, also called credit scores. What's that, you say? The Fair Isaac Corporation invented the FICO score. You need to understand FICO scores in order to understand how interest rates work on P2P lending sites.

When you understand how FICO scores work, you can work on getting the best interest rate for yourself when you borrow money. And if you're lending money, this knowledge is equally important. Choosing an appropriate interest rate nets you the best return. Remember that when it comes to credit, knowledge is power.

Banks and other financial institutions and businesses use FICO scores to decide whether potential borrowers are good credit risks. According to Fair Isaac's myfico. com site, here's some information about average consumers:

- The average consumer has a total of 13 credit obligations.

- Only 30 percent of consumers have been more than 60 days overdue paying a debt.

- Fewer than 20 percent of consumers have had a loan or an account closed by a lender due to default.

- Forty percent of credit card holders have balances less than $1,000.

- Fifteen percent of credit card holders have balances greater than $10,000.

When considering all credit obligations (credit cards plus lines of credit, auto loans, and so on) other than mortgages:

- About 48 percent of consumers have less than $5,000 of debt.

- Almost 37 percent of consumers are more than $10,000 in debt.

What's a FICO Score?

You may have heard that a high FICO score is really, really important. But many of us don't understand exactly what the term "FICO score" means. A FICO score is calculated using various credit data that's reported by *credit bureaus*.

Here's the breakdown of a FICO score:

- Payment history: 35 percent

- Amounts owed: 30 percent

- Length of credit history: 15 percent

- New credit: 10 percent

- Types of credit used: 10 percent

We'll go into more detail about what FICO scores are and what affects them, both positively and negatively. Keep in mind that the breakdown of FICO scores can change depending on individual circumstances.

def•i•ni•tion

A **credit bureau** is an agency that functions like a clearinghouse for credit information. Credit bureaus collect and rate consumers' credit information. The three largest credit bureaus in the United States are Equifax, Experian, and TransUnion.

This means that one factor, such as payment history, may have a little more weight on one person's score than on another's. For example, if someone has a history of late payments and he or she has turned this around, a creditor might give more weight to the more positive parts of his or her report. It's impossible to predict, though, whether a creditor will take that into consideration. This is because the creditor may decide to look only at your score and ignore the details.

One thing's for sure, though. You don't need to worry about someone on a vendetta calling the credit bureau to badmouth you or accuse you of being late on a debt. If it's not on your credit report, it doesn't factor into your score. Creditors report an individual's payment history to the bureaus. The bureaus also collect information, such as bankruptcy proceedings, from public records.

Good Cents

Here are two websites to check out if you want to educate yourself further about FICO scores and credit in general: from the original FICO score company, Fair Isaac Corporation, www.myfico.com; and www.CardRatings.com.

Payment History

As you'd expect, the history of making timely payments (or not, if that's the case) makes up the largest part of a FICO score.

Following are some of the questions that are considered for this part of a FICO score:

- Did you make timely payments when paying specific types of accounts, such as mortgages, installment loans, or credit card accounts?

- Have you ever been through bankruptcy or had your wages garnished?

- How long has it been since you have been through a serious situation that's part of the public record?

- If applicable, how severe are your payment delinquencies?

♦ What amount is currently past due?

♦ How many past-due items are on your report?

♦ How many accounts have you paid as agreed? (Finally, a positive question! And hopefully your report shows a positive answer to this one.)

Amounts Owed

Okay, this can get a little tricky. Yes, it has to do with the amounts you owe on your accounts. But it also covers these areas:

♦ The amounts you owe on specific types of accounts. Example: You owe $250,000 on your mortgage.

♦ In some cases, the lack of a specific type of account. Example: You have no revolving accounts.

♦ The number of your accounts that have balances. Example: You have five accounts and four of them have balances.

♦ The proportion of your balances to your total credit limits (on some types of revolving accounts).

♦ The proportion of your balances owed when compared to the original loan amounts on *installment loans.*

All this talk about different types of loans can get confusing, so here's an example to make the last bullet point a little clearer. An installment loan is a debt that is paid at a regular interval over a period of time. So if you got an installment loan for a new car for $10,000 (good deal!) and you've paid off $5,000, then the "proportion" you still owe on this type of loan is 50 percent.

def•i•ni•tion

Installment loans are paid at regular intervals over predetermined periods of time. Mortgages and car loans are good examples.

If you originally owed $40,000 on another installment loan for a sailboat (after all, you saved a lot of money on your car!) and have paid off $10,000, then the proportion on your installment "type" loans is:

Original loan amount:	$10,000 + $40,000 = $50,000
Amount owed:	$5,000 + $30,000 = $35,000
Proportion of amount owed:	$35,000 ÷ $50,000 = .70, or 70 percent

So in this example, the proportion of your balance owed to the original loan amount on installment loans is 70 percent.

Length of Credit History

This one is pretty direct and answers the following questions:

◆ How long is your credit history? There's no absolute answer to how long is long enough, but if you've had credit for a few years, that's helpful.

◆ How long have your accounts been open?

◆ How long have *specific* accounts (such as revolving accounts or installment loans) been open?

◆ How much time has passed since there was any activity in your accounts?

New Credit

This part of your score is concerned with how many accounts you've opened recently. Also included is the following:

◆ The proportion of accounts you've recently opened (by type). For example, you've opened three accounts recently, two credit card accounts and one installment loan—two thirds of the accounts you've recently opened were for credit cards.

◆ The amount of time that has gone by between account openings (again, listed by type of account).

◆ The number of recent *credit inquiries*. This shows if you've been applying for a lot of new loans or credit card accounts.

◆ The amount of time that has gone by since the last credit inquiry.

◆ If you've rebuilt your credit, the amount of time that has passed since you had a poor credit history.

You probably didn't realize how complicated this part of a FICO score is. Many people think that just opening new lines of credit and getting more credit proves they are good credit risks. In reality, some of these decisions can give a FICO score a nice little ding in the wrong direction.

def•i•ni•tion

When someone applies for credit, the business that is considering lending the money sometimes contacts a credit bureau and asks for the borrower's credit report. This is called a **credit inquiry.** Only the inquiries that are related to credit applications (a "hard" inquiry) have the potential to reduce your score. So if you apply for a department store credit card, this results in a hard inquiry. A hard inquiry reduces your score a little. Note that the score is the result of a complex algorithm, so it's impossible to determine just how much your score will go down with each inquiry.

Types of Credit Used

A FICO score is affected by the number of different types of accounts a person has (for instance, consumer finance accounts, credit cards, mortgage, installment loans, or retail accounts). People who have credit that includes different types of loans (credit cards, car loans, and a mortgage) tend to have higher scores.

At the beginning of this chapter, we noted that the average consumer has 13 credit obligations. Typically, this number is comprised of nine credit cards and four installment loans.

Credit Reports Free to a Good Home

Yes, few things in life are free, but this is one of them!

There are three main credit bureaus: Equifax, Experian, and TransUnion. You're entitled to receive one free report every 12 months from each of the credit bureaus. AnnualCreditReport.com is a good site to visit to request your free reports because it is sponsored by all three credit bureaus.

You can request your report online, download a request form and then mail it in, or call a toll-free number, 1-877-322-8228. A report request by mail or phone takes a few weeks. An online report request is usually immediate once you've given identifying details about yourself.

Order a copy from each bureau. You want to check all three of them to see whether your credit information is correct across the board. Many times there are errors, which can give you an undeserved, lower FICO score. In fact, a 2004 study showed that 25 percent of credit reports contained errors serious enough to cause a consumer to be denied credit.

Note that your credit report does not contain your FICO score. For $47.85, you can order your FICO score (from all three credit bureaus) at myfico.com. And check out CardRatings.com for information on free credit score offers.

Your Rights and Your Credit Report

The Fair Credit Reporting Act (FCRA) was enacted to make sure that credit bureaus provide accurate information when a potential lender wants to review a report. The FCRA gives borrowers the right to get copies of their credit reports.

More rights under the FCRA are as follows:

◆ You have the right to know who has received your credit report in the past year.

◆ If your credit application is denied, the company that turned you down must tell you which credit bureau it contacted.

◆ If your credit application is denied due to something in your credit report, the credit bureau is required to send you a free copy of your report if you make the request within 60 days of being denied credit.

◆ When you have a dispute about an item on your report, the credit bureau is required to investigate the matter (unless the bureau considers the claim frivolous).

Mistakes on a Credit Report

How do mistakes creep into credit reports? It's sometimes a case of mistaken identity. Let's say that you applied for credit using names that don't exactly match. For example, you may have used "Jen Appleby" on one application but listed "Jennifer G. Appleby" on another one.

Maybe you wrote down your Social Security number wrong (it happens). Or perhaps the clerk at the lender's office entered it into the computer wrong. The same thing can happen with your account numbers. Human error can occur on either side of the lending equation.

In the Red

Don't assume that your credit reports are error-free. One of the reasons to check your reports regularly is so you can detect any errors as soon as possible. Under the Fair Credit Reporting Act of 2003, both the credit bureau and the organization involved with the errant report are responsible for fixing the mistake.

Fixing Mistakes on a Credit Report

If you find a mistake on your credit report, you should take action quickly so that it gets fixed before it causes a credit problem. Contact the credit bureau that made the error. Myfico.com recommends that you also contact the lender involved and make it clear that you're disputing the information in the report.

Here's where the Fair Credit Reporting Act is your friend. The credit bureau and the lender are responsible for investigating the error within 30 days. You must contact both parties in writing and be very clear about the data that you believe to be inaccurate. Then request the information to be either deleted or corrected.

Are you feeling intimidated about how to write a letter such as this? Lots of people feel the same way. Myfico.com will help you write the letter. There's a sample dispute letter on its website that guides you through the points you need to make.

> **Good Cents**
>
> Send your dispute letter by certified mail to both the credit bureau and the lender. Remember, the credit bureau and the lender have only 30 days to investigate your claim and let you know the outcome.
>
> By using certified mail, you'll know the exact date when it was received. If you aren't satisfied with the resolution, ask the credit bureau to include your statement about the dispute in your credit report. Experts say, though, that inserting this statement may not make a difference in the way lenders view your report. If this is a situation that's causing you harm, you may need to get a lawyer to resolve it.

What Else Is in a Credit Report?

Aside from the FICO score, there's personal information such as your name, address, birth date, and Social Security number. This comes directly from the information that you give to potential lenders or creditors when you apply for credit.

Other items in a credit report include:

- The lowdown on your accounts. This includes the types of accounts, when they were opened, your balance, and your payment history. You already know that this data is reflected in your score, but it's also listed in your report for lenders to see.

- All the credit inquiries. When you apply for credit, lenders look at your credit report. Your report shows who accessed this information within the last year.

The report shows "voluntary" and "involuntary" inquiries. Voluntary inquiries are those that you initiated yourself. For example, you wanted to buy a car and the inquiry was triggered.

Involuntary inquiries are performed by companies who want to give you credit although you didn't ask. You know those credit cards you get in the mail telling you that you've been preapproved for a $100,000 credit limit? We're exaggerating a little for effect, but you know the ones to which we're referring.

> **Hidden Treasure**
>
> Getting tired of all those preapproved credit cards you get in the mail? You can have your name removed from their lists by calling 1-888-567-8688.

◆ Anything on your public record. Credit bureaus get public information from state and county courts as well as from any records of overdue accounts that have been sent to debt collectors. This data includes bankruptcy proceedings, liens, wage garnishments, foreclosures, and judgments.

Scores Across America

The higher the score, the better. Scores greater than 720 are considered quite good. According to myfico.com, here's how scores look nationwide:

◆ Under 499: 2 percent

◆ 500–549: 5 percent

◆ 550–599: 8 percent

◆ 600–649: 12 percent

◆ 650–699: 15 percent

◆ 700–749: 18 percent

◆ 750–759: 27 percent

◆ 800 and higher: 13 percent

There's no particular low score that makes every lender always say, "No way!" But you can see that only 7 percent of America is in the "under 550" category. That's not a fun category to be in when you're trying to get a loan.

This is also true for P2P loans. In fact, Prosper doesn't allow anyone with a credit score less than 520 to borrow money. We'll cover the specific requirements for the P2P lending sites when we get to Part 2.

Hidden Treasure

Are you in the armed forces? When you're deployed, request for an active-duty alert to be placed in your credit report. This alert will keep you safe from identity theft while you're away.

All you have to do is call the toll-free number for one of the credit bureaus. (There's no need to call them all.) They're required by law to notify each other of changes in someone's credit report.

Equifax: 1-800-525-6285

Experian: 1-888-397-3742

TransUnion: 1-800-680-7289

How a FICO Score Affects Interest Rates

Let's take a look at how FICO scores impact interest rates for two different buyers, Sue and John. They each want to buy a new car. Sue has a credit score of 610. On a three-year, $25,000 loan, Sue pays around 14.11 percent interest with a monthly payment of $856. Yikes!

John, on the other hand, has a credit score of 750. On the same three-year, $25,000 loan, John gets an interest rate of 6.376 percent interest with a monthly payment of $765. That's $91 a month less than what Sue is paying. Over the course of the three years, John pays $3,276 less than Sue.

Check out the difference with a $300,000, 30-year fixed mortgage. Sue gets a 9.45 percent interest rate with a $2,512 monthly payment. John gets a 6.4 percent interest rate with a $1,807 monthly payment.

A great FICO score saves you money by helping you get a lower interest rate when you need a loan. As you'll see, this is also the case with P2P loans. Lenders will view you as a better risk, and you'll get better interest rates.

In the Red

If you're contacted by a company that claims to be able to fix a credit score, be wary. The Federal Trade Commission says these companies, often called credit clinics, charge for many things that you can do yourself—for free—to repair your credit. These credit clinics may also make fraudulent claims, such as saying they'll remove late payment histories. Some even offer to create a new identity and credit file for you. Run—don't walk—away from these companies.

Improving Your FICO Score

You can't fix your FICO score overnight, contrary to what some credit clinics claim. But you have to consider this challenge as a work in progress. There are steps to take to improve your score over time. If you're thinking about getting a P2P loan for something that's not absolutely necessary, such as remodeling your bathroom, and your FICO score is less than ideal, work on raising your score first. That way, you'll get a better interest rate and pay less for your new bathroom.

So you can't just say, "Sorry! I promise not to pay late ever again!" Just start paying your bills on time and you might see an improvement in a few months. But be aware: accounts that have gone to collection agencies stay on your report for seven years.

Try these tips for improving your score:

- Remember all that talk about proportions? Here's where you can use that to your advantage. Keep low balances on your cards, and ask for increases in your credit limits. The proportion of debt to your credit limit can raise your score. Remember, though, that you must have the discipline to not use that extra credit!

- If your payment history is the problem, pay your bills on time. If you can't meet your current expenses on your salary, then consider getting credit counseling (from a reputable counselor) and develop a plan. For help, check out the National Foundation for Credit Counseling's website at www.nfcc.org.

- Don't close credit cards thinking this will raise your score. It usually lowers your score because it adversely affects the proportion of your debt to your credit limits. Also, a closed account still shows up on your report.

- Don't suddenly open a lot of new credit card accounts. This approach can lower your score—especially if you're new to the credit world and don't have a solid credit history.

◆ If you get a P2P loan and successfully pay if off (with no late payments), it helps to improve your score over time.

Good Cents _____

If you're in debt way over your head, consider going to a credit counselor before you try P2P loans. A counselor can help you decide whether a P2P loan is a good risk for someone in your situation.

And even better, getting credit counseling does not affect your FICO score. Here's one caveat, however: the steps you take based on the advice of your counselor may affect your score. But just getting counseling so you can make an informed decision does not.

The Least You Need to Know

◆ A FICO score is comprised of your payment history, amounts owed, length of credit history, new credit, and types of credit used.

◆ You can obtain free credit reports from all three credit bureaus once per year.

◆ Credit bureaus and businesses that supply erroneous information on an account are obligated to investigate the situation and report to the person within 30 days.

◆ A higher credit score results in a loan with a lower interest rate.

◆ Don't get advice from credit clinics. Go to a reputable credit counselor for solid advice.

◆ Closing or opening accounts to improve a score can backfire. Improving your FICO score can take many months (sometimes years) and persistence.

Chapter 6

Beyond Your FICO Score: Interest Rates and More

In This Chapter

- ◆ Some basic facts about interest rates
- ◆ How the Federal Reserve's rate affects you
- ◆ Interest rates and state regulations
- ◆ How debt-to-income ratio is calculated and what it means to lenders
- ◆ Calculating estimated ROI

You now have a sound working knowledge of how a FICO score can affect someone's available interest rate—sound enough to entertain co-workers at your next company picnic! On second thought, you're not likely to have a captive audience unless you're the boss.

Now let's take one more step and examine how national interest rates affect the rate a person gets on a P2P loan. If you're a borrower, you want the best rate. If you're a lender, you want the best return. Once you have a good idea of how the system works, you can use that information to help you make the best financial decisions.

Interest Rates 101

There are so many rates to think about. Nothing involving the government is ever easy, right? It's easy to get confused, so here's a straightforward guide to help you keep track.

Hidden Treasure

In 1791, Treasury Secretary Alexander Hamilton urged Congress to establish the First Bank of the United States. But many Americans were uncomfortable with the idea of a large, powerful bank.

In 1811, its charter was revoked. In 1816, establishing a large U.S. bank was tried again and also failed. Apparently, Americans were still uncomfortable with a central bank having so much power.

In 1914, what we now know as the Federal Reserve was finally born. Later that year, 12 U.S. cities were chosen as sites for regional Reserve Banks just as Europe was entering World War I.

How the Federal Reserve Rate Affects You

Banks sometimes lend money to other banks, but don't let this worry you. This happens because the *Federal Reserve*, also known as the Fed, has the authority to decide how much money a bank has to keep in cash reserves. This is how the Federal Reserve controls the money supply. Relax—you don't have to put on your "economics" hat to understand how this game is played.

The interest rate that banks charge each other is called the *federal funds rate*. When banks have to borrow from the Fed, this rate is called the *discount rate*.

def•i•ni•tion

The **Federal Reserve** is the central bank of the United States. The Fed sets monetary policy by controlling the money supply and interest rates. Through controlling the money supply and interest rate, the Fed dampens inflation and improves recessions. Sometimes banks lend money to other banks. The rate that banks charge for this service is called the **federal funds rate.** And sometimes banks have to borrow money from the Fed. The Fed gives other banks a special interest rate, called the **discount rate.**

When the Fed raises or lowers its rate, it has an impact on the rate at which people can borrow money. When the Fed changes the rate, it affects the economy. And that affects you and your wallet.

Here's how it works when the Fed wants to raise interest rates:

- ◆ The Fed sells *bonds* in the open market, causing the supply of bonds to increase. This causes the supply of money to go down because money has been spent on the bonds. When the supply of money goes down, the banks have less to lend. So the banks raise their rates and borrowing money becomes more expensive.

- ◆ The Fed also raises the discount rate and the federal funds rate. Together, these actions cause banks to have less money to lend—which makes it more expensive for the bank to lend money. Thus, borrowers have to pay a higher interest rate.

Here's how it affects you. Let's say the Fed's rate is 2 percent. For banks to make money, they have to charge higher than the 2 percent rate that they have to pay.

When the funds rate or the discount rate starts to rise, this usually affects interest rates you pay on your credit card (which probably has a variable interest rate). You still want to buy that new car? Well, now it costs more because you'll have to pay more in interest.

def•i•ni•tion

When a corporate or governmental entity needs money, it sometimes sells **bonds**. People purchase bonds for a specified amount of time and at a fixed interest rate. These features make bonds a fixed-income security. The bond holder also receives interest income.

This technique is used to battle inflation. In this situation, a lot of people simply decide not to buy that car. Demand decreases, and so do prices.

Hidden Treasure

On September 11, 2001, the Fed played an important role after New York City, Washington, D.C., and Pennsylvania experienced terrorist attacks. The Fed lowered interest rates and loaned more than $45 billion to financial institutions.

By the end of September, this action had stabilized U.S. financial markets. This was no small task, considering the extent of the crisis.

Here's how it works when the Fed wants to lower rates:

- The Fed buys bonds in the open market, causing the supply of bonds to decrease. This causes the supply of money to go up because people and banks now have fewer bonds and more money.

  When the supply of money goes up, the banks have more to lend. So the banks lower their rates—and borrowing money becomes less expensive.

- The Fed also lowers the discount rate and the federal funds rate. Together, these actions cause banks to have more money to lend. So the money they have to lend becomes less expensive (hence, a lower interest rate for you).

- Here's how it affects you: with more cash available to banks for lending, the Fed's rate falls and so do the interest rates on most loans and credit cards. More people start spending again because goods cost less.

This technique is used during a recession to get people spending. When people spend, companies start hiring, too. Everyone's happy—at least until all this good fortune creates inflation!

Hidden Treasure

How does excessive spending create inflation? When people start spending their money, supplies of goods decrease. For example, let's assume that everyone suddenly wanted to buy a Porsche (well, we can all dream, right?). During a recession, no one is buying Porsches, so the price goes down in order to sell the cars in inventory. People then start buying Porsches at low prices.

This makes the supply of Porsches go down, so the car dealers start raising the prices so they can meet the demand. Those willing to pay more get the cars. This causes inflation to hit the price of Porsches.

You've probably seen the term *prime rate* as well. This is the rate that banks charge their best customers—the customers who have really good credit. These customers get a better rate because they're dependable and the banks trust that they'll get their money back.

If you're a *default risk*, however, you don't get a prime rate. You'll end up paying more. The bank is taking a risk on you, so it charges you a higher rate. Well, guess what? This is also how rates work in P2P lending, but because the arrangement is between a borrower and a lender (or 10), there's a chance for a better rate. You're kind of outsmarting the banks.

def•i•ni•tion

If you're a credit-worthy customer, your bank will charge you the **prime rate.** Your **default risk** can determine your interest rate. You get a higher rate if the bank believes you'll default on, or fail to pay back, the loan.

What This Means for P2P Loans

If you're the borrower, you might be considering a P2P loan because your credit card interest is too high. The interest rate on your credit card typically hinges first on the Fed's rate and second on your credit rating.

A lender, on the other hand, wants to get a decent return—unless you're getting the loan from Aunt Lucille. Hopefully Aunt Lucille likes you enough to give you a minimum rate.

Anyway, the Fed does set the rate upon which all other rates are based—which in turn affects how P2P lending decisions are made. And like the bank, if you're the lender, you can ask for a higher rate if you think the borrower's credit is suspect.

But don't fret if you're the borrower in this situation because even then, you're likely to get a better rate than you would from your bank.

Good Cents

Check out Bankrate.com's Interest Rate Roundup every week for the latest rates on mortgages, CDs, auto loans, home equity products, and credit cards. The numbers are based on Bankrate's national surveys of large banks and thrifts (smaller community banks focused on taking deposits and lending money for home mortages; also known as "savings and loan" associations). Visit Bankrate at www.bankrate.com/brm/static/rate-roundup.asp.

If you're looking specifically for credit card rate information, visit CardRatings.com.

How State Usury Laws Affect Interest Rates on P2P Loans

In Chapter 4, we discussed state usury laws in the context of how some of these laws protect consumers. Remember that not all states have these laws, and some that do have umpteen exceptions. In some cases, how a borrower's state operates regarding usury limits can prevent someone from getting a P2P loan.

For instance, Pennsylvania's usury laws cap interest rates for loans under $50,000 at 6 percent. That sounds good on the surface if you're the borrower. But these days, try getting a loan from a bank at 6 percent. (And it's tough getting a rate like that on a P2P site, as well.) In such a case, the borrower is out of luck and can't get a loan—not even if he or she is willing to pay a higher interest rate to get that loan.

Banks are getting stingy these days and are less willing to take a risk if they are unsure the consumer will repay the loan. The bank may decide that a loan with 16 percent interest is worthless if the consumer defaults. In that case, the bank forgoes lending the money.

These usury laws differ by state, and in many cases there are multiple exceptions to the rule. Sometimes you need to consult with an attorney to sort through the legal exceptions to see what the rate actually is. As we discussed in Chapter 4, these rates tend to change quite a bit, so always follow up and see if your state's laws have changed or been updated. Whether you're the borrower or the lender, be aware of your state's usury laws. As a lender, these rates are important so you can determine if it limits your opportunity for interest income.

What's Your Debt-to-Income Ratio?

The debt-to-income (DTI) ratio compares the amount of money earned to the amount of money owed to creditors. This number is mainly used to determine mortgage eligibility, but lenders on P2P sites also look at this number along with credit rating.

What do lenders see with this ratio? The DTI ratio paints a picture of spending habits. This ratio is the opposite of the FICO score in that a lower DTI ratio is better. Lenders prefer a score of 36 percent or less. But some P2P lending websites require a minimum DTI to qualify for a loan.

Good Cents _____

Visit www.bankrate.com/brm/calc/ratio-debt-calculator.asp to use Bankrate's DTI calculator and get your ratio in seconds. The lower you keep this number, the more attractive you'll look to lenders.

For example, Lending Club now requires borrowers to have a DTI of less than 25 percent. You may see other sites moving toward a DTI requirement. This is a way that sites can help protect their lenders. A low DTI sometimes (although not always!) decreases risk.

For this calculation, add all of your monthly obligations—focusing on recurring expenses such as mortgage payments and loans. This calculation doesn't include expenses such as entertainment or groceries. Having to buy a new dishwasher doesn't fall in this category, and neither do the new clothes you bought for vacation.

We're just talking about recurring, monthly obligations. Let's examine James, for example. James makes $72,000 per year as a manager for a paper products company. Here's a simple way to calculate his DTI ratio:

◆ Gross monthly income: $6,000

◆ *Recurring debt* expenses: $2,200

◆ Debt-to-income ratio: 36.7 percent ($2,200 ÷ $6,000)

def•i•ni•tion

A payment on a debt that occurs on a continuing basis is called a **recurring debt**. Examples include child support, mortgage payments, and installment loans. The more recurring debt a borrower has, the higher his or her DTI ratio will be.

An acceptable ratio is less than 36 percent, so our pal James is doing pretty well. There are more complicated ways to calculate this. For instance, some formulas use net income because gross income exaggerates the amount of money you actually have to spend. But for getting a P2P loan or, if you're the lender, analyzing a borrower's loan request listing, the basic formula suffices.

How does this affect your ability to attract loans? Well, if your ratio is more than 40 percent, lenders will worry that you might not be able to meet a monthly loan obligation. At 50 percent, you're living pretty dangerously. There's not a lot of room for error there. What if you lose your job or have a health crisis? If you're the lender and you see a high DTI ratio, these are the kinds of questions that should cross your mind—and rightfully so. And if you're a lender on a P2P lending site that allows you to question borrowers, ask the borrower why his or her DTI is so high.

In the Red

A DTI ratio of greater than 36 percent sends a warning signal to lenders. This tells lenders that your spending habits are too high for your income. When you want to borrow from P2P lenders, they will be looking at this ratio.

When you add another recurring debt, your ratio creeps even higher. Consider what James's ratio would be if he got a $4,500 loan for a monthly payment of $146.49:

- Loan request: $4,500

- Gross monthly income: $6,000

- Recurring expenses: $2,346.49 ($2,200 + 146.49*)

- Debt-to-income ratio: 39.11 percent ($2,346.49 ÷ $6,000)

Assuming James has an A credit rating and gets a 10.61 percent interest rate (per Prosper's average rates for an A credit rating in the $1,000 to $5,000 range).

This puts James in marginal territory. Even with good credit, a DTI ratio this high will likely drive up his interest rate a little. And if you're the lender, you'll see this high ratio and be concerned that James might end up skipping out on the payments. If James can lower this ratio a bit, he'll get a better deal with a P2P loan. And he'll certainly be more attractive to you, the lender.

You can make a ton of money and still have a poor ratio. Or you can make only $30,000 a year, borrow sensibly, and have a great ratio. So take a look at your DTI ratio before you ask for a P2P loan. Lenders will definitely be looking at your ratio.

If your FICO score is a little iffy, a healthy DTI ratio might work in your favor. How can you get a better DTI ratio? Don't *add* more recurring debt, for one thing. Paying down the debt you currently have will help.

Here are a few more tips:

- Your car broke down and you're thinking of buying a new one. If your old car is salvageable, get it repaired and don't take on a new recurring debt.

- Step away from the credit card—far, far away. When you're trying to decrease your DTI ratio, you don't need to put a new red sofa on your credit card.

- If you've gotten into credit card debt, keep making your payments on time. And when you can, throw some extra money at paying down your accounts. Cut corners in other areas, such as driving expenses. Walk instead of drive to save on gas. The sooner you pay down your cards, the sooner your ratio will rise. Visit CardRatings.com for more helpful tips on this subject.

- Save for a rainy day. This might sound trite, but having some money socked away for an emergency can mean the difference between paying cash to get the old car repaired instead of having to charge the expense.

If you're a lender, looking at the borrower's DTI ratio should be an important part of reviewing a loan listing. We'll get into that in more detail in Chapter 18 when we talk about checklists, but for now, just know that this number can be very revealing of a person's spending habits.

What's Your Return on Investment?

Return on investment (ROI) is another complex-sounding term that's actually not complex at all. In the world of finance, ROI is known as a "performance measure." ROI is a ratio that measures the benefit of an investment. If the ROI is positive, it's a good investment. If it's negative, it's not a good investment. See how easy that is?

Here's the basic calculation:

$$\text{ROI} = \frac{(\text{Cost} + \text{Gain from Investment}) - \text{Cost of Investment}}{\text{Cost of Investment}}$$

The ROI formula has been known to be meddled with a little. That is, the flexibility that makes the ROI formula so easy to use also makes it easy to manipulate.

Good Cents _____

Calculating ROI is a valuable tool for lenders. As a lender, you'll most likely invest in several different loans—maybe even on several different P2P lending websites. Take the time to calculate the ROI for every loan. The results give you valuable information to use while making investment decisions on P2P loans in the future.

For instance, depending on what you include in "gains" and "costs," the number may vary. But as a lender, you can use this as a tool to help you decide whether your P2P loans are bringing in returns.

For instance, you loan a borrower a total of $500 and get back your money plus $25 in interest. Your ROI is 5 percent ($25 ÷ $500 = .05, or 5 percent). You can calculate the ROI for your entire portfolio.

At the time this book was written, the average yield on a money market account and savings account was around 3 to 4 percent. So in the example, 5 percent is a better return than what you can currently get in a money market or savings account in a bank.

What's the bottom line for lenders? You want to make sure you're coming out ahead. Otherwise, P2P lending isn't worth the risk. Remember, when your money is in the bank, it's FDIC insured, so there's little risk you'll lose your funds.

The Least You Need to Know

- ◆ The Fed's rate affects the rate you can get if you borrow money.

- ◆ The Fed sets monetary policy by controlling the money supply and interest rates.

- ◆ State usury laws affect interest rates.

- ◆ The debt-to-income ratio reflects a person's spending habits.

- ◆ The return on investment calculation helps a lender decide whether he or she is getting a good return on an investment.

Part 2

Prime-Time Players in the P2P Marketplace

Now it's time to plunge into P2P lending websites. You'll see that there's quite a bit of variety in the way these sites are set up. Some sites are general and welcome all types of loans, while others specialize in certain kinds of loans.

In Part 2, you learn about the most popular P2P websites on the Internet. To make the choice easier for you, we end this part with advice on how to pick the site that best meets your needs and financial goals.

"Try Googling 'fairy godmother' and 'college loan.'"

Chapter 7

Prosper.com

In This Chapter

- ◆ How Prosper.com makes money
- ◆ Borrowing on Prosper.com
- ◆ Making loans and bidding on Prosper.com
- ◆ How late fees and defaults are handled on Prosper.com

Okay, now let's dive in and take a close look at the major players in the P2P lending marketplace. First, we take a look at Prosper. Prosper.com began in 2006 under the guidance of CEO Chris Larsen, formerly the cofounder, chairman, and CEO of E-LOAN. Prosper offers "direct" loans and is the largest of the current slate of P2P lending sites.

How does the P2P loan process at Prosper work? Let's say that Lauren is an entrepreneur who needs $2,500 to expand her bakery business. She becomes a member of Prosper, and her loan request gets funded by a number of different lenders. Prosper processes the loan and sends the money to Lauren's bank account.

This scenario is considered a direct loan because the lenders set up accounts with Prosper that contain funds for lending. When the borrower's loan gets funded, the cash from the lender's Prosper account gets transferred to the borrower's bank account. Technically, Prosper is the go-between, but compared to some other methods of P2P lending, this approach is pretty direct.

Borrowers create listings requesting loans. Lenders look at the loan listings and decide which loans they're interested in funding. We'll look at the borrowing and lending process at Prosper from both perspectives so you have a clear vision of how it all works. Frequently, borrowers also become lenders (and vice versa).

We've mentioned how fast the P2P lending industry is growing. On Prosper's website, go to the Help page, look for the Other Topics section, and click "What's new on Prosper?" Here, you'll find recent financial updates as well as other new, important updates that you might need to know.

Eligibility Requirements

To be a borrower on Prosper, you have to be a U.S. resident, have a FICO score of at least 520, have a bank account, and have a Social Security number. Once your identity is verified by Prosper, you may borrow between $1,000 and $25,000. The loans are unsecured, so no collateral is needed.

> **Hidden Treasure**
>
> You can also join a Prosper group or even start your own. Groups can consist of borrowers, lenders, or both. Groups have higher funding rates and are rated by the group's collective performance on repaying loans. We go into detail about groups on Prosper in Chapter 16.

To be a lender on Prosper, you have to be a U.S. resident, have a bank account, and have a Social Security number. You also have to prove your identity, just as the borrower does. And once that step is done, you may become a lender. Note that the loans are unsecured, which increases your risk.

You can lend as little as $50 or as much as $25,000. But we certainly don't recommend lending $25,000 to one borrower. In fact, we encourage you to spread out your risk and bid around $50 to $100 for each loan. You'll find out about all the risks involved with P2P lending and take a quiz to help you decide how much risk you can tolerate in Chapter 23.

How Prosper Makes Money

Remember talking about how people like the transparency in P2P lending? Prosper makes it clear that there are no hidden charges for lending or borrowing through the site. What you're charged as a borrower depends on your credit grade and the loan amount. Lenders pay an annual servicing fee. Let's take a look at Prosper's charges for borrowers first.

Borrower Fees

You knew there was no such thing as a free lunch, right? Still, this isn't too bad. There's a *closing fee*, and how much you pay depends on your credit rating. Prosper has its own rating system that corresponds with the borrower's FICO score. You've read the chapter on FICO scores, so you're kind of an expert now.

def•i•ni•tion

The loan **closing fee** is what borrowers pay as the cost of obtaining a loan.

Prosper's credit rating system is as follows:

Grade:	AA	A	B	C	D	E	HR
Score:	760 and higher	720–759	680–719	640–679	600–639	560–599	520–559

Note that if your score is below 520, you're not eligible to borrow money on Prosper. A 520 score qualifies you for the HR category, which stands for "high risk."

Your closing fee is $25 or a percentage based on credit rating, whichever is higher. The percentages are as follows:

- AA: 2 percent closing fee
- A–B: 2 percent closing fee
- C–HR: 3 percent closing fee

Here's an example of how it works:

Maggie has a C credit rating and wants to borrow $5,000 to pay off high-interest credit cards.

Maggie will be charged $5,000 × .03, or $150. This means that the loan amount she'll receive is $4,850, not $5,000. If that extra $150 is vital to Maggie, she should ask for a loan amount that covers the closing fee.

Let's look at Sam, who has an A credit rating. Sam wants a loan for $17,000 to consolidate his credit card debt. He'll pay $340 in closing costs ($17,000 × .02). If he needs exactly $17,000 to consolidate his debt, he should ask for around $17,340 to cover closing costs.

What about other costs? If you ever have insufficient funds in your account to make a payment, then you'll be charged $15 for a failed payment fee. If your payment is 15 days late, you're charged a late fee, the greater of $15 or 5 percent of the unpaid installment amount; this amount is passed on to the lender. Prosper maintains a strict "late fee" schedule.

On the other hand, you get a 1 percent discount if you pay your loan via electronic funds transfer (EFT).

Lender Fees

On Prosper, lenders pay a 1 percent *annual serving fee*. A lender's annual serving fee is accrued daily and is based on the current outstanding loan principal. This amount changes daily because the fee is based on an amortized amount over the life of the loan. Amortized loans are those that require payments to include both principal and interest.

def•i•ni•tion

The **annual serving fee** is what lenders pay to reimburse Prosper for collecting loan payments.

There are also collection agency recovery fees. If one of your loans becomes more than a month late, Prosper sends the loan to a collection agency to collect the debt. Fee structures for agencies vary, but count on agencies taking between 15 and 30 percent of the funds they recover on your behalf.

How Prosperous Is Prosper?

When it comes to financial stuff, it's usually easier to see the big picture with a chart. Here's a snapshot of Prosper's financials since it opened its virtual doors in 2006:

Prosper.com	May 2008	Since Inception
New members	33,050	725,763
Funded loans	$9.6 million	$147 million
Number of loans	1,603	23,302
Average loan size	$5,989	$6,303

It's easy to see that Prosper is experiencing continual growth in P2P lending. Note that although a borrower can get up to a $25,000 loan, the average loan size has stayed around $6,000 since inception.

So, You Want to Borrow Money?

If you want to borrow money via Prosper, start by going to Prosper's webpage and clicking "Join Now." Like most P2P sites, Prosper does not charge a membership fee. You'll be asked to give your name and e-mail address and to choose a screen name and a password. Once your registration is confirmed by e-mail, you're eligible to be either a borrower or a lender.

What about privacy? Prosper and WebBank both have privacy policies that protect your identity. You can decide how much private information to disclose. Prosper does show data regarding a borrower's credit score and anything else that might be pertinent to the borrower's credit history. This is necessary for lenders to make decisions about their funding choices.

Here are some of the legal agreements you'll be asked to review and agree to before becoming a borrower:

◆ Borrower registration agreement. This agreement is pretty long and comprehensive. Some of the points covered include giving Prosper the right to obtain your credit report, what it means when you make a loan request, and what your obligations as a borrower are.

◆ A *promissory note*. This comes at the end of the borrower registration agreement. The promissory note signifies your commitment to repay any money that you borrow.

def•i•ni•tion

Each borrower on Prosper signs a **promissory note**, which is basically an agreement to repay the loan.

◆ Credit profile authorization. This provides Prosper and WebBank with the authorization to view the borrower's credit report.

◆ Debit authorization. This authorizes Prosper to debit your account for the monthly payment on your loan. It spells out the amount and the date your account will be debited. Double check your bank account number.

Requesting a Loan

You must be approved by Prosper's anti-fraud and identification systems before you can proceed. Once that's done, you can ask for a loan. Here are the terms of the loans available on Prosper:

def•i•ni•tion

A **fully amortized** loan involves scheduled regular payments that include both interest and principal.

◆ Length: 3 years

◆ *Fully amortized* loan

◆ Unsecured, no collateral needed

◆ Amount: $1,000 to $25,000

Creating a Listing

Never divulge your full name and street address when you create your loan listing. Lenders will have access to your financial information, and that's what they need to make a decision. When you create the listing, you'll decide how much money you want to borrow and what interest rate you're willing to pay.

Many of the attributes that make a loan listing successful are common across the P2P lending sites. That's why we give this topic extra special attention in Chapter 13.

Signing for Your Loan

If all goes well, you'll get an e-mail from Prosper notifying you that your loan is ready to be funded. Follow the link in the e-mail *within seven days*. If you don't sign the loan within this time period, your loan gets cancelled. That would be a bummer.

Good Cents

How do you sign an e-mail? When you click "Sign and fund loan" in the e-mail message, you'll see a Truth in Lending Disclosure statement for your loan. You'll then confirm your bank account number where the money will be deposited before electronically signing each of the promissory notes for your loan.

So, You Want to Lend Money?

First, you have to be a registered member with Prosper to bid on loans. So if you haven't already registered, click "Join Now," which is conveniently placed on every page of the site. You have to set up your lender account so that your funds are available for loans. Once you've transferred funds, you're ready to bid (well, after you read the next section!).

Hidden Treasure

As we were finishing up this book, Prosper announced it had filed a registration statement with the Securities and Exchange Commission (SEC) to offer (and sell) promissory notes to lenders on its website. Remember the secondary lending market we mentioned in Chapter 1? This registration is a requirement for entering that arena. During the quiet period, Prosper isn't allowed to speak with the press or accept new lenders. But by the time you buy this book, Prosper will most likely be out of its quiet period and have a platform to accommodate secondary lending.

As we mentioned in Chapter 1, in a secondary lending market, lenders are allowed to buy and sell loans to other lenders on the site. This is a new trend in P2P lending. It gives lenders a way to get their money back before the maturity dates of borrowers' loans.

First, you have to browse the loan listings. Here's a sample of what they look like on Prosper:

LISTING SUMMARY

PAYING MY PARENTS BACK
$4,000 @ 12.45%

FUNDING: 17% funded
BIDS: 4 bids

CREDIT PROFILE

| A credit grade | 29% DTI |

LISTING SUMMARY

DEBT CONSOLIDATION
$3,000 @ 9.25%

FUNDING: 7% funded
BIDS: 2 bids

CREDIT PROFILE

AA credit grade	32% DTI

LISTING SUMMARY

REMODELING OUR RESTAURANT
$10,000 @ 19%

FUNDING: 75% funded
BIDS: 25 bids

CREDIT PROFILE

C credit grade	39% DTI

Note that in the first loan, it says the loan is 17 percent funded. On Prosper, there's a bar graph that shows how much of the loan is funded.

def•i•ni•tion

The **annual percentage rate (APR)** differs from the borrower's rate because it includes one-time fees. The APR measures the cost of credit at an annual rate.

When you click on a loan, you get more details. You see how many hours are left to bid, the borrower's *annual percentage rate* (*APR*), a funding forecast, and a rate comparison chart. The funding forecast shows the level of funding the loan has received each day. The rate comparison graph shows the listing's interest rate and compares it to a 90-day history of other loans with similar attributes, such as the same amount, credit grade, group memberships (if applicable), and so on.

If you're a registered lender, you're able to see what questions were asked by other potential lenders and how the borrower answered them.

Start the Bidding!

Prosper uses an auction-style platform for bidding on loans. If you're a veteran of eBay, you already understand this concept. But don't worry if you've never made a bid on a piece of popcorn that looks like New England quarterback Tom Brady (which, by the way, would probably cost a lot).

After you select a loan you want to bid on, you need to decide what rate you'll bid. Uh, how do you decide that?

First, take a look at the maximum rate the borrower is willing to take. Then, you need to take a look at the borrower's credit rating. Remember Lauren the baker? Let's say you want to bid $100 on her $2,500 loan. Lauren has a B credit rating. According to Prosper's "Marketplace Performance" information page, B borrowers with loans less than $5,000 …

- ◆ Have a net default rate of 2.48 percent.

- ◆ Get an average lender rate of 11.79 percent.

- ◆ Earn an average annual return of 8.41 percent for their lenders.

Prosper notes that these numbers are based on historical data and your experience may not mirror these numbers. Remember, lending is a risk. But this information enables you to make an educated decision about the risk. This information also gives you an idea of what's an appropriate rate to bid.

But you also want to check out the borrower's other financial information before placing a bid. Does the borrower have a debt-to-income (DTI) ratio of more than 36 percent? If so, that could increase the risk of default. On Prosper, you can send the borrower questions about his or her finances. Don't hesitate to do so. The borrower's answers can help you make a better decision. If the person doesn't respond, well … maybe that tells you something, too!

Two Ways to Bid

Bidding on loans is an easy concept to master. There are two ways to go about this. You can make manual bids or use a portfolio approach.

If you use a manual bid:

- ◆ Click the "Bid Now" button.

- Enter the amount you want to bid, which will be somewhere between $50 and the entire amount of the loan.

- Enter the minimum rate you're willing to bid. Note that if you're one of the winning bidders, the interest rate you receive will likely be higher than the one you bid. Prosper bids down the rate on your behalf, so that's why this happens.

Now when you bid, funds from your account are set aside. You can't change your mind about the bid once you've entered it. But if your bid isn't chosen as a winning bid, the funds are available once again and you can bid on another loan. Other lenders' bids aren't shown, so there's no way to know when you make the bid whether you're outbidding someone else. Make the bid you're comfortable with. If you're not a winner, move on to another loan.

It's possible to be a partial winner. This probably seems like a strange concept to you because we're all used to winning or losing. On eBay, for instance, you don't get to partially own that antique table. You either win the auction outright or you lose.

Being a partial winner on a Prosper bid means that you were outbid for the most part—but that part of your bid is being used to fund the loan. If you bid $100 and $50 of your bid is being used to fund the loan, then the remaining $50 goes back into your lender's fund to use on another loan. So congratulations—you're a partial winner!

If this manual process seems like a headache to you, then try the portfolio approach. In Prosper's world, a portfolio plan is a tool you can use to automatically bid on listings that contain your predetermined criteria.

For example, you can set up your criteria so that you don't bid on anyone with a credit grade of less than A or with a DTI ratio greater than 35 percent. Or you can set it up so you go as low as C-grade borrowers but only those who have DTI ratios of less than 30 percent. Pretty cool, huh?

More benefits of using the portfolio approach include the following:

- Obviously, this saves you time.

- You have control over the criteria.

- You can build a portfolio of loans quickly.

- You can diversify with smaller loans.

Prosper has templates you can use that range from conservative to aggressive. Here's how the estimated returns work out with portfolio plans:

- Conservative (very low risk): 5.4 percent

- Balanced (low risk): 7.82 percent

- Moderate (medium risk): 8.78 percent

- Aggressive (high risk): 9.69 percent

- Start from scratch (unknown risk): you can devise your own criteria; your estimated return is unpredictable

Notice that the higher the risk, the greater the return. But the higher the risk, the greater the chance of default. You know how this works from our earlier discussion about interest rates, so this isn't a surprise. It's just another situation where you have to decide what's best for you.

Nothing is written in stone, either. You have control over your portfolio, and you can make changes whenever you want. You can even override your portfolio plan and make a manual bid on a loan that didn't meet your specified criteria. But remember, once a bid on a loan is made, you can't take back the bid. You have to wait and see whether you're one of the winners before you can use that money anywhere else.

Bid Histories

You can follow the funding process of a loan on Prosper.com. You can view the bid history and see how much of the loan is funded and what the bid amounts are.

Here's an example from Prosper's website: the borrower has requested $1,000 with a starting rate of 9 percent. The loan got funded by three lenders at a rate of 8 percent.

Take a look at the bid history:

Lender	Rate	Bid Rate	Amount Bid	Winning	Status
#1	8 percent	6 percent	$250	$250	√
#2	8 percent	7 percent	$500	$500	√
#3	8 percent	8 percent	$400	$250	√ (and X)
#4	9 percent	9 percent	$500	$0	X
Starting rate	9 percent				

Remember that bids aren't actually shown in real listings. We show them here to give you an idea of how this auction system works. In reality, you bid and then have to wait and see whether your bid wins. You never know the rate of the winning bids.

Look at Lender #3's row. This is an example of a lender partially winning a bid. The lender participates in the loan with an 8 percent rate. Now, because this is the first bid to "lose," the rate is set at 8 percent.

This is the opposite of eBay in that the highest bid (in this case, the rate) doesn't win. The system favors lower bids and gives a nod to lenders who jump in early with bids. Lender #4 bid a 9 percent rate. That's higher than the 8 percent set by the losing bid.

Don't spend time trying to beat the system. Give an honest bid, and move on if you don't win. There are many variables involved, but the system is set up to achieve fairness for the borrower and the lenders.

When you do win, your funds are transferred from your Prosper account to the borrower's account. This doesn't occur until the borrower signs the promissory note. Prosper then transfers the loan amount to the borrower using the Automated Clearing House banking system.

Your loan begins accruing interest on the business day following the funds transfer, which is considered the origination date of the loan. The monthly payment date is the same day of the month as the origination date. For example, if the origination date is August 15th, then the loan payment will be due every month on the 15th. The borrower will make payments on September 15th, October 15th, and so on.

What if the origination date is August 31st? The payment dates are the day closest to that date. So the payment in September is due on the 30th.

Payment Status

No one wants to be on either end of a late payment. If you're the borrower, you have a big problem if you signed a promissory note and now can't deliver the goods. If you're the lender, well … it's annoying if the payment is a little late. And it's beyond annoying when it's more than a month late.

Prosper classifies payments as follows:

- ◆ Origination delayed: The funds transfer didn't go as planned, and it will be delayed a day or two. If problems remain, your funds are returned to your account and you can use them on a new loan. Not a big deal.

- Current: The borrower is current, and everyone is happy.

- Late (less than 15 days): The borrower is in the grace period. It's too early to get nervous (or annoyed).

- Late: The borrower is between 15 days and 1 month late and is charged a late payment fee. It's okay to start frowning at this point.

- One month late: The borrower is between one month and two months late. Prosper sends the loan to a collection agency. Go ahead and get annoyed.

- Two months late: The borrower is between two months and three months late. Time to start worrying.

- Three months late: The borrower is between three months and four months late.

- Four or more months late: The borrower is between four months and five months late.

- Defaulted: This is a word neither borrowers nor lenders like to hear. The loan is now written off for nonpayment.

- Payoff in progress: A good sign! A payment has been made to start the payoff process.

- Paid: A beautiful-sounding word for both sides of the deal. The loan is paid in full.

- Cancelled: The loan was cancelled or repurchased from the lenders by Prosper. One situation that would trigger a repurchase of the loan is if the borrower committed identity fraud.

Prosper sends monthly statements as well as year-end statements to borrowers and lenders. Hang on to any documentation you receive. We discuss the tax implications in detail in Chapter 17 (for borrowers) and in Chapter 24 (for lenders).

The Least You Need to Know

- Prosper.com is the largest P2P lending marketplace.

- You must have a FICO score of 520 to be eligible for a loan on Prosper.

- Your identity will be verified before you're allowed to borrow or lend money.

◆ Borrowers are charged closing fees based on their credit ratings.

◆ Lenders are charged a 1 percent annual servicing fee.

◆ Prosper uses an auction-style format for bids on loans.

◆ Late fees are given to the lenders, but collection fees for defaulted loans come from the lender's pocket.

8

P2P Lending Sites and Microfinance

In This Chapter

◆ How P2P lending is connected to microfinance

◆ Lending money through Kiva.org

◆ Why MicroPlace.com refers to lenders as "retail investors"

◆ Lending money on MicroPlace.com

◆ Learning about microfinance on MicrofinanceGateway.org

In this chapter, we take a look at how P2P lending has become a part of microfinance. What is microfinance? It's a way to help entrepreneurs in poor countries. It's based on the concept that if you give someone a little help, that person will be motivated to do what it takes to improve his or her life. The loan amounts are small, hence the term *microfinance*.

It's a powerful tool that's believed to be helping those in undeveloped countries. You'll learn about microfinance and how P2P lending is involved as we discuss Kiva.org, MicroPlace.com, and MicrofinanceGateway.org.

Kiva.org

Looking at Kiva's mission statement is a good way to get a feel for its priorities: "Kiva's mission is to connect people through lending for the sake of alleviating poverty."

Kiva, Swahili for "unity," launched in October 2005 and calls itself "the world's first person-to-person microlending Web site." *Microlending* is a part of microfinance. This is also known as *microcredit* because the loans are so small.

On Kiva, you'll find entrepreneurs from developing countries. You'll find men and women who run butcher shops, clothing stores, and grocery stores in places such as Peru or Cambodia.

Kiva partners with *microfinance institutions* (MFI) to make these small loans to entrepreneurs. The MFIs are responsible for choosing entrepreneurs for Kiva loans. The MFI partners send the entrepreneurs' profiles to Kiva's website, where lenders can read about them and decide whether they'd like to help.

def•i•ni•tion

Microfinance involves giving small loans or financial services to the poor. A **microfinance institution (MFI)** is an organization that provides microfinance services.

Getting a small loan is also called getting **microcredit**, and giving a small loan is called **microlending**.

Lenders don't make money lending on Kiva, but we've included a discussion about Kiva because the driving force behind Kiva is also at the very core of P2P lending. The reason lenders come to sites such as Kiva is because they want to do something meaningful with their money. And Kiva is a P2P lending site where a lender can make a difference with a small amount of money.

Kiva is a U.S. 501(c)3 nonprofit organization. This means it is recognized for tax purposes as a nonprofit organization. This certainly makes sense because the goal of Kiva is to help the working poor.

Target Market

Unlike most P2P lending sites, Kiva is for lenders only. So if you have a few bucks to spare and you'd like to help someone in a developing country, you might consider becoming a lender. Loan amounts are small ($25, for example), so you don't have to be Warren Buffett or Ted Turner to get in on the action.

Basically, you need an Internet connection and a credit card to qualify as a lender on Kiva.

Hidden Treasure

The World Bank defines poverty as living on less than $1.25 per day. Current estimates show that 1.4 billion people are below this poverty line. On the positive side, the World Bank says that the fight against poverty is showing some progress.

This is why microlending can have a huge impact on entrepreneurs in poor countries. For those living on $1.25 per day, receiving $25 from a lender can help them succeed and make better lives for themselves and their families.

How It Works

The MFIs are considered "field partners," and Kiva has more than 90 field partners in 43 countries. The field partners not only find the entrepreneurs who are good risks for Kiva loans, but the partners also frequently help the entrepreneurs. For example, they might provide some kind of training that will help an entrepreneur succeed.

As you can imagine, these field partners are important to your success as a lender. In fact, when you browse the listings, you'll want to check out who the field partners are. Risk ratings are maintained on the field partners so you can get an idea of which MFIs have chosen successful entrepreneurs.

Good Cents _____

You can also help out Kiva by getting a credit card called the Kiva Advanta BusinessCard. If you make a grant using the card, Advanta matches your grant dollar for dollar (there is a monthly limit on the matched amount). Visit CardRatings.com or Kivab4b.org for more details.

So, You Want to Lend Money?

When you lend money to an entrepreneur on Kiva, you're taking a risk on the borrower, first of all. The field partner has screened the borrower, but loans are always a risk. Kiva reports that in a total of $10,969,060 in loans, there's only a 1.8 percent default rate.

If you've decided you want to give to an entrepreneur, here's how to start. Go to an entrepreneur's full listing and click the "Field Partners" link to review its risk ratings.

Following is a sample.

ABOUT THE FIELD PARTNER

FIELD PARTNER:	Field Partner #1
COUNTRY:	Bolivia
RISK RATING ON KIVA:	★★★★★
TIME:	12 months
TOTAL LOANS:	$1,122,000
DELINQUENCY RATE:	0.00 percent
DEFAULT RATE:	0.00 percent
FUNDRAISING STATUS:	Active

Each MFI, or field partner, is listed, and you can see the country in which the MFI is located. You'll also see a number of stars in the "Risk Rating" column. A field partner with five stars is a keeper. Between one and five stars are given to show how reliable the MFI's entrepreneurs are when it comes to paying back the loans.

Hidden Treasure

Kiva recently started promoting the concept of lending teams. This is similar to the group concept on Prosper, but on Kiva it's related to microfinance. On Kiva, the teams still lend as individuals, but each lender can count his or her loan toward the team's total. This way, team members can evaluate the overall effectiveness of their team.

At the time this book was written this was a new concept on Kiva, so check its website, www.kiva.org/community/explore, for the latest information.

Field Partner's Repayment Reliability

Very Significant	★★★★★
Significant	★★★★
Moderate	★★★
Limited	★★
Very Limited	★

A one-star partner is usually an MFI that has little experience selecting successful entrepreneurs. Kiva keeps the two- and three-star partners around because it's letting them develop experience and gain track records. Kiva recommends sticking with the three- to five-star partners if you want a lower-risk investment.

Either before or after you review the field partner's risk ratings, you can browse the borrower's listings. You actually get quite a lot of information from the listings on Kiva.

In the Red

When loaning money internationally, you must consider the macrolevel risks involved. There's an economic risk because a currency devaluation could happen, a political risk because governments could change hands, and a natural risk (such as a tsunami or earthquake).

Here's a sample of what you might see on a Kiva entrepreneur listing:

Grace

ACTIVITY:	Clothing Store
LOAN INFO:	$900.00
COUNTRY/PARTNER:	Uganda/SACCO (MCDT)
DESCRIPTION:	Grace is 25 years old and leads a group of clothing retailers who need to buy merchandise.

Lucia

ACTIVITY:	Farming
LOAN INFO:	$500.00
COUNTRY/PARTNER:	Dominican Republic/Esperanza
DESCRIPTION:	Lucia is a 47-year-old single mom. She needs to raise money to buy equipment for her farm.

Jose

ACTIVITY:	Taxi service
LOAN INFO:	$1,200.00
COUNTRY/PARTNER:	Guatemala/FAPE
DESCRIPTION:	Jose is a 40-year-old father of four. He drives a taxi and needs money for repairs.

You may see something you like on the first page you view, or you can sort the listings by different categories.

Here are your sorting options:

♦ Status: Fundraising, raised, active, paid back, defaulted, or all (to look at all of them).

♦ Gender: Self-explanatory.

♦ Sector: Choose from a wide range of occupational areas, such as transportation, food, health, or agriculture.

♦ Region: Africa, the Middle East, South America, Asia, Central America, Eastern Europe, and North America.

♦ Sort by: This option enables you to search for new loans, old loans, and loan amounts. Or you can simply choose the "Popularity" option and see the ones getting the most activity.

Good Cents

An easy, safe way to loan money on Kiva is via PayPal. This service allows you to make online payments using credit cards or bank accounts. Check it out at www.paypal.com and follow the site's instructions for establishing an account.

Once you make a payment with PayPal or with your credit card, Kiva passes the money on to the field partner who's associated with your entrepreneur. The borrower then starts repaying the loan, and you can see updates on Kiva or receive e-mails if you like.

When you receive your money back, you can either relend the money to the same entrepreneur or lend it to someone else who needs your help. Either way, pat yourself on the back for doing a nice thing.

MicroPlace.com

MicroPlace's mission is "to help alleviate global poverty by enabling everyday people to make investments in the world's working poor." MicroPlace considers itself a social business, which it defines as a financially sustainable company that has a social mission.

MicroPlace is owned by eBay, the online marketplace where people and businesses buy and sell goods using an auction-style platform. MicroPlace is a registered broker with the Securities and Exchange Commission (SEC) and also a member of the Financial Industry Regulatory Authority (FINRA).

Good Cents _____

You can tell your friends about MicroPlace by sending them eCards. Just click on "Send an eCard" from the "Community & Blog" page. You can choose from one of MicroPlace's themes: Small change, Big change; Microfinance and MicroPlace; Microfinance in Latin America; Microfinance in Southeast Asia; Microfinance in Africa; Microfinance in South Asia; and Microfinance in Eurasia.

You then just fill out the e-mail recipient's information. Send your card and spread the word!

Target Market

Like Kiva, MicroPlace targets entrepreneurs in undeveloped countries. Sites such as MicroPlace.com don't specifically target women, but a 2007 report from the Microcredit Summit Campaign showed that 85.2 percent, or 79.1 million, of those who received microloans were women.

The lenders on MicroPlace are called "retail investors" and they are people just like you. Lenders are called investors because the online platform involves purchasing *debt securities.* All you have to do is open an account on MicroPlace and you can loan money via PayPal or your bank account.

How It Works

On MicroPlace, your loan is considered a socially responsible investment. You're required to make an initial investment of $100, and this amount is invested with one of MicroPlace's microfinance *security issuers.* After your initial investment, you can loan in $50 increments.

The security issuers, which currently are Calvert Foundation and Oikocredit, bear the risk and protect investors if the selected MFI defaults. Investors (lenders) generally receive a rate of return of around 1.25 to 3 percent. The average maturity rate of your investment is around 27 months.

As you can see, you're not loaning directly to a specific entrepreneur (or a specific group of entrepreneurs) as you are on Kiva. But as you'll see in the next section, you can decide what country you want to support.

def•i•ni•tion _____

A **debt security** represents borrowed funds that must be repaid on a specific date and at a specified interest rate. A **security issuer** sells debt securities. The investor (in this case, you, the lender) purchases a debt security from the security issuer. The investor decides which microfinance institution receives the funds. From there, the loans are distributed to poor entrepreneurs.

MicroPlace also has arrangements with two MFIs in the United States. If you prefer to help out America's working poor, you also have that option on this website.

So, You Want to Lend Money?

After you register, you can get down to business. Click on "Find Investments" and start your search for the entrepreneur you want to help.

MicroPlace's website is set up a little differently from Kiva. On the loan listing, you'll see the face of someone who represents a sample of their borrowers. Here's an idea of what you might find in the loan listings:

 ◆ Name of the MFI.

 ◆ Last day to invest.

 ◆ Photo of a sample borrower.

 ◆ Financial data: Your financial return (for example, 2 percent per year); repayment terms (for example, due in six months—on September 27, 2009); type of institution (single or multiple).

 ◆ Locations that your MFI covers. For instance, you might see "Investment enables loans to the working poor in India."

 ◆ Social data: The poverty level, which ranges from poor to extremely poor; there's also a flag when the listing focuses on women.

Just as on other sites, you can click on the loan listing and get more details. Underneath the "sample" borrower's photo, you'll get specifics on the individual. For instance, he or she might be a chicken farmer or operate a fruit stand. You also get to read a bio.

Now keep in mind that this entrepreneur is part of the MFI's sponsored group of borrowers. In fact, the total number of borrowers is listed and sometimes it's a pretty high number.

When this book was written, there was an MFI that had over 720,000 borrowers. But do you know what the repayment rate was? 100 percent! It's a different concept to think in terms of your investment going to a huge group instead of to an individual, but you just have to consider the success rate of the MFI involved.

Anyway, on the second page of the listing you'll also find bios of a few others who are represented in that group of borrowers. What's interesting on this site, too, are the comments from investors. That's a nice touch that helps to personalize the process.

But to make it even a little more personal, you can narrow your search in a variety of ways. There are three main categories: social, financial, and geographic.

The social category gives you options to search using the following parameters:

  ◆ Level of poverty: You'll see options for poor, very poor, and extremely poor.

  ◆ Focus on women: Click on this to see listings that benefit poor women.

  ◆ Serves rural areas: Click on this and you'll get results of listings from only rural areas.

The financial category gives you options to search using the following parameters:

  ◆ My financial return: Your options are less than 2 percent or 2–3 percent.

  ◆ When I get repaid: Your options are less than two years, two to three years, and longer than three years.

  ◆ My money is going to: Your options are single institution or multiple institution (MFIs).

The geographic category gives you options to search using the following parameters:

  ◆ Geographic: Your choices are Latin America, Eurasia, Africa, South Asia, North America, Southeast Asia, and Middle East. From there, you can even break down these categories into countries.

It's clear that getting a return on your investment depends somewhat on the reputation of the MFI. On Kiva, you saw the rating system that it uses on its site.

MicroPlace uses MicroRate (www.microrate.com), which is a rating agency for microfinance. Note that the reports are pricy. It's not something you'd want to purchase on your own.

Good Cents

If you decide that microfinance isn't something you want to get involved in, that's okay. But if you'd like to make an outright contribution, check out GlobalPartnerships. org. This website focuses on poor entrepreneurs in Latin America.

Global Partnerships hooks up with MFIs like other microfinance organizations do. But in this instance, your "loan" is considered a donation and it's distributed to an MFI who then loans the money to a poor entrepreneur.

MicrofinanceGateway.com

Let's be clear from the start that the Microfinance Gateway isn't a P2P lending site. The Microfinance Gateway, or the Gateway, is based in Washington, D.C., and launched in June 2000. The website bills itself as "the most comprehensive online resource for the global microfinance community."

According to its website, the Gateway features over 7,000 online documents, lists over 1,000 microfinance-related organizations, and has a database that contains over 400 consultant profiles. There's even a section for microfinance-related job listings. The Gateway welcomes contributions to the vast library, but also notes that documents are approved by the staff before being included.

This is a great place to do some research if you're considering getting involved in microfinance. You'll find the microfinance version of "Headline News," industry announcements, a discussion forum, and a wide variety of resources. You can also subscribe to an RSS feed.

Hidden Treasure

NextBillion.net is another website that offers information on the microfinance industry. The name, NextBillion.net, refers to the "next billion people to rise from the base of the economic pyramid (BOP), and the next billion in profits for businesses that strive to fill market gaps by integrating the BOP into healthy economies."

The objective of this site is to bring together those who want to explore the relationship between development and enterprise in poor countries. It's another good resource if you'd like to explore how microlending affects the entrepreneurs.

The Least You Need to Know

◆ Microfinance is a way of giving financial help to entrepreneurs in poor countries.

◆ Kiva offers loans to entrepreneurs in poor and developing countries.

◆ A person can become a lender on Kiva with as little as $25 because the loan amounts are small.

◆ MicroPlace calls its lenders "retail investors" because its platform involves purchasing debt securities.

◆ On MicroPlace, you can't choose an individual to lend to, but you can choose the country and the level of poverty, and even choose to focus on women.

◆ The Microfinance Gateway is an online resource where you can gather current information on the microfinance industry.

9

Lending Among Family and Friends

In This Chapter

- How Virgin Money got started
- How Virgin Money makes money
- Borrowing and lending on Virgin Money
- How lending and borrowing works on LoanBack
- Navigating Nolo's website and ordering documents

Most of us have been told that it's a terrible idea to loan or borrow money from family or friends. It's just too easy to miss a payment when you only owe it to your cousin Albert. And it's so easy to pay it on the 20th instead of the 15th. You've got a lot going on, and it's hard to keep track of the payments. You've also started wondering whether the interest rate he gave you is fair.

And if you're Cousin Albert, it's so awkward to say (gently, of course), "Hey! Where's my money?" Maybe you're flush with cash and don't need the money back quickly. But that isn't the point, is it? You want to help your cousin, but you want to be treated fairly, too.

Enter P2P lending websites that specialize in helping you avoid these awkward moments when you borrow from family or friends. These sites help you set up payments so that the borrower has a payment schedule and the lender has everything in writing. The best way to avoid a family squabble when it comes to money is to have plenty of structure.

VirginMoneyUS.com

When Richard Branson was getting started in the record business, he got a loan from his Aunt Joyce, which he says kept his business—a little company called Virgin Records—afloat. So maybe it's not surprising that he liked the concept behind CircleLending (incorporated in 2002) enough to acquire a majority stake in the company.

CircleLending was the first to offer unsecured loans between family and friends. In 2007, the company was renamed Virgin Money, to rebrand the company. Over the years, Virgin Money started promoting mortgages and student loans. In the first quarter of 2008, the company's loan volume exceeded $300 million.

Target Market

Virgin Money is for people who want to loan or borrow money and keep it in the family or between friends. If you're in a position to give a family member or a friend a loan or to help out with his or her mortgage—or you need some help from a relative or friend in this way—then you're Virgin Money's target market. Virgin Money also encourages student loans.

There are also areas on the website that encourage real estate and financial professionals to get their clients to use Virgin Money instead of going the traditional borrowing route.

How It Makes Money

Virgin Money offers packages with varying degrees of service. There are packages for personal loans, student loans, business loans, and real estate loans. Virgin Money also makes money through monthly servicing fees. We take a brief look at each one so you can get an idea of the level of service that goes with each price.

Remember that in the world of Internet-based business, the names of products and the pricing structure can rapidly change. So to get the latest, up-to-date information, visit the website at www.virginmoneyus.com.

For the most part, the lowest-price packages on its website include basic documentation. If you can swing it, upgrade to the package that includes servicing the loan via electronic fund transfers. Whether you're lending or borrowing money for a personal loan or a mortgage, make it as easy for yourself as you can afford to.

At the time this book was written, there were several choices for personal loans. Here they are in a nutshell:

♦ Handshake Basic: This includes basic documentation with promissory notes and repayment schedules. Virgin Money doesn't participate in collecting the money. This means that the borrower and the lender are on their own as far as actually exchanging money. The borrower should pay according to the payment schedule.

♦ Handshake Plus: This includes basic documentation with promissory notes and repayment schedules. Virgin Money provides loan servicing, which includes electronic fund transfers, e-mail reminders, online account access, and year-end reports.

For student loans, Virgin Money recommends going for the free money first: scholarships and grants. Do your due diligence before asking for money for college expenses from relatives. If you think about it, the relatives will be a lot more willing to trust you with their money if they can see how resourceful you are.

Once you've exhausted the scholarship/grant/federal aid route, then give some thought to whom you might ask for additional aid. Then you're ready to look at the packages offered.

Good Cents

Chapter 11 focuses exclusively on websites that specialize in student loans, such as Fynanz.com and GreenNote.com. These sites have a different approach, so investigate all your options before choosing the P2P lending site for financing your education.

♦ Student Payback—single-use only: There is no loan servicing. Use this option if you're borrowing only one time, because new loan amounts can't be added. For instance, you may need a total of $5,000 and that's it. You know you won't be coming back to your grandmother and asking for $5,000 more in six months.

♦ Student Payback—loan documentation and servicing: This price includes documentation plus loan servicing, including legal promissory notes, payment schedules, electronic fund transfers, and more. Use this option if you're most likely to borrow more than once during your college years. Additional loans are easily added when you use this package.

Business loans are often made between family and friends. It can be really tough to get a bank to finance your dream. Your family, on the other hand, has insight into your character and may be willing to take a chance.

Hidden Treasure

There's a nifty tool for students on Virgin Money's website called the Lender Blender. Yes, it's an actual graphic of a blender. You're given funding alternatives and you choose how you want to compile the funds you need for school.

For example, if you want to combine a Federal PLUS loan with a loan from a family member, you click on the buttons representing those options and drag them to the blender. The blender then "mixes" these options and offers suggestions on what your rates might be for the different sources. It may not solve all your problems, but it is kind of fun and may help you generate some ideas on how to proceed to fund your education.

Loans to family and friends can be made through the Business Builder package:

- Basic Services—Standard: You get loan documentation.

- Basic Services—Secured: You get more loan documentation and there are additional security measures for the borrower and the lender.

- Full Service: Virgin Money documents and services the loan.

- Full Service Security: Virgin Money documents and services the loan. There are additional security measures for both the borrower and the lender.

With the mortgage crisis, expect an upswing in real estate loans among family members. For some, this may be the only way to become a homeowner. Here's the deal if you go through Virgin Money: it offers a family mortgage plan that's a private loan for use toward a home or for refinance of an existing mortgage.

- Family Mortgage—Basic Package: This includes documentation of the loan agreement.

- Family Mortgage—Full Service Package: This includes documentation of the loan agreement and loan processing with electronic payments.

- Family Mortgage—Full Service with Escrow: This includes documentation of the loan agreement. There is loan processing with electronic payments, and this package also includes an escrow account.

- Family Mortgage—Full Closing: This includes documentation services, which includes promissory notes, mortgage recording services, and more. Virgin Money handles the closing, including the title search and funds disbursement. There is also loan processing with electronic payments.

- Family Mortgage—Full Closing with Escrow: This includes all the services that come with the Full Closing package. This package also includes an escrow account.

> **Hidden Treasure**
>
> If you're already partially supporting an elderly relative financially, consider a retirement mortgage through Virgin Money. Your loved one gets the money to stay in his or her home, and you get paid back with home equity. It can be set up as a reverse mortgage, which lowers the mortgage payment for the homeowner.

So, You Want to Borrow or Lend Money?

It's pretty simple. If you're the borrower, choose the type of loan you need and the generous friend or relative from whom you want to borrow. For example, if you want a personal loan to pay for your wedding, choose either the Handshake Basic or the Handshake Plus. Go to www.virginmoneyus.com and follow the instructions.

If you're the lender, work with the borrower and choose the package that makes sense for both of you. Consider that the more structure the loan has, the better off you'll both be.

Virgin Money has some nifty tools on its site that you can use to estimate the cost of the loan. Click "How It Works" and then "Tips & Tools" to calculate how much money you'll be keeping in the family by borrowing money from Uncle Ted. There's also a payment calculator to help you figure what your payment would be with a given interest rate, loan amount, loan period, and frequency of payment.

Making a Loan, Not a Gift

When you choose an interest rate, consider the current *Applicable Federal Rate* (*AFR*). The AFR is the interest rate set by the U.S. Treasury to calculate interest charges. There are also federal guidelines that determine whether a loan is considered a gift. If you're the lender, you must charge an interest rate that meets the minimum rate required by the federal government.

def•i•ni•tion

The **Applicable Federal Rate (AFR)** is the interest rate set by the U.S. Treasury to calculate interest charges. When lenders try to give their relative an interest rate that's below the AFR, it causes problems for the lenders. So lenders must be sure to charge an interest rate that meets the AFR. The "lost" interest, also known as the foregone interest, on a loan below the AFR will be considered a gift to the borrower.

Good Cents

If your loan is less than $10,000, you can use any interest rate you like. There's no need to worry about the AFR. Some folks on Virgin Money even set up the loan with zero interest charged.

Charge less than the minimum on a loan greater than $10,000, and you may find the government views the foregone interest (the interest you lost as a result of your lower rate) as a gift. In this case, the lender would be assessed a gift tax. The rates are published monthly in the Internal Revenue Bulletins at IRS.gov. Note that the rates change every month, so it's imperative that both the borrower and lender check the IRS website to know the current rate.

For instance, in July 2008, the AFR for long-term loans (greater than nine years) was as follows:

- Annual rate: 4.6 percent

- Semi-annual rate: 4.55 percent

- Quarterly rate: 4.52 percent

- Monthly rate: 4.51 percent

And don't forget about the usury laws of each state. You can look up the laws for your state in Chapter 4 or find a list on Virgin Money's website.

LoanBack.com

LoanBack's homepage shows a counter with the amount of P2P loans it has handled.

And at the time of this writing, that's more than $1 billion. (That's a lot of loans!) LoanBack offers its services if you're trying to loan or borrow money from family members or friends.

Target Market

As you've probably already guessed, LoanBack targets the same folks who might use Virgin Money. But with LoanBack, there's less formality (less service, too)—but you have to make your own decision about what works best for you and for the person with whom you're dealing.

How It Makes Money

LoanBack offers two packages: Loan Forms and LoanBuilder™. With both, you get promissory notes and loan schedules.

- ◆ Loan Forms: Choose from various types of promissory notes, including those for secured and unsecured loans. Forms are downloadable into Microsoft Word files.

- ◆ LoanBuilder: Choose from various types of promissory notes, including those for secured and unsecured loans. Forms are formatted as Adobe PDF files.

LoanBuilder also includes repayment schedules plus e-mail notifications.

So, You Want to Borrow or Lend Money?

Like most of the P2P websites, you must register to participate. You can play with LoanBuilder before you sign in, but to move forward with the loan, you have to register with the site. Once you've signed in, you can choose how you want to proceed.

You have the option of using the site's LoanBuilder form if your main objective is just to get something in writing. It's really a cool tool. Here's how it works:

- ◆ Choose your role. Are you the lender or the borrower?

- ◆ Enter the amount of the loan.

- ◆ How will the loan be used? There are several options to pick from, including a generic "I'd rather not say."

Let's say you want to lend $2,000 to your nephew, David. David needs the money to attend the state university. You key in these parameters into LoanBuilder, and you see something like the following.

Loan Calculator

Amount to lend	$2,000
Annual interest rate	5 percent
Payment frequency	Monthly
Payment type	Interest and principal
Repayment period	2 years
Loan start date	*Today's date*

Loan Summary

Payment amount	$87.84 (monthly)
Total number of payments	24
Total of all payments	$2,105.83
Total interest paid	$105.83

Then you can click "View Payment Schedule" and get a nice little spreadsheet:

Payment #	Due Date	Payment	Interest	Principal Amount	Outstanding Principal
1	8/10/08	$87.74	$8.33	$79.41	$2,000.00
2	9/10/08	$87.74	$8.00	$79.74	$1,920.00
3	10/10/08	$87.74	$7.67	$80.07	$1,840.85
4	11/10/08	$87.74	$7.34	$80.41	$1,760.78
5	12/10/08	$87.74	$7.00	$80.74	$1,680.37
6	1/09/09	$87.74	$6.67	$81.08	$1,599.63

Isn't that cool? You could just print this schedule and give it to David, telling him that you expect him to pay on the due dates. This gives David structure to pay back the loan and also gives him experience paying interest. (Not that anyone wants that experience, but it's a part of life when you get a loan or buy on credit.)

But there's nothing in writing, is there? So you take the next step on the screen (it's encouraging—saying that you're almost finished!). Remember, you started this loan as the lender, and here you're asked to key in your information (including name and address).

Next, LoanBack wants the borrower's information, so be sure you have it handy. The last step asks a few important questions. Some of these you'll want to discuss with David ahead of time:

> **Good Cents**
>
> Be sure that you have a signed promissory note from the borrower. If the borrower defaults, at the very least you can write it off as a bad debt. But you *must* have the promissory note to prove to the IRS that there was a loan.

- Where do you want the payment sent?

- Will late fees be charged? (You can get tough with David!)

- Will the loan be secured by collateral? You have the choice to make it a secured or unsecured loan.

- Do you want to be able to transfer this loan?

- In which state are you executing this loan?

- Do you have any additional terms to add?

After you've answered all the questions, you can print your documents at home. This is a pretty simple approach, so if you're intimidated by some of the other sites, this might be a good option for you.

Nolo.com

Nolo.com is a huge legal site. It took us a while to find the right spot for P2P lending on Nolo's site, so we'll save you the trouble. From Nolo's homepage, click "Property & Money," and then in the Main Topics box, click "Credit Repair & Debt." No, you're not there yet!

Now in the Main Topics box, click "Making and Repaying Debts"—and you're almost there. In the Related Articles box, click "Promissory Notes: Personal Loans to Family and Friends." You're there. Whew!

Target Market

Nolo is for those concentrating on family and friends but who also like the prospect of all that legal advice waiting in the wings. That said, this is the do-it-yourself P2P lending version. Nolo also publishes books on a variety of legal-related topics that you might find helpful, especially if you run a small business.

On its website, Nolo says, "If we ran the American legal system, we'd make it simpler, fairer, and more accessible to ordinary individuals and businesses." Well, that sounds pretty good, doesn't it?

How It Makes Money

Like LoanBack, using Nolo is pretty easy to explain. You want the documents only? Just pay for them. Nolo has a vast number of promissory notes to suit your needs. Most of them are around $7.49. For example, you can buy:

♦ A promissory note for a personal loan (installment payments without interest)

♦ A promissory note for a personal loan (installment payments with interest)

So, You Want to Borrow or Lend Money?

Nolo sells promissory notes and gives advice on how to fill them out. And it also gives advice on whether or not to charge interest to a family member or friend. There's a reminder that you need to be aware of the AFR if you try an interest-free or low-interest loan.

There's also a reminder to pay attention to state usury laws. Nolo gives advice on several options and offers promissory note packages to help document loans, including the following:

♦ Installment payments in equal amounts: In this plan, the borrower makes equal payments over a set period of time. This can be set up either with interest or without.

♦ *Lump sum payment* of principal and interest: The borrower pays off the loan all at once and on a specified future date.

♦ *Balloon payments:* Nolo says this is rare among family and friends, but it does happen. The borrower makes equal monthly payments for a specified time, and then there's a large "balloon" payment at the end when the borrower pays off the principal and interest (if it's charged).

def•i•ni•tion

A borrower who pays off a loan all at once is making a **lump sum payment.** A borrower who makes equal monthly payments and then makes a large payment at the end of the loan term is making a **balloon payment.** The balloon payment pays off the remaining principal and any charged interest.

♦ Secured loans with property: Most personal loans are unsecured, but if you choose a secured loan, Nolo has advice for the type of collateral used. For tangible personal property (such as a car), complete a security agreement along with a promissory note.

For real estate, you need a mortgage or deed of trust. Consult a real estate attorney to do this properly. For intangible personal property (such as copyrights), you also need an attorney for the proper paperwork.

Nolo can work for families who don't mind spending time on its site to determine which documents are the best for their situations. But be sure to carefully read all the fine print in the documents.

In the Red

Don't try to get by with a promissory note and a security agreement if you're using real estate or intangible personal property for collateral. Consult with an attorney who specializes in either real estate or intellectual property.

The Least You Need to Know

♦ Virgin Money offers families and friends packages for personal loans, mortgages, student loans, and business loans.

♦ Be aware of the AFR if your loan exceeds $10,000.

♦ LoanBack offers documentation services for loans among family members or friends.

♦ Nolo is a large legal site that offers many types of forms to document loans among family members and friends.

The Best of the Rest

In This Chapter

- ◆ How Lending Club got started
- ◆ Borrowing and lending on LendingClub.com
- ◆ GlobeFunder.com and direct-to-consumer lending
- ◆ Borrowing and lending on Loanio.com

The founder and CEO of LendingClub.com, Renaud Laplanche, started a company in 1999 and over the course of a few months had put $20,000 worth of expenses on his credit card. Although he had a great credit score, Laplanche was paying 18 percent interest. He decided to get the money he needed from friends at 10 percent interest.

The loans he got from friends helped him create a successful software business, Matchpoint, which was later acquired by Oracle. A few years later, Laplanche created Lending Club so others would have access to better interest rates when they needed loans.

Let's take a look at LendingClub.com first. Then we'll look at two other interesting P2P networks, GlobeFunder.com and Loanio.com.

LendingClub.com

Lending Club refers to itself as a "social lending network that lets borrower members borrow money through personal loans, and lenders fund these loans by investing in notes. Each note corresponds to a portion of a borrower loan." The concept of purchasing "notes" to lend money is a little different, so let's take a brief look at how this approach to P2P lending evolved.

Laplanche started the site on Facebook in May 2007. Then in September 2007, LendingClub.com was launched and became available to the public. Lending Club partners with WebBank, and it's regulated just like other sites.

Lending Club distinguished its service by offering LendingMatch to help lenders find loans based on a predetermined set of criteria. Lending Club calls it "affinity-matching technology," and it can be used by a lender to find borrowers who, for instance, might have grown up with the lender in a certain area, who went to a particular college, or who have a particular occupation.

As of June 30, 2008, Lending Club had issued more than $17 million in loans with a default rate of 0.36 percent. The stats are updated daily, so you can check out the current numbers on its website.

Hidden Treasure

In June 2008, Lending Club filed a registration statement with the Securities and Exchange Commission (SEC) under the Securities Act of 1993 to issue up to $600 million "Member Payment Dependent Notes" with the intent to offer them on its website. Lending Club was in a "quiet period" for months while waiting on approval from the SEC. During the quiet period, Lending Club was not allowed to speak with the press and it was required to stop accepting new lenders. In October 2008, the SEC registration was approved and the quiet period ended. Lending Club resumed regular business activities and began offering lenders an opportunity to enter the secondary lending market.

On Lending Club, each loan corresponds to a series of notes (basically like a promissory note). Lending Club offers these notes via a prospectus, which you can read on its website. The prospectus is a legal document and it describes the investments that are being offered to lenders. Read it carefully!

Target Market

Borrowers who are at least 18 years old and are U.S. residents can apply for three-year unsecured personal loans between $1,000 and $25,000. On Lending Club, you can be both a borrower and a lender.

To be a borrower, you also must have a credit score of at least 640, no current delinquencies, a credit history of at least one year, and a debt-to-income (DTI) ratio lower than 25 percent. You must also meet the following requirements:

- You must have had no more than 10 inquiries on your credit report in the last six months.

- You must use revolving credit accounts at less than 100 percent.

- You must have more than three accounts in your credit report, with at least three of them open.

To be a lender (also called an "investor" on the website), you must have *one* of the following: a gross annual income of at least $70,000 or a net worth of at least $250,000. Plus, a lender cannot purchase notes that exceed 10 percent of the lender's net worth. For more details on the calculation of net worth, review the prospectus on Lending Club's website.

How It Makes Money

Lenders pay a monthly 1 percent processing fee of all amounts paid by the borrower to the lender. The fee is collected to cover the management of loan payments and lenders' portfolios. If a lender sells a note using Lending Club's trading platform, the lender must pay a 1 percent trading fee (the trading platform is discussed in the next section).

Borrowers pay a processing fee between 0.75 and 3.0 percent of the loan amount. This fee is assessed right before the borrower receives the loan proceeds. Borrowers receive a loan grade of A–G on their listings, and the fees are assessed by grade.

A	B	C	D	E	F	G
0.75 percent	1.50 percent	2.00 percent	2.50 percent	2.75 percent	3.00 percent	3.00 percent

Okay, so if you want a $2,000 loan, you need to consider the fee. If you have an A grade, you'll pay $15. The amount you'll receive is $1,985.

So, You Want to Borrow Money?

Once you join Lending Club, you can apply for a loan online. You'll be notified about your loan grade and what interest rate you qualify for.

We mentioned that Lending Club uses a loan grade system for determining the processing fee. Here are a few of the grades and corresponding interest rates just so you can get an idea of how they match up. (Note that the interest rates given are subject to change.)

Loan Grade	Interest Rate	Loan Grade	Interest Rate	Loan Grade	Interest Rate
A1	7.37 percent	C1	11.78 percent	F3	17.15 percent
A3	8.00 percent	C5	13.04 percent	F5	17.78 percent
A5	9.38 percent	D2	13.70 percent	G1	18.09 percent
B1	10.20 percent	D5	14.62 percent	G3	18.72 percent
B4	11.14 percent	F1	16.51 percent	G5	19.36 percent

This chart certainly drives home the fact that a good credit rating is a thing of beauty. What a difference between A1 and G5. We hope you're closer to A1 than to G5!

When you apply for your loan, you'll be asked information to verify your identity. Your grade is determined by many factors, including the loan amount and what's in your credit report. Loans are generally funded by several lenders. When your loan is funded, money is transferred to your account via the Automated Clearing House System (ACS). Lending Club withdraws your monthly payment from your account on the day it's due.

So, You Want to Lend Money?

After you join as a basic member, you can become a lender member after you provide Lending Club with information about your identity and finances. After these steps are successfully completed, you can start browsing the notes that are listed. Each note is simply a description of the borrower and his or her loan. When you choose a loan to fund, you're actually investing because you're buying the note that is associated with a specific loan. For instance, if you invest $100 in Loan X and $50 in Loan Z, you'll own a note worth $100 (Loan X) and a note worth $50 (Loan Z). Purchasing notes is all done online and, in general, you won't receive actual hard copies of the notes.

You can either fund loans one at a time or ask for a portfolio recommendation. Notes are available to purchase for as little as $25, and in $25 increments. So, for example, you could decide to lend $75 to fund a borrower's loan. In this case, you'd purchase a note worth $75.

If you go through the portfolio matching system, LendingMatch, you can build a diverse portfolio of loans in a fairly short amount of time. It saves time because LendingMatch hooks you up with loans that meet your predetermined criteria.

Here's an example of what the loan requests might look like on Lending Club:

Title	Loan Amount	Interest Rate	Connections*	Left to Fund	Time Left
Buying a used car	$7,500	B2: 10.51 percent		$1,350	6 days
Paying off credit cards	$4,800	C3: 12.41 percent		$800	3 days
Relocation expenses	$4,950	A2: 7.68 percent		$2,500	7 days

*Key to Connections

 = Geographic affiliations

 = Company affiliations

 = School affiliations

 = Association affiliations

We really like the Connections tool. When you're browsing loans, you can hold your cursor over one of the icons and see where the borrower went to school or where he or she lives.

In the Red

If you have a security freeze on your credit file to prevent identity theft, the credit bureaus can't access your information. To become a lender, you need to temporarily remove the freeze. Once you're registered, you can refreeze your account.

You can click the title of the loan and get more information. Next, you see the borrower profile (if you're registered as a lender), the borrower member loan number, and a description of the loan. This sometimes includes the reason for the loan.

For instance, in the first loan in the preceding listing, the borrower is buying a used car. In the loan description section, he or she might write, "I'm buying a good, used car so I can get rid of my expensive, gas-guzzling SUV."

Note also that in the listings, the Loan Rate column shows the loan grade and the interest rate. A B2 grade means that the borrower has a B loan with a subgrade of 2. Lending Club reviews financial information from a borrower and determines the subgrade, which is an adjustment for risk and volatility.

When the borrower makes payments on your loan, the money is transferred to your lender account. Most borrowers' loan payments are made via electronic funds transfer. If the borrower doesn't have enough money in the account to make the loan payment, then Lending Club's member support team contacts the borrower. If attempts to get the money (for whatever reason) are unsuccessful, then Lending Club turns the account over to its internal collections department. Members should not seek collections on their own. It's important to let Lending Club handle these matters, because there are legal issues involved.

The Secondary Lending Market

Lending Club is the first P2P lending website to offer a secondary lending market to lenders. The secondary lending market allows lenders to buy and sell notes associated with borrowers' loans on Lending Club's trading platform. If the term "trading platform" conjures up images of frantic stockbrokers on Wall Street, you can relax. It's nothing like that. In fact, it appears to be a nice addition to the P2P lending marketplace because it gives lenders a little more flexibility.

Lending Club uses a Note Trading Platform that's operated by FOLIO*fn* (a provider of online brokerage services). If you're a Lending Club lender, you'll need to open an account with FOLIO*fn*. Just follow the instructions on Lending Club's website to do so. It's easy to go back and forth between Lending Club's main website and the Note Trading Platform.

Here are some advantages to buying and selling notes on the Note Trading Platform:

◆ If you're a buyer, you can buy a note on the Note Trading Platform that has a shorter maturity date than the new loans on Lending Club's website. For example, a borrower may have already paid through the first year of the loan. If you buy this note, you're funding a loan for only two more years as opposed to three years (the term on original loans). So you get the money you're lending to this borrower back sooner.

◆ If you're a seller, having the option to sell your notes makes your investment more "liquid." This means that if you find another investment opportunity you'd rather pursue—or you have a financial emergency and need your money back—you can sell the loan and get your cash back before the maturity date.

It's not a free service. If you're the seller, there is a 1 percent trading fee (equal to 1 percent of the resale price of the note sold) that is taken from your Lending Club account. And lending on this site is risky, like all other forms of P2P lending. Don't become a lender and think you'll get your money back in a hurry by selling it on the trading platform. The note may or may not sell.

Remember that the secondary lending market in the P2P lending industry just began in late 2008. It's imperative that you read Lending Club's prospectus to get up-to-date details on its trading platform. In fact, if other P2P lending websites start offering a secondary lending market, make reviewing the prospectus a priority.

GlobeFunder.com

GlobeFunder.com launched in January 2008 and says its mission is to "lower borrowing costs for *every person on the planet* by driving capital through an efficient, online marketplace." Like Kiva, GlobeFunder likes the microfinance concept of lending and wants to spread P2P lending to entrepreneurs in developing countries. GlobeFunder also uses microfinance institutions to find worthy borrowers around the globe.

But GlobeFunder is a little different from other sites, too. It recently partnered with CalSpas, a manufacturer of luxury home products such as spas and saunas. This partnership was created so that consumers could obtain better financing—when a consumer wants to buy a product from CalSpas, GlobeFunder acts as the middleman and offers financing.

GlobeFunder created direct-to-consumer (D2C) lending to get better financing rates for consumers. D2C lending includes consumer loans through retailers, direct loans to consumers who want to consolidate credit card debt, and small business loans.

GlobeFunder is regulated and is a licensed consumer lender. According to its website, it's also a registered money service business (MSB) with the U.S. Treasury Department's Financial Crimes Enforcement Network (FinCEN).

Target Market

Borrowers can apply for unsecured loans up to $25,000. A minimum FICO score is required, but this number is determined by current market conditions and loan performance experience.

So, You Want to Borrow Money?

Borrowers pay loan closing fees. To borrow money, you need to register, of course. Fill out the loan application online.

At the moment, lending opportunities are not available. They're making changes to the site. A spokesperson says GlobeFunder is active at the moment recruiting banks and retailers for partnerships. It's definitely a site to check into when it's further established.

Loanio.com

Loanio is a relative newcomer to P2P lending. Founded in 2006 by Michael Solomon, it's based in Nanuet, New York. The website launched in September 2008 and uses an auction-style P2P lending platform. Loanio is currently in a quiet period (see Chapter 1).

Compared to other P2P lending websites, Loanio has a few unique, patent-pending features. For instance, borrowers can opt in to a Platinum Verification designation to enhance their funding chances.

Note that Loanio had just recently launched when this book was written. At the time, loans weren't open to borrowers from all states. With the exception of Pennsylvania and South Dakota, Loanio was open to lenders from all other states. From Loanio's website, click on "State Licensing and Rates" to see if your state is approved for you to be a borrower on Loanio.

First let's take a look at Loanio's target market. Then we'll discuss how it makes money and how the unique features, such as the Platinum Verification designation, work.

Target Market

To become a borrower, you must be a resident of the United States and be at least 18 years old. There are requirements for FICO scores. Loanio relies on VantageScore from Experian to confirm the borrower's FICO scores. Borrowers must have a FICO score of at least 501 to qualify for a loan.

Hidden Treasure

VantageScore is a credit score that was developed by Experian in cooperation with the other major national credit reporting companies. It's the first credit score to be developed jointly by Experian, TransUnion, and Equifax.

VantageScore uses a scoring formula that grades the credit scores with letter grades from A down to F. Still, there's room for interpretation among lenders. A 901 is considered an A by VantageScore, but some lenders might decide an 880 is good enough to be an A.

Borrowers have the option of having a co-borrower. The co-borrower is legally obligated to pay off the loan if the borrower fails to do so. To be a co-borrower, you must be a resident of the United States and at least 18 years old. You must also have a Social Security number and a Loanio credit grade that is greater than E (569).

To become a lender, you must be a resident of the United States and at least 18 years old. You must also have a Social Security number and a bank account. Lenders also must pass Loanio's identity and fraud verification systems.

How It Makes Money

As on most P2P lending websites, borrowers are charged a fee at the time the loan is originated. The origination fee equals a percentage of the loan, which is based on these two things:

- Your credit score
- Your decision to have a co-borrower

Your VantageScore credit grade determines your fee. You get a more detailed explanation of how your credit score translates to your Loanio credit grade in the next section, but for the purpose of determining the origination fee, here's what you need to know.

- If your credit grade is A+, A, B+, or B, your origination fee is 2 percent.

- If your credit grade is C+, C, D+, D, E+, E, F, or NC (no credit), your origination fee is 3 percent.

- If you have a co-borrower, add 1 percent. This means that you add 1 percent to your origination fee.

- The minimum origination fee is $95. But you're required to pay whichever is greater: the $95 fee or the calculation of your fee based on your credit grade and whether you have a co-borrower.

Remember we mentioned that Loanio has a special Platinum Verification plan? Here's the scoop:

- It's an optional (prepaid) feature that gives your loan request more credibility.

- To qualify, you must provide additional financial and identification documents.

Loanio determines the additional documents that are needed. Here are some examples of what you might need and why:

- To validate your ID with photo identification, you might be asked for a driver's license and/or a passport.

- To prove your income, you might need to provide W-2s, IRS materials that show your adjusted gross income (AGI), and 1099s (if applicable).

- To prove you have a checking account, you'll provide a recent checking account statement.

- To prove your employment and salary, you'll submit pay stubs.

- To prove you live where you say you live, you'll need to submit a recent utility bill that shows your current address. Loanio says that it then conducts database searches to confirm your address.

- To prove homeownership, you don't have to do anything. No, that's not a typo. This information comes from your credit summary report. If you've paid off your home in full (lucky you!), you'll need to provide evidence of this to Loanio.

So there you have it. If you jump through these hoops and get approved, you can get the coveted Platinum Verification Box, which is placed in your listing. Collecting and processing all of these documents from borrowers does come with a cost. The borrower pays $35 extra for the designation; with a co-borrower, the cost is $45.

You have to be the one to decide if this is worth the time and effort. As you know from previous discussions in this book, the more transparent you come across with your financial information, the more lenders are likely to trust you.

Lenders on Loanio pay an annual servicing fee of 1 percent. The fee is accrued on a daily basis. Although Loanio collects late payment fees on borrowers' loans, Loanio does not keep the collected late fees. These amounts are distributed (on a pro-rata basis) to the lenders who funded the loan.

So, You Want to Borrow Money?

After you register as a borrower and have your identity verified, you receive your credit grade. Once you have that, you create your loan request.

Here are a few facts about borrowing money on Loanio:

♦ Loans are unsecured

♦ Length of loans: 36, 48, or 60 months

♦ Minimum loan amount: $1,000

♦ Maximum loan amount: $25,000

Now you know enough about the P2P lending websites to know that your credit score impacts your credit grade. The only difference on Loanio is that the score it uses is VantageScore instead of the FICO score the other sites use. Let's dive into the details of the way Loanio uses your credit score to decide your credit grade. Take a look at this chart:

Experian VantageScore	Loanio Credit Grade
784–990	A+
728–783	B+
692–700	B
668–691	C+
660–667	C
633–659	D+
624–632	D
604–623	E+
569–603	E
501–568	F
No score	NC

If you have no credit score, you'll need a co-borrower. As on most P2P lending websites, you can set your maximum interest rate for your loan. Loanio does offer these suggestions based on your credit grade:

Credit Grade	Suggested Maximum Rate
A+, A	7 percent–14 percent
B+, B	12 percent–16 percent
C+, C	14 percent–19 percent
D+, D	15 percent–24 percent
E+, E	22 percent and up

These are just suggestions, of course. But realistically, if you have a D credit grade, it's hard to get a great interest rate. On the other hand, if you have an A grade, you're in line for a pretty good rate.

Okay, so you've been through identity verification and you're ready to roll. Get started by creating your loan request. You need to know the amount you want to borrow, the maximum interest rate you're willing to pay, and the length of the loan. Remember, on Loanio, you choose to pay off your loan in three-, four-, or five-year terms.

Here's an idea of how listings look on Loanio:

	Loan Title/ Description	Amount/Lender Rate/Grade	% Funded	No. of Bids Time Left
	Business Improvement Normal Loan	$4,000 @ 5% A+	25%	10 Bids 8 days, 2 hrs, 2 mins

See where "Normal Loan" is listed under the listing title? If this were a loan in the Platinum Verification category, the Platinum Verification Box would show up here in place of Normal Loan.

If you clicked on the loan title in the preceding example, you'd go to the borrower's loan profile, where you'd see these line items:

◆ Amount Requested: $4,000

◆ Rate: 5 percent

◆ APR: 5.97 percent

◆ Term: 60 months

◆ Loan Purpose: Increasing inventory to expand my business

◆ Time Left: 8 days 2 hrs 2 mins

◆ Percent Funded: 25 percent

◆ Estimated Monthly Payment: $75.48

◆ Monthly Income after Expenses: $1,344

◆ Debt-to-Income Ratio: 28.9 percent

You can use Loanio's handy loan calculator to determine your APR, monthly payments, finance charges, and loan origination fees.

Below the Loan Profile section you see the bid listings. The process of getting your loan funded is similar to Prosper's platform. It's an auction-style platform, so the bidding drives down your interest rate. Here's what the bid history section looks like:

Amount Bid	Winning Amount	Current Rate	Lender	Time of Bid
$100	$100	5%	Lend22	4-04-09 07:24:22 AM
$100	$100	5%	Money7	3-29-09 09:07:52 PM

What if you don't get all the funding you need? On Loanio, if more than 35 percent of your loan gets funded, then you can opt to take that amount for your loan.

In the preceding example, the borrower who wants to expand her business can accept $1,440 ($4,000 × .36) in lieu of her original amount requested. For some borrowers, this may be a better choice than starting over either at this website or on another P2P lending website.

So, You Want to Be a Co-Borrower?

Congratulations on being a supportive family member or friend! That said, take a moment to make sure you know what you're getting into.

Loanio will take a look at your credit summary as well. This is a soft inquiry and it won't affect your credit report or your score. However, after the co-borrower gets his or her loan funded, Loanio conducts a hard inquiry and this does go on your credit report. It may not affect your score, but it's impossible to predict because so many factors are involved in the scoring process.

Okay, let's get right to it: what happens if your co-borrower doesn't pay? If your co-borrower is more than 15 days late, your friend/family member will be charged a late fee that's based on the laws in his or her state. There's also a $15 fee for NSF.

Attempts are made to collect the late payment and associated fees from the borrower's account, but if Loanio is unable to collect from the borrower's account, then your (the co-borrower) account is charged around the 26th late day. Please check with the website, though, to make sure the terms haven't changed or been updated.

In the Red

If you're the co-borrower and you can't make the payments either, the loan becomes delinquent and can eventually become a defaulted loan if neither of you can make payments. If it gets past 120 days late, the loan is sold to a debt purchaser. The delinquency and the subsequent sale to a debt purchaser is reflected on your (the co-borrower) credit report as well as the borrower's. So don't take on the legal obligation unless you're sure you can come through in the event that the borrower doesn't come through.

So, You Want to Lend Money?

After you register, get your identity verified, and deposit some money into your Loanio account, you're ready to lend. The money that's in your Loanio account is a non-interest-bearing account, and it's FDIC-insured up to $100,000. After the money leaves your account to fund the loan, it's no longer insured.

The minimum amount you can bid on a loan is $50. The maximum is $25,000, but we don't recommend that! It's important to spread out your risk over many loans. Remember that P2P lending involves unsecured loans that carry risk.

In the preceding borrower's section, you learned that Loanio uses an auction-style platform similar to Prosper. Borrowers provide you with a maximum rate they're willing to pay. You can choose to bid that rate or bid one that's lower than that rate. Your chances of possessing a "winning" bid increase when you bid a lower rate.

After you place a bid, you can't say "Never mind!" The bid stays in place and funds in your account are set aside until bidding is closed. At that point, if you don't have a winning bid, the money you bid becomes available in your account again.

At the time this book was written, Loanio was fairly new. There weren't many Platinum Loan listings (listings that have been through Platinum Verification). But if you're interested in lowering your risk, look for Platinum Loans. If you don't find any that interest you, start at the top of the credit grades (A+) and work your down until you're no longer comfortable with the risk.

And remember, some folks on this website have co-borrowers on their loan listings. This gives you a little security if the borrower has little credit (or poor credit).

Late Fees on Loanio

This section should interest you whether you're a borrower or a lender. Let's take a quick look at the late fee schedule so you know where you stand in case you have some bad luck (as a borrower or as a lender!).

- Failure to collect funds through automatic debits: The borrower is charged $15 every time Loanio attempts to collect funds from the borrower's account.

- More than 15 days late: Borrowers are charged a late fee according to the laws of their states.

- After 45 days, 75 days, and 105 days: Late fees continue to pile up based on this schedule. After the loan is 60 days late, it gets reported to the credit reporting agencies.

- More than 120 days late: The loan is no longer delinquent, but in default. The loan is sold to a debt purchaser at this point. The default gets reported to credit reporting agencies and will remain on the borrower's credit report for seven years.

It's a good idea to check Loanio's website as well as the other P2P lending websites every now and then—maybe every month for good measure. The industry sometimes changes quickly and this may result in changes to a lender's policies. Also, be sure to sign up for e-mail news if that's an option on the site. Most of the P2P lenders have this option because they want you to be informed.

The Least You Need to Know

- Lending Club requires borrowers to have a FICO score of 640 or higher.

- Lending Club uses a matching system that enables lenders to choose borrowers by specific attributes.

- GlobeFunder's approach is unusual in that it finances loans between consumers and retailers.

- Loanio is a recent addition to the P2P lending industry and uses an auction-style lending platform.

- Loanio allows borrowers to use co-borrowers if they have little or poor credit.

Head of the Class: P2P Lending Websites for Student Loans

In This Chapter

◆ The rising costs of a college education

◆ How to get student loans on Fynanz.com

◆ What you need to know before becoming a lender on Fynanz.com

◆ Connecting with lenders when you get a loan through GreenNote.com

◆ What you need to know before becoming a lender on GreenNote.com

◆ How other P2P lending sites compare to Fynanz.com and GreenNote.com for student loans

If you're not an heir or an heiress, paying for an education is getting more and more difficult. Take a look at these numbers from the National Center for Education Statistics:

◆ Average annual cost at a public four-year institution:

1985–1986: $3,859

2005–2006: $12,108

Increase: 313.8 percent!

- Average annual cost at a private four-year institution:

  1985–1986: $9,228

  2005–2006: $27,317

  Increase: 196 percent!

Is it any wonder that students and their parents are getting creative in their search for education dollars?

On top of that, the economic fallout from the subprime mortgage crisis has resulted in a decrease in the number of loans that are available to students. The banks (and other lenders) that are remaining in the student loan business are setting the credit bar high for borrowers. Mark Kantrowitz, publisher of FinAid.org, predicts that such high standards could leave around 200,000 students ineligible for private loans in the near future.

Fortunately, P2P lending sites are thinking of ways to capitalize on this niche market. So this chapter is for borrowers—both students and parents—who are looking for an alternative in the loan market. It's also for lenders. Contributing to someone's education and getting interest income in the process seems like a win-win situation for all involved.

Let's take a look at the P2P sites that specialize in student loans. We review Fynanz.com and a new one, GreenNote.com.

Fynanz.com

As you've already deduced, P2P lending is taking off quickly. New websites are popping up all over the place. Fynanz is a newcomer that focuses on loans to finance education.

Fynanz, based in New York City, has an OpenLoan program that can be used to pay for qualified (by Fynanz) expenses, such as tuition fees and books. Fynanz uses an auction-style marketplace that's designed to get good interest rates for borrowers and for lenders. A borrower posts a loan listing and then lenders bid to fund the loan. On Fynanz, the term "lender" is used, but the loans are financed by Fynanz. The lender is actually a "loan purchaser."

Fynanz has created a model, the Fynanz Academic Credit Score (FACS), which it uses to grade the loan listings. The grade is based on the borrower's academic attributes.

Some of the attributes considered are grade point average (GPA), types of courses taken, and class standing. Fynanz believes that these characteristics help predict whether or not a borrower is a good risk.

Target Market

Just like on other P2P lending sites, to become a lender you must register on the website. After a lender's identity and account information is verified, a lender can link a bank account to his or her Fynanz account. Some lenders are parents, but some are other family members or friends.

In order to borrow on Fynanz, you must be enrolled in an approved school and be at least a half-time student. You must be a U.S. citizen with a Social Security number. And if you're younger than 21, you need a *cosigner*. Either you or your cosigner must have some income and two years of uninterrupted employment.

If you're a junior or senior in college, you may apply for a loan without a cosigner if you meet these qualifications:

- ◆ You're enrolled in a degree program at a four-year institution.

- ◆ You have a good credit report. This means that your history is free of delinquent payments.

- ◆ You're not requesting more than $7,500 per year or $15,000 over the course of two years.

Like Virgin Money, Fynanz encourages borrowers to first look for scholarships, grants, and other sources for federal funds. That money is, well, free!

def•i•ni•tion

A **cosigner** is responsible for paying off a loan if the primary debtor doesn't pay. The cosigner basically guarantees that the lender will get his or her money back, even if the cosigner is the one who pays it.

How Fynanz Makes Money

A borrower pays fees based on his or her loan's FACS grade. That fee is added to the loan amount. Fynanz maintains a "Default Prevention & Guarantee Fund," and a portion of the borrower's fee goes into this account to cover defaults.

Lenders pay a 1 percent servicing fee. The fee is based on the initial loan amount.

So, You Want to Borrow Money?

When you've passed Fynanz's anti-fraud procedures, you can create a loan listing. When the loan is completely funded, you'll receive your money in less than two weeks.

The loan check may have both your name and the school's name on it. If this is the case, you need to endorse the back of the check and give it the appropriate department at your school. If some of the money needs to go directly to you and not to the school (for example, money to buy books), you need to work directly with the school to get the proper amount refunded to you.

Here's a word about the FACS grades (and you thought you only had to worry about grades in school!). There are six grades:

FACS Grade	Base Rate	Margin Range (set by marketplace auction)
Platinum Honors	2.63 percent	2.50–3.70 percent
Platinum Plus	2.63 percent	3.50–4.70 percent
Gold Honors	2.63 percent	4.50–5.50 percent
Gold Plus	2.63 percent	5.40–6.40 percent
Silver Honors	2.63 percent	6.30–7.10 percent
Silver Plus	2.63 percent	7.10–7.90 percent

Your loan interest rate works out to this:

Base Rate + Margin + 1% Guarantee Fee

Be sure you take a close look at the annual percentage rate (APR) that Fynanz gives you on your loan. You'll have an opportunity to approve it before your listing becomes visible.

How do you repay the loan? Well, like most of these sites, your payment is taken from your bank account by automatic transfer.

Good Cents

Try to pay off 10 percent of your loan as soon as you can. When you get 10 percent of the loan paid, Fynanz rewards you by dropping the interest rate by 1 percent.

There are a few repayment options to consider:

◆ Deferred repayment option: There's a six-month grace period after the student leaves school, but monthly $25 "Good Faith" payments are required. This shows lenders that you're financially disciplined and expect to repay the loan in full.

◆ Interest paid option: While you're in school, you pay the amount of the monthly interest on your loan. If necessary, you can pay only the interest expense during the first two years of the repayment period.

Your interest expense may qualify as a deduction because it's for educational purposes. We devote an entire chapter to borrowers and taxes later (see Chapter 17), but we mention this now to give you a heads-up.

So, You Want to Lend Money?

You can make loans starting at $50 on Fynanz. This is an auction-style marketplace when it comes to bidding. Bids are given priority as follows:

1. Interest rate: Priority is given to the bids with the lowest interest rates.

2. Type of lender: The next priority is given to the relationship between the lender and the borrower. Highest priority is to family and friends. Next priority is to alumni of the borrower's school and then to Fynanz.

3. Time of bid: If a tiebreaker is necessary at this point, then the earliest bid wins. So if two lenders tie on interest rates and are both alumnus of the school, then whomever bid first is the winner.

Fynanz allows lenders to bid on individual loans to set up a "Smart Bid" portfolio approach with a predetermined set of criteria.

Also, you should know that Fynanz sometimes bids on its own loans. Why? They sometimes do this to get bidding started on a loan. But note in the preceding list that Fynanz is given last priority when it comes to the type of lender who wins the bid if there's an interest rate tie.

Following are a few examples of Fynanz loan listings.

LISTING SUMMARY

FLORIDA STATE UNIVERSITY
SILVER HONORS
$2,700 @ 8.93% INTEREST PAID

MAJOR: Education
YEAR: Junior

LISTING SUMMARY

NEW YORK UNIVERSITY
GOLD PLUS
$5,800 @ 7.33% DEFERRED REPAYMENT

MAJOR: Pre-Med
YEAR: Sophomore

LISTING SUMMARY

DEPAUL UNIVERSITY
GOLD HONORS
$7,900 @ 7.03% DEFERRED REPAYMENT

MAJOR: Computer Science
YEAR: Senior

Note in the listing that the repayment option is listed. You also can see their FACS grades. Click one of the listings and you'll go to a page where the borrower describes in detail how much the school costs per year. Borrowers also might tell you what their career plans are.

You'll see the bid history, which looks something like this:

Bidder	Relationship	Rate	Amount	Bid Date
#1	Institution	---	$100	Jan-9-09
#2	Institution	---	$250	Jan-11-09
#3	Institution	---	$200	Jan-11-09
#4	Institution	---	$50	Jan-12-09
#5	Institution	---	$100	Jan-13-09

And to the right of the history, you'll find a box that shows something similar to this:

Lender Bids	5 bids
Winning	$700, 10 percent of loan
Fynanz Bids	0
Winning	$0, 0 percent of loan
Total	5 bids for $700, 10 percent of loan

When you have won a bid and funded a loan, you will get paid from your Fynanz account. Remember, this is an indirect loan. Borrowers pay Fynanz, and Fynanz pays you.

GreenNote.com

GreenNote, based in Redwood, California, launched in June 2008. It's another P2P lending site that specializes in student loans. We predict you'll see more sites specializing in student loans in the future. The amount of money that's needed for a college education will continue to increase, so it's not surprising that this P2P lending student loan niche is starting to expand.

GreenNote's lending platform is quite different from the other P2P lending sites we've examined. Read on and you'll see why.

Target Market

Sure, the basic target market that comes to mind is the individual who needs money for school. But the target market really includes four groups:

- ◆ Students who need to borrow money to pay for their educations
- ◆ Parents of the students who need to borrow money
- ◆ Students' relatives who are willing to lend money
- ◆ Lenders who are totally unrelated to the students

GreenNote's online platform differs from the more general sites where a FICO score and credit history can stand between a borrower and the money he or she needs. And unlike Fynanz, borrowers younger than 21 don't need a cosigner. What does GreenNote look for? Character!

The World According to GreenNote

Lately, you've probably heard TV pundits and experts talk about how difficult it is to find a job in the current economy. This can be especially tough on kids just graduating from college. The problem is that there are so many graduates hitting the job market at the same time. Are there that many jobs available every June?

No, there aren't. But take solace in knowing that, in general, college graduates are unemployed for a shorter amount of time than nongraduates. Why bring this up? Because there's a chance a borrower won't be able to make loan payments right away after graduation. If a student gets a loan through a website that requires immediate payback or gets a short-term loan, he or she may not be able to pay it off on a timely basis.

def•i•ni•tion

A **deferred payment** is a loan option that allows you to receive funds in the present and postpone repayment until a stated time in the future.

That's why it's a good idea to take a look at sites such as Fynanz and GreenNote. They include *deferred payment* terms, and the payback terms of the loans are also longer because they recognize that getting a job doesn't always happen right after a student graduates.

Here's a list of the terms for the student loans through GreenNote:

- ◆ Minimum loan amount: $1,000

- ◆ Repayment terms: 10 years

- ◆ Fixed interest rate: 6.8 percent

- ◆ Deferred payments: Up to five years while the student is in school; interest accumulates during this time and is added to the loan balance at the time of repayment

- ◆ No cosigner required

- ◆ Grace period: The first six months after leaving school

- ◆ Repayment: Includes principal and interest

- ◆ Borrower's fees: 2 percent of loan (or a minimum of $49)

Okay, you haven't read anything yet about eligibility, so you're probably wondering what the deal is. Well, if you want to borrow, you're qualified! This P2P lending model is set up so that credit history (or lack thereof) is not a hindrance. The borrower's success in getting a loan funded has a lot to do with how hard he or she networks.

Networking for a college fund? Well, yes. The borrower asks for loans via an e-mail list of his or her possible lenders; GreenNote calls this a "Pledge Drive."

So, You Want to Borrow Money?

GreenNote distinguishes between two phases when it comes to funding your loan:

- Pledging: Students contact relatives and others to get commitments for loans.

- Funding: This is the part where the loan is documented and your school gets the money from GreenNote.

This section focuses on the pledging part.

If you're a parent who's trying to pay for your child's education, you can really help during this stage. If you're an older student, it's still a good idea to have some creative input from someone else.

Creating your profile is your first step, and you should plan to spend a lot of time on it. Before you start writing your GreenNote profile, let's take a look at each part:

- Your name: Along with your first and last name, list your location, gender, and ethnic group. The website encourages you to paint a comprehensive portrait of yourself.

- Your story: Here, you talk about your interests and past experiences. Sharing anecdotes can make this section come to life. Were you named after a relative who was a World War II hero? Explain how this trait has impacted your life and your desire to go to school. Or did you get laid off? It happens every day. Share your story and explain how going back to school will help you update your skills.

- Your loan amount: State your goal and the date by which you'll need the funds.

- Your photo: This is really important. We reviewed this site when it was fairly new, and we noticed that a lot of profiles didn't include a photo. Read Chapter 13 to get tips about using photos. Even if it's a photo of your parakeet, it will help!

- Your school choice: Here you can go into details about your major and any honors you've received.

- Your high school: Name your high school and the activities in which you participated. If you're an adult returning to college, you may want to forgo this step. But if you excelled in high school, there's nothing wrong with tooting your own horn years later!

Remember that the GreenNote platform is different. You're not being "graded" according to FICO scores or even by your grades. This is a character-driven platform. So as you put together your profile, let your values come through. Your prospective lenders will be reading your profile, so make it a great one.

Here are some suggestions—including some from GreenNote—to polish your profile for your Pledge Drive:

◆ Use a serious tone, but let your enthusiasm shine through. No slang, please!

◆ Include anecdotes that illustrate your background or values.

◆ Consider your first draft to be just that ... *your first draft!* You want to spend a few days working on it. Write it and set it aside for a day. Then reread it and revise it. If you're having trouble getting started, GreenNote has some excellent sample profiles that you can use as guides.

◆ Have another person read it for spelling and grammatical errors. Don't rely on your computer's spell-check function. Remember, "do" and "due" are both spelled correctly!

Once you're happy with your written profile, it's time to make a list of prospective lenders to include on your e-mail Pledge Drive list. Ask your family to make suggestions. There's a good chance you'll forget about some of those aunts and uncles you haven't seen in a while.

Also, think about people you know in your community. Are you a member of a church or synagogue? Do you volunteer your time in a hospital? Think about people outside your family who know you well. Make a list so you don't forget anyone when it's time to send out the e-mails. GreenNote has e-mail templates you can use to get started, but try to personalize your message so that your personality shows.

Remind lenders that they can pledge as little as $100, so if you get enough pledges, you may be able to fund your loan. Of course, if one of them wants to fund your entire loan, that's okay, too!

When your loan is completely funded, GreenNote will set up the documentation and you'll be required to sign a promissory note.

So, You Want to Lend Money?

Whether you were persuaded by the student's Pledge Drive or you've been a supporter of the student since way back, you've decided to become a lender. First, be sure you read the preceding borrower's section so you're familiar with the loan terms. Also note that GreenNote may check with a credit bureau to verify your identity. But this is one of those "soft" inquiries that won't affect your credit rating.

Here are a few more things to keep in mind:

◆ Lenders pay an administration fee of 1 percent. This fee is charged when the repayment process begins.

◆ You can become a lender with as little as $100.

◆ The loans are unsecured.

◆ The interest rate is fixed at 6.8 percent (annual percentage yield [APY] of 6.97 percent).

◆ The student pays accrued interest on the loan even if repayment is deferred for five years. The interest is accrued daily.

A word about risk: there's *always* risk in P2P lending, and helping students via GreenNote is no exception. Remember, on this site there isn't a process that reviews a borrower's credit history. If the student defaults, though, GreenNote does handle the collection phase. And this is a legally binding loan, so if the student defaults, it's reported to collection agencies and will affect the student's credit score.

Hidden Treasure

The interest rate on GreenNote is fixed at 6.8 percent. This may seem arbitrary, but it's not. It matches the Federal Unsubsidized Stafford Loan. In case you aren't familiar with these loans, Stafford loans are either subsidized or unsubsidized. For an unsubsidized loan, the limit for the first year of undergraduate education is $2,000 for dependent students and $6,000 for independent students.

The subsidized loans are based on financial need. You aren't charged interest during the deferment period. During this time, the federal government pays for the interest. On July 1, 2008, the subsidized rate dropped to 6 percent. For the 2009–2010 academic year, the rate is dropping to 5.6 percent. To find out more about Stafford loans, visit www.staffordloan.com.

When it's time to fund the loan, you'll be able to do everything online. You'll sign the promissory note via an e-signature, and you can make your funding payment online or even send a check in the mail if you prefer.

In the Red _____

Don't count on your interest income to come out to be the full 6.8 percent. Remember, you pay a 1 percent administration fee, so your rate is actually around 5.8 percent.

Working with Schools

GreenNote works with the financial aid departments in some schools. GreenNote's goal in doing this is to get colleges to educate students about the P2P lending option. It's not an endorsement or a recommendation that students pursue this option but a mention that there's an alternative for the students.

Here's a partial list of the schools that include GreenNote on their financial aid websites:

- California College of the Arts: www.cca.edu/students/financialaid/altloans

- Idaho State University: www.isu.edu/finaid/altr_loan.shtml

- Stanford University: www.gsb.stanford.edu/finaid/types/other_loans.html

- University of Texas at Dallas: www.utdallas.edu/library/resources/hot.htm#grants

- Loyola University New Orleans: www.loyno.edu/financialaid/Undergrad_Alternative_Loans.php

Considering Other Sites for Student Loans

You know that some of the other sites we've covered offer student loan options. Here are some "quick hits" to consider regarding how the others match up with those that specialize in student loans:

- Prosper: Loans are for three years, and repayment begins immediately; the borrower must have a good enough credit history to be considered for a loan.

- Lending Club: Loans are for three years, and repayment begins immediately; the borrower must have a FICO score of at least 640 to be considered for a loan.

- Virgin Money: Virgin has a "Student Paycheck" package. The interest rates are lower than 6.8 percent, and payments can be deferred until graduation.

◆ Loanio: Loans are for three, four, or five years; if you have little or no credit, you may use a co-borrower to request a loan.

So there you have it—the scoop on an alternative way to pay for an education. You're definitely encouraged to look for the "free" money first—scholarships, grants, and so forth. But isn't it nice to know there's another alternative if you get stuck?

The Least You Need to Know

◆ The average annual cost of a public 4-year institution is $12,108, which is a 313.8 percent increase over a 20-year period.

◆ To get a loan through Fynanz, the borrower needs to have good grades and a cosigner if he or she is younger than 21.

◆ GreenNote's eligibility requirement is character; neither a credit history nor a cosigner is required.

◆ On GreenNote, the borrower conducts a "Pledge Drive" to raise money.

◆ Although student loans are available on more general P2P sites, it's important to note the length of the loans and whether there are deferred payment options.

Chapter 12

Choosing the Right Site

In This Chapter

- What factors to consider when choosing a site as a borrower
- What factors to consider when choosing a site as a lender
- Handy charts to help you narrow your choices
- Educating yourself about the different P2P lending websites
- How to set up Google Alerts so you can keep tabs on changes on the P2P lending websites that interest you
- What to do if you still can't decide

There are a lot of ways to go in P2P lending. How in the world do you choose? One step at a time, that's how. We have some step-by-step guidelines for you to follow that will help you narrow down your choices. In most cases, there will only be one or two sites that work for you and your needs.

That's what great about P2P lending—you get to make your own choices.

If You're Borrowing

This question may seem really obvious, but what do you want the money for? No, seriously—we want you to think hard about this. In fact, write it down on paper and then read it out loud. Then think of every question you'd want answered if you were the lender.

You say you want to pay for your education? Okay, fine. Where do you want to go to school? How much do you want to spend per year? What field do you plan to study?

You want to consolidate your credit card debt. What interest rate can you live with? How confident are you that you won't use your card again until the debt is paid?

See where we're going with this? You need to have a clear picture in your mind of what you're going to do with that money. You need to be able to say how that loan is going to help you either in life or in your career (or whatever is important to you). When you're clear about that, you're ready to figure out which site is best for you.

We'll ask a series of questions, and all you have to do is answer them. And at the end of this exercise, you'll see a blinding light that shows the way. Okay, just kidding. But hopefully, you'll have a pretty good idea of which P2P lending site is best suited for you and your needs.

Along the way, you'll also find charts to help you pick a site.

Step 1: What Type of Loan Do You Need?

After doing your homework about why you want the loan, answering this question should be easy. A personal loan is too generic. *Be specific.* Label it as a student loan, a car loan, a mortgage, and so on.

Use the following chart to narrow down your choice by type of loan. Personal loans include debt consolidation, buying a car, wedding expenses, and so on. Note that mortgages and student loans have their own categories. If you just want documentation of a loan between yourself and someone else, then Nolo is an option.

P2P Site	Personal Loans	Business Loans	Mortgages	Student Loans
Prosper	X	X		X
Loanio	X	X		X
Virgin Money	X	X	X	X

Lending Club	X	X		X
LoanBack	X	X		X
Fynanz				X
Nolo (forms only)	X	X	X	X
GreenNote				X

Step 2: Who Are Your Lenders?

Is a family member or a friend willing to lend you money? If the answer is no (or if you're unsure), then you need to widen your net to include lenders you've never met.

According to the following chart, if family or friends aren't options, then you can remove Virgin Money and Nolo from your list. If you're looking for a deal on a mortgage, however, there are two options. In the future, it wouldn't be surprising to see other P2P sites brokering mortgage loans between people who have never met. Stay tuned for that.

P2P Site	Family/Friends	Lenders I Don't Know
Prosper	X	X
Loanio	X	X
Virgin Money	X	
Lending Club	X	X
LoanBack	X	
Fynanz	X	X
Nolo (forms only)	X	
GreenNote	X	

Step 3: What's in Your Credit Report? And, If You're a Student, What Are Your Academic Grades?

Many of the sites have minimum FICO scores, so if you don't meet the requirements for some, you can knock those sites off your list. Some also have requirements about your credit history.

If you're a student, your grades can affect the interest rates you'll get on some sites. On Fynanz, an exceptional academic record earns you a better interest rate. On GreenNote, being able to tout good grades will help you attract lenders. This is because many people believe that obtaining good grades is often a sign of responsibility.

P2P Site	FICO Score
Prosper	520 plus
Loanio	Uses Experian VantageScore (with a low score, a co-borrower is an option)
Virgin Money	N/A
Lending Club	640 plus
LoanBack	N/A
Fynanz	N/A
Nolo (forms only)	N/A
GreenNote	N/A

Step 4: What Payment Terms Do You Need?

Does it matter to you if you get a three-year or a five-year loan? Will you be happy with a lower interest rate than what you have now? Do you want a fixed-rate loan?

These are important questions to answer. As you can see in the following chart, there's a lot of variance in the term lengths of loans.

P2P Site	Loan Terms/Amounts
Prosper	3-year, fixed-rate loans; $1,000–$25,000
Loanio	3, 4, or 5 years, variable rates; $1,000–$25,000 (depending on state)
Virgin Money	You decide the length/amount; minimum AFR if loan exceeds $10,000
Lending Club	3-year, fixed-rate loans; $1,000–$25,000
LoanBack	N/A
Fynanz	5-,7-, or 10-year loans; $2,500–$40,000 annually
Nolo (forms only)	You decide
GreenNote	10-year terms with deferred payment options, 6.8 percent fixed rate; you decide amount

Good Cents _____

A loan listing on Prosper is there for seven days. If you need the funds quickly and you're willing to pay a higher interest rate, Prosper allows you to choose automatic funding. This means your loan bypasses the longer bidding process that drives down the interest rate. As soon as the loan is funded, you get the money right away.

Step 5: Do You Have a Plan B?

You're probably thinking, "What? No one said I needed a Plan B!"

You need to be prepared just in case your loan request doesn't get funded. You should have another option in the back of your mind—even if your Plan B involves trying to get the loan on a different site or trying to get the *same* loan on the *same* site six months later.

If You're Lending

We have a set of questions to help you, the lender, decide where you want to invest your money. The good news for you is that you can decide to fund loans on more than one site.

Step 1: What's Important to You?

Think about what you feel passionate about. Is it your alma mater? Do you get excited when you hear about someone's innovative business idea? Do you just adore anyone who's from the South? Or are you interested in helping your granddaughter get through law school?

Maybe you just want to make some money. Hey, that's okay, too. The reason we bring up the passion issue is because for many people, that's an important part of social lending. It's the chance to hear someone's story and then offer a helping hand.

But most of these sites welcome you regardless of whether your motive is altruism or profit. If your motives lean toward the altruistic side, Kiva is an option to consider. Lenders are drawn to this site for its unique opportunities to help entrepreneurs in developing countries.

Take some time to figure out how much money you want to lend and what kind of a return you want, and maybe you'll get a good idea of where you might want to invest your money.

Step 2: How Much Money Do You Want to Lend?

Think in terms of how much you'd like to initially invest. You can get started with a small amount, to be sure. But if you only want to lend a total of $200, you don't want to be in a situation where you have to invest all of that into one loan.

You'll learn later about diversifying, but for now, you want to choose a site where you can spread the wealth—even if it's a small amount of wealth!

P2P Site	Minimum Bid Per Loan
Prosper	$50
Kiva	$25
Loanio	$50
Virgin Money	N/A
Lending Club	$25
LoanBack	N/A
Fynanz	$50
GreenNote	$100
MicroPlace	$100 for your first loan; $50 for subsequent loans

Step 3: What Kind of Return Are You Looking For?

Are you just looking to do better than if you were to invest in a money market account or a CD at a bank? It's not possible to accurately predict what you'll make. But looking at the following interest rates can help you see what kind of interest income is typically being generated at these sites.

With interest rates, it also depends on the risk you're willing to take. The lower the credit rating, the more interest income you'll make. But then again, there's more of a risk that you won't get your money back.

In the Red

The P2P lending business is unpredictable, so don't rely on the interest rates that sites publish. Even borrowers with high credit ratings default on loans from time to time. Be sure you use these rates as a guideline and not as an absolute measure of your return on investment (ROI).

Here is an estimate (subject to change) of what to expect on a $4,000 loan:

P2P Site	Estimated Interest Rates
Prosper	AA credit grade: 8.15 percent C credit grade: 18.66 percent
Lending Club	A1–A5 grade: 7.37–9.38 percent C1–C5 grade: 11.78–13.04 percent
Loanio	A+, A credit grade: 7–14 percent C+, C credit grade: 14–19 percent

Here's a word about default rates as well: default rates can be misleading because your results may depend on the specific type of borrower you choose. For instance, Prosper's net default rate over all credit grades was 4 percent in July 2008. But if you chose only AA grade loans, the default rate was only .56 percent.

At the time this book was written, the economy was having a lot of ups and downs—mostly downs. So looking at an average may or may not be reflective of what you'll experience. Your experience could be better or worse. Remember, anytime you see estimated rates, you're looking at a snapshot of rates at that point in time.

Really, it's not that different from playing the stock market. You choose your risk and live with the consequences, either good or bad.

Read All About It

What you need to do now is learn everything you can about the site (or sites) in which you're most interested. With a 24-hours-a-day, 7-days-a-week news cycle like we now have, it's easy to become well-informed on just about any topic imaginable.

Magazine and Newspaper Articles

In the age of interactive websites, it's sometimes easy to forget about print media. There's a wealth of information in magazines and newspapers. The financial press, such as *The Wall Street Journal*, is writing a lot about the emerging P2P industry. But you'll also find stories in the more mainstream press. *Time* magazine ran a recent story on the increase in P2P loans.

> ### Hidden Treasure
>
> Interested in one-stop shopping for news? For a list of magazines and newspapers from all over the world, check out Newsdirectory.com. You can browse newspapers in any country or region. In the United States, you can click a state and get a list of newspapers by area code. Some you have to register with or pay a subscription, but often you go directly to the paper's site.
>
> You can also browse magazines by subject, read college newspapers, or get up-to-date breaking news.

If you don't have the extra money to buy magazines and newspapers, then go ahead and read what's available online. Some require online subscriptions, but not all of them do. You can register on *The New York Times* website and read the paper online for free. You can also read *The Atlanta Journal-Constitution* online for free. Check out your hometown newspaper online, too, and see whether it's free.

Another option is going to the library. Remember libraries? They're still there, and they're better than ever. Visit a library to read magazines and newspapers free of charge. We don't know whether libraries have Starbucks yet, but if they do, we wouldn't be surprised.

Websites

We spent a lot of time on websites while researching this book, and some of them are pretty thorough. Prosper, especially, has a well-designed site with tons of information. And Lending Club and Loanio both have user-friendly, visually appealing sites. It's a good idea when you're on these P2P sites to read about the entire process. You only plan to be a lender? That's fine, but it's a good idea to know how the borrowing side works, too.

You don't want to understand only one side of the process. When you review a borrower's listing, wouldn't it be nice to know how he or she got to that point? And when you know what kind of information the borrowers are required to give, you're more informed about the kinds of questions you should be asking.

Blogs

The number of blogs out there is more than 100 million and still counting. One reason they're so popular is because blogging is a quick and friendly way to keep readers informed about a topic.

There are lots of individual blogs dedicated to P2P lending. But first, read the official blogs of P2P sites before branching out. Out of 100 million blogs, you know there must be a few clunkers. Be sure you have a good knowledge base so you can tell the difference between the good, the bad, and the downright ugly blogs.

Let's take a look at the P2P blogs that are associated with P2P lending sites.

♦ The official Prosper blog is at www.blog.prosper.com. It's an excellent resource with numerous categories to choose from, such as academics, business development, and Prosper news. It's updated frequently.

♦ Find Loanio's blog at www.blog.loanio.com. This is a fairly new site and at the time we looked, the content was fresh and helpful.

♦ Lending Club's blog is at www.blog.lendingclub.com. It's an active blog with categories and archives.

♦ LoanBack has a blog at www.loanback.blogspot.com, but there were no current entries when we looked.

♦ MicroPlace has a blog that covers the microfinance industry. It appears to be updated frequently and is very informative.

♦ GreenNote's blog has helpful information, but when we looked, it wasn't being updated frequently.

♦ Fynanz's blog appears to be updated a couple times a month. The content includes the impact of current events on student loans. For instance, an October 30, 2008, entry compared the views of the presidential candidates on the topic of college affordability.

Forums

Forums are a great way to get a feel for how a site works. You can also get a vibe about the culture and how satisfied the users are. Like blogs, forums are not all created equal.

♦ Prosper's official forum is located at https://connect.prosper.com. There are five of them: lenders, borrowers, groups and friends, bug reports, and developers. You do have to register to enter the forums.

♦ CardRatings.com has tons of activity, and P2P loans are frequently discussed. This is a good place to get some objective feedback from informed users.

♦ Lending Club has a discussion board on its Facebook page, which we discuss next.

Facebook

It shouldn't surprise you that P2P lending is alive and well on Facebook. Social lending goes hand in hand with social networking. And this is a good way to give details in a casual environment.

◆ Prosper invites anyone to join its group on Facebook. There's a discussion group and a chance to virtually mingle with other P2P lenders and borrowers.

◆ Lending Club got its start on Facebook, and it hasn't abandoned its roots. It still has a Facebook presence. There's a discussion board where you have a chance to talk with members (both borrowers and lenders).

◆ GreenNote has a page, but there was very little activity when we looked. It's a fairly new website, though. Sometimes Facebook pages pick up new members when the websites become more visible and popular.

◆ Kiva is also on Facebook. There's a discussion group, and everyone is welcome to join.

◆ Virgin Money has a page, but at the time we looked there was minimal recent activity. There were about 60 fans, so maybe it's starting to generate some activity. Virgin Money does update the page with company news and videos.

◆ Fynanz is there, but at the time we visited its page, it was just getting started and there wasn't much going on.

◆ MicroPlace has a page on Facebook, and at the time we looked, it was pretty active. It's an open group, which means anyone can join.

These groups are easy to find on Facebook. Just do a search on the P2P website's name. Click on the name and you're there!

Set Up Google Alerts

P2P lending is a rapidly changing industry, so if you want to know the latest happenings, set up a *Google Alert* on the topic. Go to www.google.com/alerts and set up search terms in its Create a Google Alert box.

Set up a few variations of P2P lending. Try these:

◆ "Person-to-Person Lending"

- "Peer-to-Peer Lending"
- "Social Lending"
- "Social Finance"
- "P2P Lending"
- "P2P Loans"

Get the idea? You never know how this subject will be referred to within a blog or an article, so requesting a few different variations increases your chances of Google grabbing it for you and sending it to your inbox. And don't forget the quotation marks, or you'll get an unbelievable amount of irrelevant—and possibly very strange—e-mail.

You can also do Google Alerts on the P2P sites you're most interested in keeping up with.

For type, ask for "comprehensive"—and for frequency of the updates, that's up to you. You can receive e-mails once a day, as they happen, or in one lump e-mail at the end of the week.

If you haven't already registered with Google, you'll need to do that so you can manage your alerts.

def•i•ni•tion

Google Alerts are e-mail updates that Google finds based on search terms you've requested. There are six different types of alerts: news, web, blogs, comprehensive (this option includes all the types), video, and groups. You can also decide how frequently you want to receive this information.

The Winner Is ...

You probably have a much clearer picture now of which site is best for you. But if the type of loan you're looking for is pretty generic, such as credit card debt consolidation, and you have an excellent credit rating, then you may still have a lot of options.

Don't worry. Remember, P2P lending is about making your own choices. There's no pressure from banks to take their rates. Just take your time and keep reading. Learning how to write your loan request and how to manage photos on your loan profile might help you decide which site is best for you.

The Least You Need to Know

- If you're borrowing money, think carefully about what you want the money for.

- You can narrow down your borrowing choices considerably by the type of loan you desire or just by the credit score requirements.

- If you're lending money, think first about what your objectives are—both socially and from a financial standpoint.

- Set up Google Alerts so you can learn more about P2P lending.

- If you're still undecided, take time to learn more about the process of P2P lending; keep reading this book and you'll learn more that may help you make a decision.

Part 3

Borrowing Money

Much of the advice in this book applies to both borrowers and lenders. But in this part, we focus on special issues that apply just to borrowers.

Do you feel a little intimidated at the idea of writing a loan listing? Learn how to create a listing that gets a lender's attention—and receive practical advice for setting up a budget so you make your loan payments on time.

Part 3 also describes how to get a second loan from a P2P lender, the advantages and disadvantages of being part of a borrower's group, and what to look for when you receive your account statements.

"I just don't think it's necessary to write 'I like long walks on the beach.'"

Chapter 13

Attracting Lenders with Your Listing

In This Chapter

- ◆ How to write a compelling loan listing
- ◆ Choosing the right photo
- ◆ Answering questions from lenders
- ◆ Getting endorsements
- ◆ Advertising suggestions
- ◆ Joining P2P lending groups on Facebook

You may have never created a loan listing before, so it's normal to feel like a fish out of water. As you work on your listing, remember that this is more like the gentle art of persuasion, not selling.

There's no need to worry. As in all things, the more you learn about a technique, the better you become at it.

Relax and read on. In this chapter, we share tips from the various P2P lending sites to get you started. And if your listing doesn't seem to be getting attention, you can always tweak it. We'll give tips for that, too.

Brother, Can You Spare $5,000?

We've already covered the process of registering and proving your identity, so we'll get right to the goods here. What's the best way to inspire lenders to flock to your listing?

If you expect lenders to give you $5,000, you need to write a compelling—but truthful—story. The sites vary a little on format (and of course, if it's a loan from family or friends, this section isn't a hot topic for you), but you'll need to explain the following in some form.

The Purpose of the Loan

What will you use the $5,000 for? Don't say you're planning to bum around Europe for the summer to find yourself. And don't try to be witty, or you'll come across as someone who's not taking the loan seriously.

If you answered the questions in Chapter 12, this is a piece of cake for you. Here's an example of a good way to state your purpose:

"I will use the $5,000 to pay off my credit card debt. With the money I'll save on interest, I'll also be able to put away a little money and get back on my feet financially."

This statement says to the lender: "I'm trying to make my life better, and you know you'll get repaid because I'm even going to be saving money during the term of the loan." Ka-ching!

Your Financial Situation

Don't panic and say, "If I had a good situation, I wouldn't be asking for a loan!" Every day, people from all walks of life get into tough financial dilemmas. In today's economy, this isn't going to be a shock to anyone. You just need to explain what happened with your finances.

Here's what you do: calmly state what's going on in your life. You don't have to give a lot of details unless you think it will make a difference and you feel comfortable sharing.

Do not give information that reveals your identity. Don't give your name, address, phone number, and so on. We mentioned this before, but it bears repeating: revealing your complete identity can make you susceptible to identity theft. You can make your loan listing seem "personal" without disclosing your city or your phone number.

Your Income and DTI

If the site allows, list your income and expenses. If your debt-to-income (DTI) ratio is high, explain how that happened and how you plan to pay back the loan. Lenders want to help, but they want reassurance they'll get their money back. Give them reasons why you're a good risk although your financials may not look good in black and white. A DTI ratio of less than 36 percent is considered okay, but Prosper recommends adding an explanation if your DTI ratio is higher than 20 percent. Your objective is to assure lenders that you can make the payments.

Read over your explanation and then put it away for a few days. Then read it again and see how it sounds. Have a friend read it. And please don't misspell words, use slang, or use poor grammar.

Funny, but we see this all the time in listings and it does not engender confidence in the lenders. Your job is to make sure (to the best of your abilities) that you come across as intelligent and responsible—which is exactly what you are!

> **Good Cents** _____
>
> If you're self-employed, then it may be difficult for you to pinpoint your DTI ratio. Use an average, if you can. Simply explain that you're self-employed and the DTI percent you're stating is an average of the previous year (or explain whatever steps you took to get an average DTI ratio).

Let Me Explain ...

Hey, no one's perfect. You don't need to apologize for that time in 2004 when you lost your credit card bill in your messy apartment for two months and had two delinquent payments. But you *do* need to explain these things in a reasonable way and make sure it's clear that it was just a blip on your otherwise stellar credit history.

There are a couple situations in particular that you should address. Prosper reports that listings that address interest rate, loan amount, and the number of delinquencies (and any other public record issues, such as bankruptcy) have the best chances of receiving funding.

> **Good Cents** _____
>
> If you're having trouble getting funded, call a few friends or a family member and ask whether one of them will make the first bid. Prosper says that sometimes getting the first bid is the toughest, and once you get it, the bids often start coming in.

Problems on Your Credit Report

You need to specifically explain a low credit score and any delinquencies that are current or that have occurred in the past seven years. In many cases, a low score is explained by the delinquencies. But other issues can cause a low score, too.

For instance, opening new accounts, closing accounts, or a shopping spree that decreased the ratio of your debt to your credit card limits can cause a low score. So address the low score in whatever way seems appropriate for your situation.

How to Word It

If you have a low score, don't say you don't know how it happened. (Yes, we've seen this in listings!) Would you loan money to someone who had *no idea* why his or her FICO score was 540? No, we didn't think so.

Good Cents _____

Don't worry about your loan listing affecting your credit score. Your FICO score is not dinged when you publish a listing. If you do get your loan funded, the details go into your credit report—but not until you actually have a successful loan request.

So what's the best way to explain some of your financial tribulations? Relax—we have some suggestions that may help. Here are a few ways to address some sticky situations:

◆ Low FICO score:

"My score is a little low because I made two late payments on my credit card bill. I've paid all my bills on time since then and will have no problems in the future."

"My FICO score is low because an error was made in my credit report. I've contacted the credit bureau and the creditor, and they are currently investigating the matter. I expect the error to be corrected soon and my FICO score to return to normal."

"My FICO score is low because I was unemployed for three months and had to charge a lot of necessities. During this time, I often had to charge up to my credit limit. I've been employed for the past six months and my job is going well. I'm paying down my credit card bills. I'll use my loan to consolidate my debt and get back on the right track."

- Late payments:

    "I made some late payments last year because I lost my job. I'm now employed again and have a DTI ratio of 35 percent."

    "I haven't made any late payments in the last five years. I have steady employment and expect to continue to have an excellent record."

    "I made a few late payments last year because I had some unexpected medical expenses. I've paid off my medical bills and will have no problems keeping up with payments."

- Public record issues:

    "I declared bankruptcy in 2002. I lost my job and lost my house. I'm now successfully employed again and rebuilding my credit. I've made all my payments on time in the last few years."

    "There was a lien on my house three years ago because I paid my property taxes late. The taxes went up considerably that year. But I now make more money and have no problem paying my taxes on time."

    "I lost my house in foreclosure last year. I've saved money since then and am living in an apartment. I now have a DTI ratio of 20 percent."

You want to make sure that you've given reasonable explanations to lenders. They have many other borrowers to choose from. Don't give them a reason to go on to the next listing.

A Picture Is Worth Thousands of Dollars

If you're planning to use a site where photos are commonplace, then having a photo on your listing is crucial. What people love about social lending is the feeling that they're dealing with a real person and not a marble-floored bank. A photo is a nice touch and makes it personal.

Hidden Treasure

If you have a digital camera, it's easy to get great shots even if you're an amateur! Visit Kodak's website at www.kodak.com to get some great tips on how to take professional-looking photos: take photos at eye level, beware of what the background looks like, watch the light, and wait for the focus to lock in.

Get comfortable, grab a cup of coffee (or tea, if you prefer), and view the photos in borrower listings on Prosper, Fynanz, Loanio, and GreenNote. Take some notes. Here are a few questions to keep in mind while you glance through the listings.

♦ Which photos draw you in?

♦ Do you prefer photos with one subject or with families?

♦ Are you more likely to read a listing that has a face attached to it rather than a photo of a boat?

♦ Which photos give you a yucky feeling? It's just as important to identify what *doesn't* work so you stay away from that approach.

There are a wide range of photos on Prosper—everything from newborn twins to pets to sailboats. We saw a listing where the borrower used a photo of a newborn *and* a really cute puppy. On Fynanz, borrowers are asked to upload three photos for their listings. Fynanz encourages borrowers to use photos containing the school's mascot or something that shows a connection to the school they attend. You can use this approach on GreenNote, too.

In fact, most of the P2P lending sites encourage photos. You can get creative, if you like. Are you planning to start your own nursery and sell trees, plants, and flowers? Take a photo and show a beautiful plant in your listing.

Love My Dog? Then Lend Me Money!

One thing you'll notice right away is that borrowers love to showcase their pets. It's not just dogs, either. You'll see cats, birds, iguanas, you name it. You'd have to be a reptile lover to be drawn to an iguana photo, but on the other hand, it would grab your attention.

You can't go wrong with a dog or a cat. You'll see lots of dogs with big eyes, such as pugs and shih-tzus. There are plenty of kittens, too. A couple Siamese kittens may have nothing to do with how you got into credit card debt, but that doesn't really matter. You want lenders to stop scanning and click your listing.

Using a pet photo is also a tactic people use when they don't think they're photogenic or because they're not comfortable using photos of their kids.

Conveying the Right Image

The other element of selecting photos involves the attitude and tone the photo conveys. Keep a few of these things in mind when you're picking your photo:

◆ Don't appear as if you're posing for a listing in a singles magazine. Keep your appearance businesslike (because this *is* a business transaction).

◆ Don't offend anyone. Avoid photos that contain curse words or offend a particular group of people. Likewise, don't wear shirts that show you're a proponent of a hot-button issue. Yes, you have freedom of speech, but this isn't the place to make political statements.

◆ Do use a high-quality photo. The image should be easy to see. If we can't tell that there's a person standing next to the Alps, then your photo is useless.

◆ Do smile if you're using a photo of yourself. In other words, look like the happy, well-adjusted person that you are!

If you don't have a current photo you can use, have a friend take a casual photo. You don't need to spend the money for a professional photographer. Save that money to repay your loan!

Answering Lenders' Questions

On Prosper, lenders can ask you questions about your listing. If lenders are asking you questions, then congratulate yourself on a listing well done. It's doubtful they'd take the time to learn more about you and your loan unless there was strong interest.

You'll get an e-mail when a lender asks you a question. Answer these promptly, because the lender may be anxious to make a decision. Again, don't reveal your actual identity. On P2P sites, everyone's Clark Kent!

Your response is sent directly to the lender. You have the option of including this question and answer on your listing.

Now, you don't have to answer any of these questions. But unless there's something offensive about a question, it's in your best interest to

> **Hidden Treasure**
>
> Even if you choose to have all questions and answers visible, casual visitors to Prosper can't see them. A lender must be registered to see this part of your listing. You can also choose to keep all questions and answers invisible on your listing—even for registered users.

answer it. Answering questions may also keep other potential lenders from asking you the same questions over and over. And if that is happening, then revise your loan listing so it's more complete.

By the way, if you do get offensive questions report them to the P2P lending site.

Getting Endorsements

If you were considering hiring someone for a job, what would you do? You would get a reference. If you're thinking of loaning someone money, seeing an *endorsement* might sway you in his or her direction.

Prosper encourages endorsements because it shows evidence of real relationships in your life. Social lending may happen online, but there's still an important psychological connection that lenders want to make with borrowers.

def•i•ni•tion

On a P2P lending site, an **endorsement** is a written recommendation by someone who knows the borrower very well. Getting endorsements helps persuade lenders that you're a good risk.

On Prosper, endorsers aren't required to bid on your loan—so be sure you explain that in case your endorser isn't in a position to bid. But endorsers do need to sign up as either a borrower or a lender on the site.

This process verifies the endorser's identity. Once he or she is registered, your endorsers will get updates on the funding process. It's usually fun for the endorser to be involved in the funding process of your loan.

Here are a few tips to make the "endorsement approach" a successful strategy:

◆ Ask family members and friends to give you endorsements. Make it easy for them to register on Prosper by explaining the process and why it's necessary.

◆ An endorsement needs to include the person's relationship to you and a statement that says your friend (even if it's your mom) knows that you will pay back the loan.

◆ If you can get your endorser to bid on your loan, that's also a good sign to the lender.

◆ You have to publish the endorsement for it to appear on your listing. If you didn't receive a message that the endorsement was received, then it didn't go through.

If this is the case, go to the endorsements received page and click "Publish" next to your endorsement. If this doesn't solve the problem, then contact Prosper for help resolving the issue.

In the Red

When you receive an endorsement, double-check it to make sure your first and last name isn't mentioned. If the lender learns your identity, it can put that individual in a precarious legal position. As a result, the lender will move on to another listing and not bid on your loan.

For some, it can be a little daunting to come up with a good endorsement that sounds sincere. Here are a few examples to help you—and the endorser—get started:

- "Kerrie is one of the most responsible people I know. I've worked with her for five years, and I have no doubt she'll pay back the loan. Everyone at our company respects and trusts her."

- "Thomas is an exceptional person. He volunteers his time as a soccer coach for his child's team. We've been friends for years, and I know I can always count on him. He's a very good risk to take on this loan. He'll pay you back without a problem."

- "Sara is a talented salesperson. She always meets her quotas. She works hard until the job is done. She's the most reliable person I've ever met. She does what she says she'll do."

- "This borrower has always been there for me. When I needed a small loan for college, he helped me out. Now I want to help him. He's an honest guy who cares about others. Take a risk on him, and you won't regret it."

There you go. Hopefully these endorsement templates will get you and your endorser started. But we're guessing that it will take only a little prodding before your endorser comes up with his or her own glowing review of your many attributes.

Shout It from the Rooftops

Okay, not literally. But don't be shy. Tell everyone you know about your loan listing. You may not be used to being your own publicist, so here are some suggestions on how to proceed.

◆ Blog all about it. Put a link on your blog that connects to your listing. If you don't have a blog, start one that chronicles your journey toward getting funded. Do you have friends with blogs? Comment on their blogs and show a link to your listing. (And ask your friend whether it's okay before you do it.)

If you frequent certain blogs, sign up for *blog feeds* so you can keep up with opportunities to comment on blogs and perhaps plug your loan request. Or be sure your own blog is available as a blog feed.

def•i•ni•tion

A feed, like a **blog feed,** is a data format used for publishing frequently changing content. It's also sometimes called a syndicated feed. When you update your blog, the notice goes out to subscribers.

◆ Use the Facebook page if your site has one. You can discuss your listing on this page. And don't forget to advertise it on your own Facebook or MySpace page.

◆ On Loanio, you can add photos. Are you starting a gift basket business? Show yourself putting together gift baskets for your new business.

◆ Let's say you're going to school. On GreenNote and Fynanz, you use a photo of the campus if you're not comfortable with using a photo of yourself. And don't forget photos of your pets. Photos of pets seem to work well for most loan listings!

◆ Tell everyone you work with. If they aren't familiar with the concept, explain it. Chances are you'll see a few people have "Aha!" moments, and they may want to invest in your loan.

◆ Go through your contact database and send e-mails to those with whom you're still in touch.

◆ Encourage your family and friends to tell their friends about your listing and which site it's on.

You can join a P2P group on Facebook and still maintain your privacy. Facebook's default settings allow all of your networks to view your listing.

Do this to restrict access on your Facebook page:

1. Go to your "Privacy Settings for Your Profile" page.

2. Choose an access level you're comfortable with. You can choose "Only friends."

3. Click "Save" at the bottom of the page or your settings won't be kept.

What If Your Loan Doesn't Get Funded?

As you can see, there really are lots of ways to attract lenders. Sometimes you'll request a loan that gets funded quickly, and sometimes you won't. Even then, there are some options.

If you receive only partial funding, it's possible on some websites to relist your loan. You'll have to check with the individual sites to determine their policies. Some sites offer an option to accept partial funding instead of the full amount of your loan. You'll have to make decisions based on what seems right for you. It depends on what you need the money for and how quickly you need it.

Good Cents

On some sites, you can opt to take partial funding on a loan. Check with each individual site. If this is an option, think about it. Also look into the option of relisting your loan or even listing your loan request on another P2P lending website.

The Least You Need to Know

◆ Writing an effective loan listing is more about the art of persuasion, not sales.

◆ Don't reveal your identity in your listing or you may make yourself vulnerable to identity theft.

◆ It's vital to explain any problem areas in your credit report.

◆ Photos can be a very effective tool for getting a lender's interest.

◆ Answer questions from lenders promptly, or they may move on to the next listing.

◆ Getting endorsements from family and friends can persuade lenders that you're a good risk.

◆ Advertise your loan request in as many places and ways as possible.

Chapter 14

Show Them the Money

In This Chapter

- ◆ Why you need to stick to a budget
- ◆ Low-tech solutions for budgeting
- ◆ High-tech solutions for budgeting
- ◆ Paying off your loan early
- ◆ Staying motivated

You want to make sure that when you get your loan, you're able to pay it off. We all have good intentions, but without proper planning it's possible that something unpredictable could happen.

So when you get your loan and you know what your monthly payment is, set up a budget. Start saving a little every month if you can. If you stick to a budget, you're more likely to pay off your loan and have money to spare.

Wouldn't it be nice if you could avoid being stressed out about money? And maybe even make a few payments early? How about paying the loan off early?

Okay, let's not get too carried away—but when you stick with a budget, you might be surprised at how much money you can save.

Don't Budge from Your Budget

You can do this the old-fashioned way and write it down on a piece of paper. Or you can use an Excel spreadsheet that you've customized for your particular lifestyle, income, and expenses.

Do a preliminary budget on paper just to get a feel for the numbers with which you're working.

Take time now and complete the following steps:

♦ Gather all of your financial statements and make a list. Find your utility bills, credit card statements, and savings account information. You want to account for everything that goes into your monthly expenses and all your sources of income.

♦ Separate expense-related information from income-related items.

♦ Use a form that's set up like the following for a basic overview.

Category	Monthly Budget Amount	Monthly Actual Amount	Difference
Income:			
Salary/bonuses after taxes	$2,900	$2,900	—
Interest income	0	0	
Miscellaneous	0	0	
Income after taxes	$2,900	$2,900	—
Expenses:			
Mortgage/rent Property taxes	$1,100	$1,100	—
Home repairs	$50	$75	($25)
Electricity/gas	$200	$250	($50)
Car payments	$150	$150	—
Total expenses	$1,500	$1,575	
Total: Income – expenses	$1,400	$1,325	($75)

How much is left? In the example, the budget shows an expectation that $1,400 will be left over each month. The actual amount remaining turns out to be $1,325. Miscellaneous expenses such as home repairs are difficult to budget for. Utilities can be difficult to budget for as well. With utilities, some months you are over budget and some months the expense is under budget.

It may take a few months to accurately estimate your expenses. Note that we've simplified this example just to make a point. As you put together your own budget, you'll no doubt come up with many other categories to include. And don't forget to include any expenses related to your children's extracurricular activities. It's amazing how quickly ballet classes and costs for baseball equipment add up.

Okay, you get the idea. Get very, very detailed and make a thorough list. Maybe you don't have a car payment and your company pays for your health insurance (lucky you!). The point is to make sure you're on top of your money situation so you don't miss payments.

> **Good Cents** _____
>
> There are lots of budgeting spreadsheets online that you can download. About.com has a similar and more detailed one than the sheet we're using here for illustration purposes. You can find it here: http://financialplan.about.com/cs/budgeting/l/blbudget.htm.
>
> Also, try downloading Microsoft Office Budget Template Worksheets at http://office.microsoft.com/en-us/templates/CT101172321033.aspx.

Free Money Management

Who says there's no such thing as a free lunch? Okay, we admit that we probably have said that before—but this time, something really *is* free. And how terrific that it's *money management.*

Check out a free money management tool on a user-friendly website called Mint.com. Mint makes recommendations for ways you can save money by using different banks or other service providers than you are currently using.

> **def•i•ni•tion** _____
>
> **Money management** refers to the process of budgeting, spending, saving, and investing by an individual.

Good Cents _____

Here are a few free online money management tools to check out:

Geezeo.com: www.geezeo.com

ClearCheckbook.com: www.clearcheckbook.com

FinancialFate.com: www.financialfate.com

If you take one of Mint's recommendations (do *not* take any of the suggestions unless it's really in your best interests), then Mint gets a commission from the company that you switched to. It's kind of like the coupons that you get at the grocery store along with your receipt for your purchases. Based on your purchases, the grocery store makes "suggestions" for other products that you might like.

How Mint Works with Your Account Information

Mint uses a clever and secure method to access your online bank accounts and credit card accounts. For Mint to be able to access your accounts, you must have online access to those accounts via the Internet.

Good Cents _____

If you don't currently have online access to your bank account, check with your bank about getting this option. Being able to view your accounts online is a great way to stay on top of your budget. It's also a good way to make sure you don't have any non-sufficient funds (NSF) charges heading your way because you let your account balance get too low.

Once you can access your bank accounts and credit card accounts online, then you simply tell Mint that you want to give it access to your checking account at, for instance, ABC Bank, and your Visa credit card with XYZ Bank.

When you set up Mint to access these accounts, you do not give Mint the account numbers at these banks or credit card companies. Rather, you tell Mint the following for each account:

- The name of the bank or credit card company

- The type of account (for example, checking, savings, or credit card)

- Your online user ID and password for that account

Mint then uses that login information to read your transactions out of your accounts. Note that Mint is one-way only. Mint only reads information out of your accounts—it never makes changes to your accounts or executes transactions of any kind.

How Mint Helps You Stop Spending

One of the hardest aspects of budgeting is to stick to it. This involves using your budget to actually prevent yourself from spending more than you should.

Hey, there probably aren't many who haven't experienced some remorse from overspending! But guess what? If you do your budget only once a month, you will only see mistakes *after* you have made them. Having something that tracks your budget against what you are actually spending every day (and when set up properly, Mint does this automatically) enables you to stop yourself when you have hit your budget for a certain category.

Say, for example, that you budgeted $300 for eating out this month. On the 15th of the month, you're looking at your Mint account and see you've spent $299. Well, that's important to know now so that you can keep from blowing your restaurant budget.

Other cool Mint features include:

♦ Graphs that enable you to see how much you have spent on particular categories over time. This is useful if you want to see how you are making progress on a month-by-month basis (or also see the bump in the road when you blew it in a particular month).

♦ Pie charts that show how your spending is broken down by category—for any month that you choose. This pie chart, along with the accompanying list of top merchants where you spent your money in that month, lets you get an instantaneous handle on your spending in a particular month.

These graphs and pie charts can be very helpful—you'll find out it can be revealing to glance at a chart and see how much money you spent at Taco Bell or Chili's. If you don't know how much you're spending, this will be an eye-opener.

How Mint Relates to P2P Borrowing

If you get a loan from a P2P site such as Prosper, Mint allows you to integrate the information about your P2P loan. Mint then allows you to track your progress while paying off your loan.

With Mint, you will get a consolidated view of the following:

◆ How much money you have in all of your bank accounts (your assets)

◆ How much money you owe, such as on your P2P loan and your credit cards (your liabilities)

◆ What your net worth is (the difference between your assets and liabilities)

If you have investment accounts for your IRA or other investment accounts, you can tie those accounts into Mint as well. This step would allow Mint to give you a better approximation of your overall net worth.

It can take time to get Mint set up in a way that's helpful to you. Now it's hard to track cash if you don't come up with a system. For instance, if you use your debit card a lot to get cash from an ATM, Mint can't break that down into categories. Mint won't know if you spent that money at the grocery store or for tickets at the movies.

If you would like to try Mint, just think about these issues. If you have the discipline to charge your movie tickets and pay that amount off at the end of the month, then Mint can keep track of that expense. When you use your credit card on a purchase, Mint can usually track that vendor and categorize it properly.

But if you don't have the discipline, be honest with yourself. You might be better off with a budgeting tool like the envelope system. The point is to pick an approach that works for you.

You can sync up your bank and credit card accounts with Mint and generate reports that show where you're over or under budget for your previously set-up categories. Once Mint is set up, you can see pie charts that show how much you spent on restaurants, groceries, and utilities.

> **Hidden Treasure**
>
> During and following the Great Depression, people were understandably uncomfortable about leaving too much of their money in banks. The envelope system was very popular during this time.
>
> Guess where people liked to keep their savings envelopes? Under their mattresses.

Another (free!) simple thing to try is the envelope system. Set up envelopes for each of your major expenses, and note how much you need to contribute to the envelope each week to meet that expense. If you get paid semimonthly, then do this every two weeks instead of every week.

Set up one envelope for the mortgage, one for the groceries, one for the car payment, and so on. Cash your paycheck and distribute the money to each envelope as needed to pay for the expenses that month.

In the envelope you've set up for your P2P loan payment, try to fill that envelope with the money you owe as quickly as possible. You don't go to the movies or eat out that month until you know you've got the money for that month's P2P loan payment.

Once it's there, don't touch that money. Just be sure it's in the bank before the automatic transfer occurs! Think of your P2P loan as your chance to get back on your feet and get control of your finances. If you think you want something more complex than the Mint or the envelope system, then check out the next section for some fun software that can help you stay on budget.

Budgeting Software

If you want to buy your own money management software, there are many options. Here are a few money management packages to try:

- Quicken Deluxe Software, $29.99 to $99.99; available at http://quicken.intuit. com/personal-finance/deluxe-money-management.jsp

- Microsoft Money Plus, $49.99 to $79.99 (not including a $30 rebate); to try it for free, go to www.microsoft.com/money/freetrial_info.mspx

- Mvelopes, membership plans starting with quarterly payments of $39.60 to a two-year plan costing $189.60; that's $13.20 per month, quarterly; and $7.90 per month for the two-year plan; offers a free 30-day trial at www.mvelopes.com/ mvelopes/service-plans.php

- Moneydance, $39.99; try a free trial version at http://moneydance.com/other

- AceMoney, $45; to find out more, visit www.mechcad.net/products/acemoney/

These are just a few of the packages from which to choose. When you're making a choice, consider the type of computer you have and if the package you want to buy is compatible with your computer's software. Look for compatibility information on each product's website. It's usually found in a section labeled "system requirements" or something similar to that.

We listed the software in this section to help get you started on your search. But with the economy sputtering the way it is, you're likely to see a lot of new money management products coming out in the next year or so.

> **In the Red** _____
>
> A lot of people get into trouble when they use their debit cards to pay for merchandise and then don't record the amount somewhere. Before you know it, you're hit with NSF charges. If you don't have a checking account register with you, keep the receipts until you've recorded the information either in the register or online if that's how you keep track of your expenses.

Staying on Track with Payments

Once you're set up with automatic transfers from your account to pay your loan installments, you don't have to worry about remembering to make a payment. But you do have to remember to put the money in the account!

Late Payment Fees

We've covered late payments in the chapters on the individual sites. Know what the rules are on your particular P2P lending site. There's usually a 15-day grace period, but never assume that. When late payments are reported to the credit reporting agencies, it usually affects your score.

If you're less than 15 days late with your payment, act quickly so your credit report isn't affected. On Prosper, after one month your delinquency is reported to Experian and TransUnion (two credit reporting agencies). When this happens, it ends up in your credit report and negatively impacts your score. If the delinquency continues, your credit report and FICO score will get worse.

On Lending Club, loans that are more than a month late are sent to a collection agency. Loanio notes that you're charged a late fee when your loan is 15, 45, 75, and 105 days late. After 120 days, Loanio considers your loan in default and sells the loan to a debt purchaser. Be sure that you know what the policies are on your P2P lending website. These sites have to protect their lenders or there will be no one to offer loans to borrowers.

Another thing to think about is how you'll feel if you encouraged friends to fund your loan. All of your lenders will get the news that you're delinquent. Yikes!

So make your payments on time and take care of your FICO score. Otherwise, you might lower your score to the point where you might not be able to get a loan anywhere. In the current economy, taking care of your credit reputation is more important than ever.

Making Extra or Early Payments

Check with the site where you got your loan funded to see whether there are any penalties for early payments. When you make an early payment, you're paying ahead of the scheduled due date for that month. When you make an extra payment, you're making more than one payment in a month.

For example, you have a $165 payment due on the 22nd of the month. If you make the payment early, you might make the payment on the 16th or so. If you want to make an extra payment, you might pay $165 on the 15th and then make your regular payment on the 22nd. The more quickly you pay off your loan, the less interest you'll pay.

On P2P lending websites, you'll be able to get information on how this affects your principal and interest. Don't be shy about asking lots of questions, either. Legitimate P2P lending websites want borrowers to feel comfortable with managing their loans and getting them paid off in a way that works for them.

Here's how a few of the sites handle extra or early payments:

- ◆ Prosper: No penalty for making extra or early payments. You're basically making a manual loan payment when you make an extra payment. You go to your account and click the "Make payment" link.

  You'll find options for making your next monthly payment (either early or on time), paying down your loan (extra payment), or paying off your entire loan. There's also no penalty for paying off the entire loan early.

- ◆ Lending Club: No penalty for extra or early payments.

- ◆ Loanio: No penalty for extra or early payments.

- ◆ Fynanz: No penalty for extra or early payments.

And kudos to you for planning on some early payments. You're on the right track!

Paying Off the Loan Early

When you've gotten a loan from a family member or friend, paying off the loan early is most likely well received. At the very least, it takes pressure off the next family reunion!

Good Cents _____

Stick to your budget, and make some early payments on your loan when you can. If you make just two early payments a year on a three-year loan, you'll pay it off around six months early.

Here's how a few of the sites handle an early loan payoff:

◆ Prosper: No penalty for paying off a loan early.

◆ Lending Club: No penalty for early payoffs. You can go online and see your loan payoff amount.

◆ Loanio: No pre-payment penalties when you pay off a loan before it's due. You are required to pay only accrued interest and other charges up to the day that you pay off the loan.

◆ Fynanz: No penalty for extra or early payments.

◆ GreenNote: No penalty for extra or early payments.

Thinking about paying off the loan early may seem like an impossible goal to you. But with the right money management, you never know.

Staying Motivated

Keep your eyes on the prize. Take a piece of paper and write down—in large letters—why you got the loan in the first place. Is it to get rid of credit card debt? Write that down and stick it on your refrigerator.

Was it for a new car? Write down how much money you were spending to maintain your old car. Write about how much safer you feel in your new car. Are you remodeling your kitchen? Write how old your appliances were and how you'll cook more instead of eating out so much. Remembering why you got the loan in the first place can keep you focused on paying it off.

Another good way to stay motivated is to participate in forums or on Facebook with other borrowers. You can also start your own Google or Yahoo! Group of P2P borrowers. These are e-mail groups that share a common interest or goal. Developing a kind of P2P support group can really help you stay motivated as you work to pay off the loan.

Good Cents _____

A great way to stay motivated while you save money is to reward yourself along the way. This sounds counterintuitive, but it's not. The key is to choose rewards that don't cost an arm and a leg.

Choose some milestones. For example, maybe you decide to reward yourself every three months for staying on budget and making your P2P loan payments on time. Have an inexpensive lunch with a friend you haven't seen in a while. Or get a pedicure, if that suits your fancy. Find a few little rewards that don't cost a lot but that keep you motivated to stay on budget.

And don't think of it as a "misery loves company" situation. Think of it as a group of hard-working individuals sprinting toward financial success—because that's what it is!

The Least You Need to Know

- ◆ Budgeting is a necessity to stay on track with your P2P loan payments.

- ◆ Start with a simple form to record your expenses and income so you can see how much you're spending and how much you're saving.

- ◆ Use software or the envelope system for staying on budget.

- ◆ Make it a goal to make extra payments now and then so you can pay your loan off earlier and save on interest.

- ◆ It can be motivating to participate in forums or a Facebbook group and associate with other borrowers.

Chapter 15

Second Helpings

In This Chapter

- Deciding whether you need a second loan
- Getting loans on more than one website
- Steps to obtaining a second loan
- How eligibility requirements differ on the major P2P websites
- Recent trends on the types of borrowers who are requesting P2P loans

There's nothing wrong with having more than one loan. In fact, some borrowers use it as a strategy.

For instance, if you need $10,000, you might have to break that amount into two different loans to increase your chances for funding (this is because lenders often shy away from funding the larger loans). You might even try to get those loans from more than one site.

In this chapter, we go through the steps you need to take to get a second loan. Because each P2P lending site has its own eligibility requirements, you get some useful advice specific to each site. And if you need any help with money management, check out Chapter 14 for some practical, inexpensive, and even free ideas.

Should You Consider a Second Loan?

Before you leap, take some time to think about how it will impact your ability to borrow in the future. Remember that your debt-to-income (DTI) ratio rises with each loan no matter where you obtain the loan. For instance, your $155 loan payment from Lending Club is factored into your DTI ratio when you apply for a loan on Prosper. com.

If your DTI ratio is lower than 36 percent and you're having no problems making your payments, then you may be a good candidate for another loan. Note that it doesn't mean that you should get a second loan—just that it's reasonable to consider one.

Here's an example of how your DTI ratio can rise when you add more recurring debt:

Let's say that you make $50,000 a year working for an advertising agency. Prior to obtaining the aforementioned $155 per month loan from Lending Club, your recurring debt was $1,345. Your DTI calculation *before* the Lending Club loan was as follows:

- Gross monthly income: $4,166.67 ($50,000 ÷ 12)

- Recurring debt expense: $1,345

- DTI ratio: 32.27 ($1,345 ÷ $4,166.67)

So your DTI ratio before your new Lending Club debt comes out to around 32 percent. Not bad. Now, let's add in the new $155 recurring debt and see what happens.

- Gross monthly income: $4,166.67 ($50,000 ÷ 12)

- Recurring debt expense: $1,500 ($1,345 + $155)

- DTI ratio: 35.99 ($1,500 ÷ $4,166.67)

Now your DTI ratio is right at 36 percent. This may be acceptable to some lenders, but with others, it's borderline high.

Let's say you do get approved for a second loan from Prosper. For the sake of brevity (and your attention span!), let's say your loan got funded and your monthly payment is $125. Now take a look at your DTI ratio.

- Gross monthly income: $4,166.67 ($50,000 ÷ 12)

- Recurring debt expense: $1,625 ($1,500 + $125)

- DTI ratio: 38.99 ($1,625 ÷ $4,166.67)

Your DTI ratio has now soared to around 39 percent. This fact should sound off some alarm bells in your head. Do you really want that second loan if it makes your DTI ratio rise to 39 percent?

When you're considering a second loan, calculate your "before and after" DTI ratios. You may be guessing a little on your monthly payment on a second loan that you don't have yet, but this exercise also might give you some insight into what dollar range your second monthly payment needs to be. That is, how high your monthly payment can go before it's too high to consider.

Good Cents _____

Even if you qualify for a second loan, give it careful thought before plunging in. Lenders may consider you a higher risk because you already have a loan obligation.

If you do decide to move forward, increase your chances of funding by making an extra effort with your new listing. Get endorsements and write an eloquent description about why you need this second loan.

How to Get a Second Loan

Okay ... you've decided to get another loan. What now?

Your next steps depend on the site you're using. The eligibility requirements that got you your first loan will, in most cases, also get you the next one. The sites do have limits, though, on the total amount of loans. Let's take a look at some of the websites and see what your next steps should be.

Prosper

At Prosper, you take the same basic steps you took when you got your first loan. You don't need to verify your identity, though, unless you've changed your name since your first loan.

Assuming you're still who you said you were when you applied for your original loan, you can concentrate on writing a new loan request, settling on your base interest rate, and then receiving bids (if you get approved to move forward with your request).

Eligibility

Prosper has certain criteria that a borrower must meet in order to qualify for a loan, including the following:

♦ Your payments on all current loans on Prosper must be up-to-date.

♦ Your current loan total with Prosper must be less than $25,000; remember, that's the loan limit on Prosper. This means that the grand total of your loans can't exceed that amount. So if you have a loan for $11,000, the maximum amount you can request is $14,000.

♦ You must request a loan for at least $1,000. Don't waste your time or theirs by asking for a $500 loan. Always know what the limits are.

♦ You must have made at least six months of consecutive—*and on-time*—payments on your first loan. This is a fairly recent change in the rules. It makes sense to see whether borrowers are successfully repaying their first loans before they're allowed to come back to the table for seconds. We describe this subject in more detail in the next section.

♦ A certain number of months must pass before you get another loan, depending on your credit grade. For example, if you have a B credit grade, you have to wait nine months before you can request another loan. But if you have a credit grade of A and you've made your loan payments for six months in a row, you're in good shape.

If you pass these basic requirements with flying colors, then you're ready for the next test. Remember the Prosper credit grades we talked about in Chapter 7? When you apply for a second loan, you have to get *regraded* by Prosper.

New Credit Grade

If only you could have gotten regraded on that geometry final in high school, right? Of course, the prospect is intriguing only if you have a chance to get a better grade.

def•i•ni•tion

When you ask for a second loan, Prosper gives you a new credit grade. It **regrades** you by looking at your most current credit report, which will include your previous P2P loan and any other credit activity that has occurred since you applied for your first P2P loan. Other P2P lending sites also do this, although they may use a different term.

Well, that's what you face when you get regraded by Prosper. You might not have given any thought to the fact that your original credit grade would influence your ability to get another loan. But if you've taken care of business on your first loan, you have nothing to worry about.

What's your credit grade now? If your credit grade is more than 30 days old, you will receive a new grade. That's why there's a column in the following chart that shows how much your credit grade is allowed to drop. If you're already a D grade or below, you can't drop any lower.

Use the following chart to see whether you've met some of Prosper's minimum requirements before you think about getting a second loan.

In the Red

Keep in mind that if you make extra payments, you don't get credit for consecutive months on that extra payment. So if you've paid your loan for five consecutive months and make the sixth payment early, you get credit for the sixth payment when the calendar says that payment is due.

Previous Credit Grade	Minimum Months Since Last Loan	Consecutive Months of Paying on Time	Allowable Drop in Credit Grade
AA	6 months	6 months	1 grade
A	6 months	6 months	1 grade
B	9 months	9 months	1 grade
C	9 months	9 months	1 grade
D	12 months	12 months	0 grades
E	12 months	12 months	0 grades
HR*	12 months	12 months	0 grades

HR stands for high risk.

Keep in mind that Prosper may turn down your request even if you meet all of the basic requirements. Just like when you applied for your first loan, many factors are considered. In this respect, it's similar to going to a bank for a loan request. Although you may look good on paper, the bank still has to say yes to the loan.

Good Cents _____

Second loans (or even third or fourth loans) on Prosper are not consolidated. There's only one situation where that might work out, and that's if your first and second loans had the same origination date. In this case, Prosper automatically consolidates the loan for you. That would be quite a coincidence, though.

It's best to plan on keeping track of more than one payment. Sure, it will be automatically withdrawn from your account just like your payment for your first loan—but you have to make sure the money is in your account.

Lending Club

As with Prosper, at Lending Club you also have to jump through the same hoops as when you got your first loan. You can have a total of two loans either concurrently or one right after the other on Lending Club. If you currently have two loans, you need to pay off one of them before you can ask for your third loan. So you can borrow money as many times as you like on Lending Club, but you can't have more than two loans at the same time.

Eligibility

Lending Club includes loans that are still in the funding process in your loan total. For example, if you've already requested a $2,500 loan and only $500 of it is currently funded, the entire $2,500 counts toward your loan limit of $25,000. So you can ask for up to $22,500 on the next loan.

In the Red _____

Although most sites don't set minimum DTI ratios, remember that Lending Club sets the bar high. You must have a DTI ratio of less than 25 percent to qualify for a loan on Lending Club.

Even if your DTI ratio made you eligible for your first loan with Lending Club, you need to recalculate your ratio to see whether it's still below 25 percent—especially if you were close to 25 percent the first time. Your current monthly loan payment may have pushed you over Lending Club's limit.

Lending Club's minimum loan amount requirement also still applies. You must borrow a minimum of $1,000.

Lending Club recently added some new requirements for borrowers, and some of the new rules are relevant to second loans as well:

- ◆ You must have no current delinquencies or collections account in the last 12 months.

- ◆ You must have no more than 10 inquiries on your credit report in the last six months.

- ◆ You must utilize revolving credit at less than 100 percent.

- ◆ You must have more than three accounts on your credit report, with at least two of them open.

Keep these rules in mind. You may have qualified for the first loan, but if you've been busy inquiring about credit in the last six months, then you may not qualify for a second loan with Lending Club.

Credit Score

Aside from needing a DTI ratio of less than 25 percent, you also need to be free of any credit delinquencies for the past 12 months.

You're required to have a FICO score of at least 640, just as you were when you applied for your first loan. You'll get regraded when you apply for a second loan. Again, your new loan grade will reflect the following:

- ◆ Your most current credit history

- ◆ Your FICO score

- ◆ The amount of the requested loan

If you want to review the loan grades and the corresponding interest rates, go back and review the section about Lending Club in Chapter 10.

When you get regraded by Lending Club, it has no effect on your FICO score. Checking your score again falls under the realm of a soft inquiry. So you don't need to worry about it lowering your FICO score. Of course, once your loan gets funded, it impacts your score because you have a new debt to repay. Once you get the new loan, your FICO score is affected as well as your DTI ratio.

Good Cents

Loans on Lending Club aren't consolidated. When you get a second loan through Lending Club, you'll be making two separate payments. You can also set up the second loan as an automatic debit from your bank account. Plan ahead and be sure you have enough money in your account to cover both payments.

Loanio

You can borrow up to two loans at a time on Loanio. Eligibility requirements remain the same as for your first loan. Remember, Loanio uses VantageScore instead of FICO scores. If you're a little fuzzy about what VantageScores are, review the discussion we had about this in Chapter 10.

Here's a quick overview of what you must have to be eligible:

- A VantageScore of 501 or higher.

- With a VantageScore less than 501, you need a co-borrower for your loan.

- At least six months of consecutive (and on time) payments on your current loan.

- The total amount of your two loans cannot exceed the maximum amount that Loanio lends in your state.

In the Red

Before you consider a second loan on Loanio, take a look at the maximum amount that Loanio lends in your state. In most states, the maximum you can borrow is $25,000. But make a point of checking the Loanio website before requesting a second loan. You don't want to waste your time if it's not an option.

Virgin Money

Whether you get a second loan on Virgin Money is between you and your family member. The benefit of using this site is that you don't have any credit hoops to jump through. But on the other hand, you owe it to your family lender to negotiate the terms of any loan in good faith.

Go ahead and calculate your DTI ratio and use this information to help you decide if you should add more debt. Just because it's easy to get a loan, that doesn't mean you *should* get a loan. Simply put, don't ask for a loan that you can't pay back—even if it's from a third cousin twice removed who you never liked.

Fynanz

These are, for the most part, loans between family and friends, but Fynanz has some restrictions on the number and the amount of loans you can get in one year.

◆ Borrowers may receive a maximum of four loans per year.

◆ There must be a minimum of 60 days between loan requests.

◆ The maximum amount is $20,000 per loan with a $40,000 annual limit.

◆ The minimum amount is $2,500 per loan, depending on state limitations.

◆ The maximum amount for an undergraduate degree is $120,000.

◆ The maximum amount for a graduate degree is $160,000.

If you needed a cosigner for the first loan, you'll most likely need a cosigner for the second one (unless, of course, you've had a birthday since your first loan and you're now 21 years old).

Cosigners must have two years of income and employment history. And, as with the first loan, if you fail to make the payments, your cosigner gets stuck with your loan.

Getting Loans from More Than One Site

You can request loans from more than one site as long as you're up front about every one of your loans, including those you got from another site. But just because you can get loans from numerous sites, it doesn't mean that you should. In general, keeping up with loans on different sites is time-consuming.

It's probably going to save you time if you stick with the same website. Here's why:

◆ You'll have to start from scratch with the identity verification process again for a new site.

◆ Within a loan site community, you can build a reputation for yourself. (And hopefully you've built a great one—one that says you pay off your loans.)

◆ You'll have to learn the ropes of the new site, because each site lists its loans differently.

If you got a loan on Lending Club and now your FICO score has dropped below 640, you may be thinking you can get a loan on Prosper. But don't let your deteriorating FICO score drive you to another site. You're headed for a credit treadmill (one that will have you running in place for years) if you go down that road.

How Recent Borrower Trends Could Affect You

Recently, there has been a trend where the P2P lending sites are attracting borrowers with higher credit scores. For some of the reasons mentioned in Chapter 3, some folks with excellent credit are finding that the P2P lending sites are a better alternative than their banks.

If this trend continues, this creates a little borrower competition. If you're a lender and you're choosing between two borrowers, you might prefer the borrower with a better DTI ratio and FICO score—unless you're a huge risk taker and you enjoy the thrill of the unknown in your search for a higher return!

Just keep in mind that the quality of borrowers has been on the rise. So, do make sure that you can absorb a second loan without wrecking your score or your credit report. Think of this potential competition as another good reason to keep your financial house in order.

The Least You Need to Know

- Consider the effect on your DTI ratio before you get a second loan.
- Eligibility requirements for second loans are defined on each P2P lending site.
- Most sites require a new credit grade when you apply for another loan.
- Check each site for limitations on the number of loans allowed as well as the dollar limits.
- You can obtain loans from more than one site if you meet the eligibility requirements on each site.
- Recent trends show that P2P lending websites are attracting borrowers with high FICO scores.
- Competition for funding loans is likely to increase as more borrowers with excellent credit get involved with P2P lending.

Chapter 16

Borrowing as a Group Member

In This Chapter

- Examples of types of groups
- How to create your own group or join an existing group on Prosper
- Qualities of an effective group leader
- Understanding group ratings
- Explaining historical default rates
- How group borrowing works on Kiva

The idea of borrowing as a group member may seem strange to you. After all, you wouldn't walk into a bank with three dozen of your closest friends and ask for a loan based on your group credit rating. But it's a nice concept if you think about it. Lenders seem to like the added security that comes from lending to someone who's a member of a successful group.

What's a successful group? It's a group whose membership pays loans on time and has a low default rate. Take a look at the kinds of groups that are out there on the lending websites. You may find one where you fit in, or you might even decide to start your own group.

Groups can be set up for the purpose of borrowing or lending money, but in this chapter we focus on just the borrowing part.

How Groups Are Defined on Prosper

Borrowing groups are popular on Prosper. These groups are comprised of people who are associated in some way. It might be a common alma mater or a common interest in bird watching. It might also just be a group of people who share the common goal of getting out of credit card debt.

Groups can be set up for different types of loans, such as personal or business loans. A group not only shares a common affiliation or purpose, but also has a designated group leader.

You'd think that the larger the group, the safer the investment. But it seems there isn't always safety in numbers. Prosper reports that borrowing groups with fewer than 50 members have a lower default rate and a higher funding rate than groups with more than 50 members.

Good Cents

A recent survey by Dale Karlan, an assistant professor of economics at Yale University, showed that groups made up of individuals who either live close together or are culturally similar are more likely to repay their loans. This is something to keep in mind no matter which end you're on. If you're the borrower, group with people who share something similar with you. If you're the lender, seek out group borrowers who seem to have a lot in common—even if just geographically.

There are lots of different things that bring people together in groups. Here are some reasons groups are formed on Prosper:

- **Social similarities:** This can include a group that is comprised of people being in a club together, such as a single mothers' or single dads' group. Or maybe they share a common passion, such as a love of Volkswagens. Yes, there's a group on Prosper called the "Vee Dubs Club."

- **Shared religion:** Some groups band together because of a common faith, such as a group of Catholics supporting each other.

- **Ethnicity:** For example, you might find a group of Asian-American educators.

◆ **Profession:** These groups are comprised of those who work in the same industries or occupations, such as retired bankers. You'll also see groups of architects, home inspectors, and law enforcement officers.

◆ **Shared affinity or accomplishment:** This is a popular concept. Alumni groups are often set up by college affiliation or fraternity or sorority. You went to Virginia Tech? There's a group for you. You were in the ATO house? Ditto. But it's not just about college buddies. There are groups of people who have past accomplishments in common. For example, Prosper has a group for Eagle Scouts.

◆ **Business ownership:** Some businesses form a borrowing group for the common objective of success. For example, there's a Prosper group that focuses on obtaining loans for start-up companies.

As you can see, groups are diverse and are based on a multitude of factors. Now that you know what defines a group, let's take a look at how borrowing groups work.

How Borrowing Groups Work on Prosper

To take a look at existing groups, you can visit Prosper's home page and click "Community." You'll see options for groups, forums, and stories (these are testimonials). Click "Groups" and you'll go to the listings for the groups. Here, you can read the listings and see whether a group interests you. You can also search for groups using keywords.

As a borrower, you can either join an existing group or start your own group. In this section, we cover the basics you need to know so you can decide the best path for yourself.

Joining a Group

When a group is set up, the leader determines whether the group will have an "open" membership policy or whether it will be "invitation only."

If there's a "Join this group" link, it means the group has an open membership policy. You'll still have to be approved by the group leader, but this means it welcomes new members.

If there's no such link, then only the group leader is allowed to invite members to join the group. Other borrowers can't invite new members; only the leader can.

Understanding Group Ratings

Here we go again with more grades. But realistically, the grades are necessary so lenders can make informed decisions. And let's face it—if you're a borrower, you need to know what the group's track record is. The last thing you want to do is align yourself with a group that has a marginal reputation for repayment.

Simply put, on Prosper, a group's rating gives you an idea of the group's performance when it comes to repaying its loans. On a more complex level, it also involves looking at the group's performance against *historical default rates* based on numbers from Experian.

def•i•ni•tion

The credit reporting agencies provide information to creditors on the **historical default rates** of consumers. This information is based on (what else?) past behavior of how consumers in each credit range have fared when it comes to repaying debt. Those with higher credit scores tend to have lower historical default rates on loans.

The Experian default rates that Prosper uses give the average of historical default rates. The information they give, though, is most applicable to borrowers who have a debt-to-income (DTI) ratio of less than 20 percent. That's a pretty good DTI ratio, don't you think?

The point is that someone who has an excellent credit rating but who sports a DTI ratio of 29 percent might be a little more likely to default. But as we've discussed, there's no sure thing when it comes to predicting someone's ability to repay a loan. These numbers give you an idea of the average default risk.

Here's a look at the default rates and how they correspond to Prosper's credit grades.

Grade	Average Default Rate
AA	.20 percent
A	.90 percent
B	1.80 percent
C	3.30 percent
D	6.20 percent
E	9.10 percent
HR	13.90 percent

Historical default rates come from data that's recorded over a 24-month period. Each credit reporting agency has its own way of calculating this risk.

How does all this affect your group ratings? First, let's understand a few terms: actual losses, projected losses, and allowed losses.

◆ Let's say a group has two borrowers who have defaulted on loans. The actual losses equal the total principal amounts on the two loans minus any amounts received from the debt buyer.

◆ Projected losses are the total of the group's anticipated losses based on the age and credit grade of the group's current delinquent accounts. Just because a loan is delinquent (late) doesn't mean it will become a default (unpaid).

◆ "Allowed losses" is basically a "loan allowance" for Prosper groups. After a group member's loan is billed for a one-month period, it qualifies for a loss allowance. Each loan in the group contributes to the loss allowance. This is calculated based on the number of one-month billing periods on the principal multiplied by the daily default rate. So the group's loss allowance equals the "loan allowances" of all the group members combined. This number helps to offset events that would lower the group rating.

The calculations of the actual losses, projected losses, and allowed losses all contribute to the rating the group receives. Like the FICO score, it's a complicated calculation, but at least now you have an idea of what's considered in the group's rating.

In the Red

Note that the average default rates listed in this section are based on those who have a DTI ratio of 20 percent or less. These default rates are just averages, and your mileage may vary. Don't develop a false sense of security just because a borrower's credit grade places him within a low default range. Use credit grades as a tool to help you determine if a borrower is a good risk, but keep in mind that default is a possibility no matter what the credit grade is.

Okay, so let's get away from mathematical equations and get back to the fun stuff—namely, grading systems dictated by the number of stars. Prosper uses a "star" rating system for groups.

Here's the skinny on what the stars mean:

◆ ★★★★★ Five-star rating

The best! This group has outperformed the historical default rates by 60 percent.

- ★★★★ Four-star rating

  Another good-performing group. This means the group outperformed historical default rates by 20 to 60 percent.

- ★★★ Three-star rating

  This group performed within 20 percent of the historical default rates.

- ★★ Two-star rating

  Uh-oh. This group underperformed by 20 to 60 percent of the historical default rates.

- ★ One-star rating

  This group underperformed against historical default rates by at least 60 percent!

- Not yet rated

  You'll see some listings with this label. This means they either haven't had a total of 15 payments yet or had at least 1 late payment.

Just for context, let's take a broad look at what's considered the great, good, and pretty bad when it comes to group ratings and the range within the historical default rates.

- Better than expected: Five- and four-star groups

- Average: Three-star groups

- Worse than expected: Two- and one-star groups

As a borrower, you want to get in a group that gives you a lift, not one that drags you down. Understanding the rating systems will help you choose a place where you can contribute to the group as well as get your loan funded.

Creating a Group

If you want to start a group, you start with the basic loan request process. Let's say you want a $2,000 personal loan for debt consolidation. You enter this reason on the screen where you request your loan and then press "Continue."

You'll see the following on the screen: "Great! Now let's get started. You're on your way to a $2,000 personal loan for debt consolidation."

Next, you're asked for the following, so think about your password and screen name ahead of time:

◆ First name

◆ Last name

◆ E-mail address

◆ Password

◆ Screen name

Don't pick a screen name such as "MillyAfromPhilly" or use your business name, such as "GreenDesignsinCA." You don't want to even slightly hint at your identity, for your own sake as well as for your lenders'. Some borrowers incorporate something that they like, such as a coffee-related moniker or something related to a favorite sports team. Or they might incorporate the purpose of the loan into a screen name, such as "This-old-home-improvement." You can always use your golden retriever's name, too.

In the Red

Do not give away too much personal information when you're borrowing. If you do, you put yourself at risk for identity theft. You also give away your right to privacy. If something unforeseen happens, such as an illness that prevents you from working, and you're late with a payment, you might be contacted by lenders. Yes, this would be an improper activity by lenders, but don't put yourself in a position that would make it easy for them to contact you.

Once you're signed in, you need to provide the following information about your group:

◆ A name

◆ A photo to represent the group

◆ A short description

◆ A more detailed, longer description

When you write your group's description, include information such as the following:

◆ A clear purpose or objective

◆ Membership requirements

- Details about how frequently the group will interact
- How the group got started
- Any affiliation (or other reason) that brings this group together
- Reasons why your group is creditworthy

After you have provided all this information, Prosper sends it to its Group Services team. This team reviews your information and decides whether or not to approve the creation of your group.

You're probably thinking that being the leader entails quite a bit of work. How much does the group leader gig pay? Uh, nothing. Group leaders do receive a finder's fee for loans posted before September 13, 2007. The rule has changed, however, so there is no compensation for being a group leader after that date.

Habits of Highly Effective Group Leaders

If you're creating a group, you probably fancy yourself as the group leader. Even if you're planning to give someone else that role, you need to educate yourself about the role of the group leader in these groups. That way, if the leader has any issues, you can at least act as a consultant to help the group run smoothly.

Not everyone is a born leader. But some of the skills involved in being a group leader can be learned. If you have good communication skills and you think you'd enjoy it, then go for it!

Prosper offers these five steps for becoming a successful group leader:

1. You must become an expert.
2. Spend time creating a memorable identity for your group.
3. Be clear about your membership criteria.
4. Get to know your members.
5. Be on the lookout for new members who will successfully fit into your group.

You can become an expert by taking advantage of the oodles of information and tutorials that Prosper offers so that you can advise your members. Find out about both borrowing and lending so you understand both sides. Read the Prosper blogs and stay up-to-date on any changes Prosper has made. Remember, this industry will probably go through several different incarnations in the next few years. Lastly, educate yourself about interest rates and credit grades. Read Chapters 5 and 6 again and look for books about credit that interest you.

Good Cents

Remember learning tricks in school so you can recall how to spell words such as Mississippi? This method works with grown-ups, too. Prosper recommends teaching your members the TIPS method:

- ◆ Tell your story. Why do you need the loan?
- ◆ Include your budget. Lenders need to know you can manage your money.
- ◆ Pictures tell a great story.
- ◆ Stick to the facts and don't exaggerate (not even a little!).

This can be an easy way to educate your borrowers. And if a group member has problems getting his or her loan funded, you can coach the borrower using the TIPS method.

You can create an identity for your group by writing a great description and using photos (where allowed) to your advantage. If your group is comprised of wine connoisseurs, for example, show bottles of the group's favorite wines. Or share links to the group's favorite wine-related websites. If your group's members are local, get together for wine tastings.

Although the membership criteria need not be written in stone, you do need to make a clear-cut decision in the beginning. Potential members need to know up front about the group's membership rules, and potential lenders want to know what the standards are. Being unclear will make lenders think the group isn't managed well.

Getting to know your group members is a key to success. Send new members a "welcome to the group" message as soon as they join. A phone call is also a good idea, but you want your new group member to have a few things in writing as well. For example, make it clear in your initial e-mail to the new member that diligently repaying a loan is necessary for the group's success. You can also make it clear that you're there for advice if any problems arise—and then be sure that you really are available to talk when a problem arises.

There are many ways to keep the channels of communication open. One way is by approving loan listings. This gives you a chance to help your borrowers from the get-go. Sometimes just a few tweaks here and there can turn a weak listing into a strong one. If a member's listing doesn't get funded, you can review the member's listing again and revise it together so it has a better chance.

You might also try sending weekly e-mails (you can set up a Google or Yahoo! Group), creating a newsletter, starting a Twitter page, or maintaining a blog about your group. Or, if you're in geographic proximity, suggest meeting for coffee or lunch once a month. Each of these suggestions gives your members an opportunity to give you feedback. Actively solicit feedback, because some people aren't comfortable voicing their opinions, particularly when it comes to criticizing someone. A good leader is always a good listener—even when receiving constructive criticism.

You want to attract new members, and there are lots of ways to do this. Put a link to your group management page in your e-mail signature or on your own website, if you have one. You can also use the invitation system that's set up for you on Prosper. It will save you time to use Prosper's invitation template, but you can also personalize it. Note that sending out the invitation via Prosper's system results in automatic approval to join your group, so be sure you're already on board with the potential member before extending the invitation this way.

Show you're a good leader who respects the process by responding within seven days when you receive a membership request from a borrower. You're free to accept or reject a member. If you need more time, you can ask for an extension. And remember that your decision to let someone into the group can be revoked later if there's a problem. Like any relationship, sometimes things don't work out. You can remove a member from your group if the individual doesn't have a current loan listing. As the leader, you want to strive for high credit standards from members, but you can't ask to see a credit report. There are state and federal statutes that protect privacy. If a borrower says that he or she has great credit, you have to decide whether it's worth the risk.

It should go without saying (but we'll say it anyway) that you can't exclude anyone based on sex, age, color, ethnicity, sexual orientation, marital status, race, religion, or military status. In other words, don't exclude anyone for reasons other than credit history or FICO score. And base your decision on the group's criteria for success, which involves paying back loans.

How Group Borrowing Works on Kiva

At Kiva, group borrowing is common. A group of entrepreneurs will band together and ask for funding for their various businesses. They get the loan as a group, and they pay off the loan as a group. Sometimes on Kiva, you'll see a listing that has a photo of the entire group. It's nice when you can associate faces with those you're helping.

One day we saw a listing for a group of businesswomen from Sudan. They ran these businesses: a bakery, a tea shop, a coffee shop, a hotel restaurant, and an ice cream shop. They wanted to borrow $1,325 as a group to expand their respective businesses. For these entrepreneurs to expand their businesses, they need to get funded by 53 lenders who each lend $25. Imagine if you could expand five different businesses with only $1,325. That loan wouldn't buy much in the United States, but a little money goes a long way in countries served by Kiva.

We talked about Kiva in Chapter 8, so you know this website specializes in microloans to borrowers in undeveloped nations. If you fit this criteria, you need to connect with one of Kiva's field partners. Check out Kiva's list at www.kiva.org/about/partners/. Or contact Kiva directly at 402-952-8811, the international number.

The Least You Need to Know

- Groups are created based on a number of factors that the borrowers have in common.
- You can create a group and become a group leader on Prosper.
- You can choose to join other groups as a member.
- Group ratings are based on the collective performance of a group's members.
- You can learn to become an effective group leader.
- Group borrowing is a common way to get a loan on Kiva.

Chapter 17

Receiving Statements and Filing Taxes

In This Chapter

- What you need to know about monthly and year-end loan statements
- What records you need to keep
- Deducting interest on your education loans
- Qualified educational expenses that you can deduct
- The rules for taking an education credit on your tax return

It can be quite boring to read financial statements. But you might find your P2P loan statements a little more interesting than most.

Why? Because getting a P2P loan is personal. You've taken a step toward being more in charge of your money. You've gotten (in most cases) a good interest rate. You made a big decision to bypass the bank. (Okay, some of you may not have had a choice.) But as we noted in an earlier chapter, there's an increase in P2P borrowers who have excellent credit scores.

So with all this personal investment in your loan, you're going to enjoy getting your statements and watching your principal go down (and down, and down!).

What to Expect

Most sites will send you monthly statements along with one at the end of the year. The monthly statements summarize the current status of your account. The year-end statement gives you detailed documentation of your loan's financial transactions for the year.

We'll cover the most popular site, Prosper, in a little more detail. But we'll also take a look at some of the other P2P lending sites.

Borrower Statements from Prosper

Prosper makes statements available about five days after your monthly loan payment date. You can view your statement from your "My Account" page. If you have two loans, you'll see two different statements.

These statements have three different summaries: loan summary, payment summary, and an overview of account activity. You'll receive similar statements at the end of the year.

Let's take a closer look at each one so you're clear about how to interpret the information. Remember, though, that over time these statements may change a little.

The Loan Summary

The loan summary is exactly what it sounds like. It gives you the details of your loan and includes the following:

- The title of your loan.
- The number of your loan, which is assigned by Prosper.
- The terms of your loan.
- The original loan amount (including closing fees).
- The *principal balance* on your loan amount.
- The annual rate of interest for your loan.
- The annual percentage rate (APR) for your loan. Remember, this includes all fees associated with your loan, so this rate is the actual cost of borrowing the money.

- ◆ The daily interest rate for your loan.
- ◆ The current amount of accrued interest. This reflects all interest accrued through the statement date.

def•i•ni•tion

The **principal balance** is the total amount of the principal that still must be repaid.

You can expect your loan summary statement to look similar to the following:

Loan Title:	Going to the chapel		
Loan No.:	123XXX	**Interest Rate:**	9 percent
Product:	3-year fixed	**APR:**	9.25 percent
Original Loan Amount:	$7,000	**Daily Rate:**	0.001726 percent
Principal Balance:	$5,756.34	**Interest Accrued This Period:**	$15.65

Pretty clear, right? Always look at your loan summary carefully and make sure the numbers look accurate to you. Hey, if there can be errors on your credit report, there can be errors on financial statements, too.

The Payment Summary

Your payment summary shows you the most current payment you've made as well as which payment is up next.

Here is what you'll see:

- ◆ Your last payment, which includes the amount, date, and status of your last payment. If you're late with the payment, you'll be notified here. You'll also be asked to make a manual payment to get your account up-to-date.

- ◆ Your next payment, which simply shows the amount and date of your next scheduled payment. Note that in the following sample illustration, there's a note that makes it clear that no action is required on your part—assuming you're using automatic debits to make your loan payments.

Here's a sample of how the payment summary part of your statement might look.

	Amount	Date	Notes
Last payment:	$255.34	January 15, 2009	Thank you for your payment
Next payment:	$255.34	February 15, 2009	No action required
Past due:	—		

In this sample summary, you can see that you made your last payment on January 15th and your next payment is due on February 15th. The "Notes" column indicates whether any action is required.

The Account Activity Section

This section gives you the nitty-gritty details on interest accrual and payments. It covers the entire month of the current period.

Here's what you'll find in this part:

- The date of each "event" that's listed. Prosper refers to each transaction as an event.

- Prosper's reference number for each event.

- Descriptions of each event. For instance, you might see some of the following:

    - Starting balance

    - Failed or late payment fees

    - Automatic payments

    - Manual payments

    - Principal payments

    - Closing balance

- Fees associated with events, such as fees for failed automatic payments.

- Fees that you have paid in regard to any delinquent fees.

- The interest paid on your loan *principal*.

- The amount of principal that you've paid.

♦ The total of fees and interest.

♦ The *principal paid.*

♦ The principal balance after all these events are accounted for.

Here's a sample of how the account activity area might look on your statement.

Date/ Reference Number	Description	Fees	Fees Paid	Int. Paid	Principal Paid	Total Paid	Principal Balance
Jan-02-2009	Starting balance						$4,288
Jan-02-2009 45299XXX	Non-payment fee	$5				$5	
Jan-29-2009 45333XXX	Automatic payment		$52	$139	$191	$4,097	
Jan-31-2009	Closing balance						$4,097
	Total payments		$5	$52	$139	$196	

At first glance, this account activity section of your loan statement can be a little confusing. Your main goal is to make sure you haven't received any improper charges. Also, make sure your payment was applied to your principal, and be sure to check your closing balance and the total payments across the bottom.

Borrower Statements from Fynanz

Because Fynanz deals with student loans, it's vital that you keep records. If you view statements online, print them out and keep track of them.

Why? There are possible tax deductions when you're shelling out dough for education. If qualified, you might be able to take a deduction for education expenses. We cover the possibilities later in the chapter.

Borrower Statements from Other P2P Lending Sites

Most P2P sites don't make the details of their statements public. If you'd like specific details, you can e-mail the websites either before or after you become a member and ask questions.

In fact, it's not a bad idea to use the statement descriptions we've given you about Prosper as a guideline for your questions.

Keeping Records

We may be living in an increasingly virtual world, but there's still plenty of paper coming our way. And when it comes to keeping records on important financial dealings, this is a good thing.

Good Cents

> To ensure you don't lose important information (and especially if you're running your own business), consider signing up with an online backup service. It protects you from disaster.
>
> Suppose you get up one morning and your computer has bitten the dust. You've lost your customer database, records of financial information, payroll data, tax information, and so on. But if you're using offsite backup, this data is backed up every single night and kept safe—just in case the unthinkable occurs. There are several providers, such as IronMountain.com and Mozy.com.

Don't get us wrong. We believe in saving trees, but unless you have surefire offsite computer backup—even if your statements are received via e-mail or you view them online—print them out and file them. In most cases, your interest expense is not deductible, but there are many other reasons to hang on to your financial details.

And when it comes to taxes, you must have documentation. In the next section, we talk more about why this is so important.

Taxing Matters for Borrowers

Wouldn't it be great if we could deduct interest expenses from personal loans? Alas, we can't.

But wait! There is a possibility you can take an education expenses deduction. If you're borrowing on Fynanz or GreenNote, you're getting loans that may be qualified educational expenses.

The IRS does limit the amount of the tuition deduction you can take. In 2007, the maximum amount was $4,000 (depending on your adjusted gross income) of qualifying tuition expenses. Be sure you find out what the limits are, because they change from year to year.

Deducting Education Expenses

So, what are qualified expenses? The IRS's Publication 970, "Tax Benefits for Education," gives all the details. You can read it online at IRS.gov from the "Forms and Publications" page.

If you'd rather save Publication 970 for a night when you're having trouble sleeping, though, we understand. Here are some highlights of the "Tuition and Fees Deduction" section:

- Your school can tell you whether it's an eligible educational institution in the eyes of the IRS. Most accredited post-secondary institutions qualify.

- Qualified related educational expenses include tuition, student activity fees, and course-related books. Supplies and equipment qualify only if they are required to attend the institution.

- The deduction is for the year in which the expenses are paid, not the year in which you pay back the loan. If you incur the expense in 2009, you take the deduction in 2009.

- If you're a parent who has paid the qualified education expenses, you may be able to claim the deductions if you claim your child as a dependent on your tax return.

In the Red

You can take the education expenses deduction only if your child is a dependent (for tax purposes) *and* you're the one who paid the expenses. If your dependent child pays the expenses, neither one of you can claim the deduction.

So plan carefully and make sure that you, the parent, are the one who is actually paying for qualified educational expenses.

Your loan and the interest payments made on the principal amount of the loan may be tax deductible if they qualify. You'll need to fill out Form W-9S, "Request for Student's or Borrower's Taxpayer Identification Number and Certification."

Good Cents _____

To save yourself time, visit this page on the IRS's website: www.irs.gov/pub/irs-pdf/fw9s.pdf. You can print out a W-9S there and fill it out.

When you complete this form, send it to your lender, which in this case is Fynanz. Fynanz will verify that your loan was used for education expenses. Remember the IRS cross-references everything! We advise you to check with a tax attorney to make sure you're properly allocating between your principal and interest expense.

Form W-9S has three parts:

◆ Part I: Student or Borrower Identification

In this section, you give your name, taxpayer ID number, and address. Students may use their Social Security number in lieu of a tax ID number.

◆ Part II: Student Loan Certification

In this section, you declare that the loan you received was indeed only for qualified educational expenses.

◆ Part III: Requester Information

def•i•ni•tion _____

The **requester** on the W-9S form refers to the lender. If you got your loan from Fynanz, then Fynanz is the requester.

In this section, the _requester_ provides a name and address. In this case, you'd list the website where you got your loan. Completing this section isn't required, by the way. The lender can always complete the section when it receives the form.

You'll also list the tuition account number and/or loan account number. This way, when the lender receives your W-9S, it's clear to which account this form refers.

Deducting Interest Expense on Student Loans

This area gets very tricky, and you're advised to consult with a tax accountant. Tax laws often change from year to year. You can find details on this topic in Publication 970 in the section, "Student Loan Interest Deduction."

But in case you want to save this material for another sleepless night, here are some highlights to help you understand what the basics are. You might be able to claim the deduction if it's a qualified student loan and if you meet the following qualifications:

◆ The interest you paid was for qualified education expenses.

◆ Your filing status is *not* married, filing separately.

◆ Your modified *adjusted gross income* (*AGI*) is less than $65,000. If filing jointly, it's less than $135,000.

◆ If filing jointly, neither you nor your spouse is claimed as a dependent by someone else.

Note that if you paid more than $600 in interest in one year on a qualified student loan, you will receive Form 1098-E, "Student Loan Interest Statement," from the place where you got your loan.

def•i•ni•tion _____

The **adjusted gross income (AGI)** is your gross income minus allowable deductions. It's also referred to as "net income."

Taking an Education Credit

There's the possibility of taking an education credit related to qualified expenses at eligible institutions. On line 49 of your Form 1040, you can take an education credit *unless* any of the following applies:

◆ You or your spouse is claimed as a dependent on someone else's return.

◆ Your filing status is married, filing separately.

◆ The amount on line 38 of your Form 1040 (adjusted gross income) is $57,000 or more or is $114,000 if married, filing jointly.

◆ You're taking the tuition and fees deduction on line 34 for the same student.

◆ Either you or your spouse was a nonresident alien during any part of the past year (unless you're married, filing jointly).

The bottom line is: no double dipping! If you're taking the expense deduction, you can't also take the education credit.

Hidden Treasure

Many high schools have programs where qualified students can take college courses at local universities. If you have a daughter or son currently taking college courses while still in high school, you may be able to take an education credit for the expenses. For more information, visit IRS.gov.

There are two education credits available: the Hope Credit and the Lifetime Learning Credit. You can get more details on both of these topics at IRS.gov. From the home page, click on "More forms and publications." From this page, click on "Form and instruction number" and then select Form 8863, "Education Credits."

The Least You Need to Know

- Carefully review all statements you receive from your P2P lending website to make sure they're accurate.

- You'll receive monthly borrower's statements from your P2P lending site.

- Keep hard copies of all statements you receive from P2P lending sites.

- If you've gotten a student loan from Fynanz, you may qualify to deduct education expenses on your tax return.

- If you deduct education expenses on your tax return, you can't also take an education credit.

Part 4

Lending Money

Part 4 gives you more information about the lending side, including whether you need a license and just how risky this P2P lending business is.

Here, you learn how to evaluate listings so you can narrow down options until you find a borrower you're comfortable with. You also get advice on how to handle tricky situations when you loan money to family members or to friends. Finally, you get a glimpse into how to handle your interest income on your tax return.

"They can't make the next payment.
Do we threaten cement shoes or mail them a dead fish?"

Chapter 18

Lending 101

In This Chapter

- ◆ Some basics about P2P lending
- ◆ Deciding whether P2P lending fits in with your financial goals
- ◆ Finding your motivation
- ◆ Deciphering the loan listings
- ◆ Evaluating new P2P lending sites

Are you trying to decide whether becoming a P2P lender is a good move for you?

It's understandable if you're unsure about lending money online to a complete stranger! Unless you're one of those people who Twitter, blog, and hang out on MySpace and Facebook, you might feel a little strange about doing something so personal online.

In Chapter 1, you read a general overview of P2P lending. Now, let's take a closer look at some of the basics you need to know to get started. It might make you feel more comfortable about the process.

Lending Basics

You now know that the P2P lending sites differ quite a bit. But there are some lending-related issues that are pretty much the same across different websites.

On all sites, you do need to understand how to read listings and what to look for. Listings differ among sites, to be sure, but understanding the concepts behind a basic listing on Prosper will be helpful to you as you read listings on other sites as well.

In the Red

Be sure to check up on the financial health of all the P2P lending websites that you are considering. In an industry that changes as fast as this one does, it's important to verify that the website you choose is still a viable, profitable website.

So in the next section, we look at a sample Prosper listing and review the important points.

Do You Need a License to Lend?

That sounds like the beginning of a James Bond movie, doesn't it? Don't worry! We're still talking about P2P lending. And to answer the question, no, you don't need a license to lend. But the site where you become a lender does. For instance, Prosper is licensed in all states where licensing is required.

You're called a "lender" on the P2P lending sites, but in actuality you are a loan purchaser on Prosper. The loans are actually originating through Prosper, and the lender is purchasing the borrowers' loans. Yes, it's a little confusing, so that's probably why Prosper and other P2P lending websites just decided to use the term "lenders."

Proving Your Identity

Borrowers have to prove their identities to make sure they're real people and that they are who they say they are. This prevents identity theft or fraud.

Lenders also have to go through *identity verification* for the very same reasons that borrowers do.

Hidden Treasure

What happens if Prosper goes out of business? Lender funds that weren't actively associated with a loan would be returned to the individual lenders. Existing loans would continue until they're repaid. They'd be handled by a third-party loan servicing agent.

As a lender, you can relax and know that borrowers would still be legally obligated to make payments on their loans. Whether Prosper is a going concern (or not, if that were the case) doesn't release borrowers from their obligations to pay back their loans.

Lenders must prove that they're real people and that they are who they say they are. There's also the goal of keeping the P2P lending community a safe and reliable place.

With lenders, though, there's the additional matter of taxes. We cover taxes more in Chapter 24, but all you need to know right now is that P2P lending sites are required to report income that lenders receive. Thus, the sites have to keep track of your personal information and your interest income.

def•i•ni•tion

When you go through **identity verification** to become a lender, P2P sites compare the information you've given them to the data from the credit agencies. If there's no discrepancy, you're in great shape.

When P2P sites collect information to verify your identity, they're also meeting anti-money laundering regulations. But don't worry. You don't have to sign over your first born or get notarized statements from your parents.

Here's what they need to verify your identity as a lender:

- Social Security number
- Birth date
- Street address
- Driver's license number
- Telephone number

Most of the sites, such as Prosper.com, compare the information you've given to the data collected by the credit agencies.

Is It Right for You?

If you've made it this far in this book, you're probably excited about becoming a lender. You've educated yourself about FICO scores and debt-to-income (DTI) ratios.

You've got money, and you're ready to roll. Just take a minute or two to do a few more gut checks before moving on.

Goal Check

Sit down and write out your financial goals for the next 20, 30, 40, or 50 years. It doesn't have to include anything fancy—although if you want to do regression analysis and fancy statistics, more power to you. This exercise is designed to get you thinking about the long term and how investing your money in P2P lending fits in with your overall financial goals.

Take a look at your goals and ask yourself some questions before you take the lending plunge:

- ◆ Does it fit in with my overall financial goals?
- ◆ Does it satisfy my desire to help others?
- ◆ Will it still work for me financially if all of my borrowers default?
- ◆ Will it affect my need for strong family relationships if I loan money to my brother and he can't pay me back?

You'll learn in the next chapter that the answers to these questions become even more important as you get older.

What's Your Motivation?

Some people are attracted to P2P lending because of the opportunity to help others. This is one reason why microlending seems to be gaining in popularity. People are finding a way to help others with small amounts of money.

But if your motivation is mostly financially oriented, that's okay, too. After all, you're taking money from other potential investments when you fund a P2P loan. And that's money that would (hopefully, at least!) be making money for you somewhere else.

See? There's no wrong answer here, as long as it's legal! Most lenders seem to find a happy marriage between these two motivations. Perhaps that's why P2P lending is such a rapidly emerging industry. And you can do both—make money and help others—by choosing the right website and the P2P lending platform that works for you.

Deciphering Loan Listings

We talked a bit about deciphering loan listings in the chapters that cover each P2P website, but it's a good idea to analyze listings in a little more detail so you can make smart decisions about your investments.

Even if you're using a portfolio system, there will be times when you want to manually choose some loans. At the very least, it's best to understand the listings so you can properly evaluate your portfolio criteria.

Take a look at this sample listing as it would appear on Prosper:

LISTING SUMMARY		
	**EXPANDING MY BUSINESS** $11,000 @ 8.90% FUNDING: 60% funded BIDS: 57 bids	
CREDIT PROFILE		
AA credit grade		19% DTI

The borrower wants money to expand a business. You can see that the loan request is for $11,000 at 8.9 percent. This borrower has an excellent credit rating and DTI ratio.

When you click "Expanding my business," you go to another screen that shows the following:

- **The listing summary.** Here, you'll see the basic information:
    - Loan amount
    - Interest rate
    - Percent of loan that's funded
    - Number of bids
    - Amount of days left to bid

- ◆ Borrower's annual percentage rate (APR)

- ◆ The monthly payment for the three-year loan

◆ **Borrower information.** This section shows whether the borrower has bids from friends and/or any questions and answers. You'll also find a handy "Forecast" chart that shows how much funding has occurred on each day and the forecast for funding in the remaining days. There's also a "Chart" that shows a graph that compares a listing's interest rate against a three-month history of loans with similar attributes, such as amount, group membership, and credit grade. This information helps you decide if this listing is offering a competitive rate.

◆ **Credit profile.** This section gives you the important numbers that help you decide whether you want to further examine the listing. Here, you'll see the borrower's credit grade, homeownership information, and DTI ratio.

Good Cents

Borrowers who are self-employed often don't calculate their DTI ratios because their incomes fluctuate. Send the borrower a question and ask whether he or she can clarify his or her financial situation. It's worth taking the extra step to do this if the business is in an area that interests you and if his or her other financial information looks promising.

◆ **Description.** This section includes the reason why the borrower wants the loan.

In the Red

If a borrower gives only skimpy information in the description section, this should give you pause.

It could very well be that the borrower is trustworthy and just didn't have time to write a comprehensive listing. But when the borrower leaves out a lot of information, it's best to assume that there's a reason why—and probably not a reason that's positive.

◆ **A statement about his or her financial situation.** What you're looking for is a few words about why the person is a good candidate for this loan. Borrowers will say things such as, "I've been steadily employed for 22 years."

◆ **Monthly *net income*.** You want to check whether the borrower has a reasonable amount of take-home pay.

◆ **Monthly expenses.** Not every borrower is going to give details, but those who do are more attractive to lenders. It's the transparency issue. The more straightforward a borrower is with his or her finances, the more trustworthy he or she seems.

def•i•ni•tion _____

Your **net income** is the amount of income you've earned after required or voluntary deductions, such as federal and state taxes and 401(k) deductions.

◆ **Friends and family winning bids.** When a borrower's friends and family members bid on his or her loan, it really helps. It's a good sign because it shows that the borrower has supportive friends. Prosper has safeguards in place to make sure the friends are for real and not from the imagination of the borrower!

◆ **Questions and answers.** This is an option you should take advantage of. If a borrower isn't giving his or her DTI ratio, ask about his or her expenses and budget. Before you ask questions, be sure you view the questions and answers on a loan listing so you don't waste either your time or the borrower's on questions that have already been addressed.

◆ **Bid history.** You got a close look at borrowers' bid histories on Prosper in Chapter 7. You can check in with loans you've bid on and see how you're doing. It can be amazing how some of these loans get funded. It's also really fun to watch and see if your bid wins.

Good Cents _____

While you're browsing through the listings on Prosper, you'll probably come across a few that you find intriguing. But maybe you need to think about them. The solution? Place the listings that interest you on a Watch List.

You can do this by clicking on the "Watch" link from any listing. You can easily remove it if you decide the listing isn't a good match for you.

Digging Deeper into Credit Data

If you're a registered lender on Prosper, you have access to even more credit data about borrowers. It's in your best interest to take advantage of the opportunity.

Here's some information on borrowers' credit reports that you can take a look at:

- **Now delinquent.** The current number of accounts that the borrower is late on.

- **Amount delinquent.** The past-due amounts that are owed by the borrower.

- **Delinquencies in the last seven years.** The number of delinquencies that are more than 90 days past due on the borrower's credit report in the last 7 years.

- **Public records in the last 12 months.** The number of public records on the borrower, such as bankruptcies and liens, over the last 12 months.

- **Public records in the last 10 years.** The number of public records on the borrower, such as bankruptcies and liens, over the last 10 years.

- **Inquiries in the last six months.** The number of credit inquiries made on the borrower's credit in the last six months.

- **First credit line.** The month and year the borrower's first recorded credit line (such as revolving or installment) was opened.

- **Current credit lines.** The number of credit lines that have been reported on the borrower within the last six months. It doesn't matter whether these lines are open or closed.

- **Open credit lines.** The number of credit lines presently open by the borrower that have been reported within the last six months.

- **Total credit lines.** The total number of credit lines appearing on the borrower's credit report.

- **Revolving credit balance.** The total outstanding balances on all of the borrower's open revolving credit lines that have been reported within the last six months.

- **Bank card utilization.** Ratios again! This is the sum of total balances divided by the sum of total limits (on all credit lines, that is).

Following is some information you can look at concerning the borrower's employment:

- The borrower's employment status. The options are:
    - Full-time employment
    - Part-time employment

- ◆ Self-employed

- ◆ Retired

- ◆ Unemployed

- ◆ The length of the borrower's current employment status.

- ◆ The borrower's current occupation.

- ◆ The borrower's stated income range (in $25,000 increments or more than $100,000).

Doing Your Due Diligence on New Sites

You learned right off the bat that the P2P lending industry is rapidly gaining strength. In the next few years, there will likely be many new P2P lending websites springing up. If, in the future, you decide to try a site that's new to the field, be sure you do your *due diligence*.

Some websites are falling into niche areas. Fynanz and GreenNote, for instance, are sites that focus on student loans. As P2P lending becomes more popular, it's likely that more websites will try to tap a niche category. For instance, you might see websites focusing on P2P loans for business startups.

def•i•ni•tion

Due diligence means to conduct a proper investigation of an entity or an investment to make sure it's legitimate before you become financially involved with it.

There are so many possibilities for P2P lending that, to protect yourself, you need to expect that some websites will be set up with a poor lending platform or an even poorer business plan.

Unfortunately, there will also probably be many websites that may not be able to run a P2P lending site efficiently or even meet the legal requirements. Just be careful and be sure you understand the sites' business models and funding sources before you commit any of your own funds. As it's said on some forums, lurk and learn before you jump into the fray.

Here are a few ways to do your due diligence:

- ◆ Send e-mails to the site and ask questions.

- ◆ Read all the FAQs that are available on the site.

◆ Browse all the borrower listings and get a feel for the type of borrower the site attracts.

◆ If there's a forum, register as a lender but then visit the forum frequently to learn more about the site.

◆ Ask about the default rate for different credit grades.

And don't forget to read all you can about new sites from other sources, such as magazines and newspapers. As you conduct your due diligence, make sure you're getting the viewpoint of those with unbiased opinions.

We mentioned in Chapters 1 and 10 that P2P lending websites have begun to enter the secondary lending market. As more P2P sites get into this area, you'll start to see news reports and articles on how this is going. Pay careful attention to what you read and follow up with the individual websites. This advice goes for new sites as well as for previously launched sites that are adding a trading platform.

This is an exciting new possibility for P2P lenders, but take your time and investigate it before you jump into it. For instance, find out if lenders have been able to sell their notes on the website's trading platform or if this has been difficult to do.

After you collect information, you'll become more comfortable with your choice. And hey, if you just can't find a comfort zone, then listen to your gut and don't use the P2P lending site that makes you feel uncomfortable.

The Least You Need to Know

◆ You don't need a license to be a lender, but your P2P lending site does.

◆ Just like borrowers, you must prove your identity to be a lender.

◆ Review your financial goals and examine your motivation before deciding to become a P2P lender.

◆ Understand how to decipher loan listings even if you plan to use automatic portfolios to choose your loans for you.

◆ As new P2P lending websites pop up, be sure you do your due diligence on new sites before becoming a member and lending funds.

◆ As some P2P lending websites enter the secondary lending market, you need to educate yourself about this process so you can ask the right questions.

Chapter 19

Is Lending a Risky Business?

In This Chapter

- ◆ Learning about risk tolerance
- ◆ Determining your risk tolerance
- ◆ Understanding risk capacity
- ◆ Decreasing risk by diversifying your portfolio
- ◆ What to do when borrowers default

Have you ever taken a glucose tolerance test? This test is used to determine blood sugar levels. The lucky patient has to fast after midnight and then report to the doctor's office the next morning to drink a bottle of glucose. If your body can't adjust its blood sugar levels, you start feeling pretty yucky—and you might get a diagnosis you don't want.

Risk tolerance is a little bit like that. If you take on more risk than you're mentally equipped to handle, you may start feeling pretty yucky. That's why it's a good idea to know up front what you can tolerate.

Types of Risk

When you talk about risk, there are really two issues to think about. First, there's your risk tolerance. If you invest $1,000 in the stock market and your investment is worth only $750 in a week, do you panic and sell the stock? Or do you wait a year and see where the market is?

If you're willing to wait a while, you have a higher tolerance for risk than the person who reacts immediately to a downturn in the market.

Second, there's the issue of your *risk capacity*. Even if you have a high risk tolerance, there are other factors to consider:

◆ Your age (and your spouse's, if you're married)

◆ Your income

◆ Your financial situation, which includes your debt-to-income (DTI) ratio, your savings, your IRA(s), and other investments

◆ The number of dependents you have

◆ Future expenses, such as college or supporting an elderly relative

◆ Your investment objectives

◆ Your retirement account

def•i•ni•tion

Risk tolerance is the amount of uncertainty that an individual can handle when it comes to negative changes in the value of his or her investments.

Risk capacity is the amount of risk you *should* take. Just because you have a high tolerance for risk doesn't mean you should go for it at the drop of a hat.

Here's an example of someone who's in a position to accept risk:

Derek is 30 years old and single. He makes $60,000 a year as an account manager at an advertising agency. He has a car loan, but his DTI ratio is below 27 percent.

If Derek has a high tolerance for risk, he's in a good position to take that risk. He's young, has no dependents, and lives within his means.

Here's an example of someone who needs to think about taking less risk with investments: fast forward 20 years, and Derek is married with three daughters. He's now 50 and is making more than $90,000 per year. His DTI ratio is still less than 30 percent, but pretty soon he and his wife will be writing checks for college tuition.

Derek is still the same guy who enjoys risk, but now he has dependents and college expenses on the horizon. He's also a heck of a lot closer to retirement now, so he needs to think about building his nest egg.

Derek may have the same risk tolerance he had when he was 30, but this is why it's important to know what both your risk tolerance and risk capacity are. Then you can assess how much risk makes sense given your current life situation.

What's Your Risk Type?

Okay, here's something fun to do. You get to take a quiz that will help you gauge your risk tolerance. When you're done, simply add the numbers next to your choices.

There's a key at the end to help you figure out whether you're conservative, moderate, or an "anything goes" kind of person.

Be honest with your answers. Your cubicle mate, boyfriend, girlfriend, ex-husband, ex-roommate, or current spouse never has to know whether you'd rather walk across hot coals than buy stocks.

Quiz: Your Risk Tolerance

This risk tolerance quiz was originally developed by two personal finance professors, Dr. John Grable at Kansas State University and Dr. Ruth Lytton at Virginia Tech. We adapted our own scoring system to make it applicable to P2P lending.

   A. How would your best friend describe you as a risk taker?

   ___ 1. A real risk avoider

   ___ 2. Willing to take risks after completing adequate research

   ___ 3. Cautious

   ___ 4. A real gambler

B. You are on a TV game show and can choose one of the following. Which would you take?

___ 1. $1,000 in cash

___ 2. A 50 percent chance at winning $5,000

___ 3. A 25 percent chance at winning $10,000

___ 4. A 5 percent chance at winning $100,000

C. You have just finished saving for a once-in-a-lifetime vacation. Three weeks before you plan to leave, you lose your job. You would:

___ 1. Cancel the vacation

___ 2. Take a much more modest vacation

___ 3. Go as scheduled, reasoning that you need the time to prepare for a job search

___ 4. Extend your vacation because this might be your last chance to travel first class

D. If you unexpectedly receive $20,000 to invest, what would you do?

___ 1. Deposit it in a bank account, money market account, or an insured CD

___ 2. Invest it in safe, high-quality bonds or bond mutual funds

___ 3. Invest it in stocks or stock mutual funds

E. In terms of experience, how comfortable are you investing in stocks or stock mutual funds?

___ 1. Not at all comfortable

___ 2. Somewhat comfortable

___ 3. Very comfortable

F. When you think of the word "risk," which of the following words comes to mind first?

___ 1. Loss

___ 2. Uncertainty

___ 3. Opportunity

___ 4. Thrill

G. Some experts predict prices of assets such as gold, jewels, collectibles, and real estate (hard assets) will increase in value. However, experts tend to agree that government bonds are relatively safe. Most of your investment assets are now in high-interest government bonds. What you would you do?

___ 1. Hold the bonds

___ 2. Sell the bonds and put half the proceeds into money market accounts and the other half into hard assets

___ 3. Sell the bonds and put the total proceeds into hard assets

___ 4. Sell the bonds, put all the money into hard assets, and borrow additional money to buy more

H. Given the best- and worst-case returns of the following four investment choices, which would you prefer?

___ 1. $200 gain best case; $0 gain/loss worst case

___ 2. $800 gain best case; $200 loss worst case

___ 3. $2,600 gain best case; $800 loss worst case

___ 4. $4,800 gain best case; $2,400 loss worst case

I. You've been given $2,000 to spend. You are now asked to choose between the following:

___ 1. A sure loss of $500

___ 2. A 50 percent chance to lose $1,000 and a 50 percent chance to lose nothing

J. A relative leaves you an inheritance of $100,000 with the stipulation that you invest all the money in only one of the following choices. Which would you choose?

___ 1. A savings account or money market mutual fund

___ 2. A mutual fund that owns stocks and bonds

___ 3. A portfolio of 15 common stocks

___ 4. Commodities such as gold, silver, and oil

K. If you had to invest $20,000, which of the following investment choices would you make?

    ___ 1. 60% in low-risk investments, 30% in medium-risk investments, and 10% in high-risk investments

    ___ 2. 30% in low-risk investments, 40% in medium-risk investments, and 30% in high-risk investments

    ___ 3. 10% in low-risk investments, 40% in medium-risk investments, and 50% in high-risk investments

L. Your trusted friend and neighbor, an experienced geologist, is putting together a group of investors to fund an exploratory gold-mining venture. The venture could pay back 50 to 200 times the investment if successful. If the mine is a bust, the entire investment is worthless. Your friend estimates the chance of success is only 20 percent. If you had the money, how much would you invest?

    ___ 1. Nothing

    ___ 2. One month's salary

    ___ 3. Three months' salary

    ___ 4. Six months' salary

To find your risk tolerance type, add the numbers adjacent to your choices and compare your score against this key:

Score	Risk Tolerance Level
12–17	Low tolerance for risk
18–24	Below average tolerance for risk
25–31	Average to moderate tolerance for risk
32–38	Above average tolerance for risk
39–43	High tolerance for risk

Grable, J. E., and R. H. Lytton. "Financial risk tolerance revisited: The development of a risk assessment instrument." Financial Services Review, *1999: 163–181.*

Let's take a closer look at the scores. If you scored 18 or lower, consider yourself conservative when it comes to risk tolerance. If you scored 19 to 28, you're comfortable with a moderate amount of risk. If you're at the high end of that range, you can stomach slightly more than moderate risk.

If you scored at least 28 points, you enjoy the thrill of a high-risk investment. You're the high-wire walker of P2P lending.

You're Conservative

If you're a conservative risk taker, you're careful with your money and don't see the point in taking unnecessary risks. To you, the "sure thing" makes sense rather than taking a big risk and ending up with nothing.

You're most likely to end up with a comfortable nest egg when you retire. You may not end up with a fortune (unless you inherit money), but you've made your money your own way and you made in a way that kept you calm and composed.

As a P2P lender, stick with borrowers who have excellent credit ratings. Don't waste your time with borrowers who are willing to pay high interest rates in return for loans. The rewards may end up being great, but the journey itself (the life of the loan) will probably give you ulcers.

You're Moderate

If you're a moderate risk taker, you enjoy a little bit of risk—but not too much. When it comes to P2P lending, stick with borrowers who have good-to-excellent credit ratings. You'll get a higher return with a borrower who has a "good" rating, but you'll be dealing with risk you can handle. Balance the risk with what you feel like you can tolerate losing.

You're a Thrill Seeker

If you're a fearless risk taker, take a deep breath! It's tempting to loan money to all those borrowers who have average (or below) credit. You're looking at the high interest rate and salivating over the potential return.

Just remember that defaults are also possible. Analyze each borrower's listing carefully before making a decision. And keep in mind that having a high tolerance for risk doesn't mean that you should take that risk.

Quiz: Your Risk Capacity

Risk capacity is all about how much risk you really ought to take. With the economy still on the downswing, being a little more cautious than normal might be a good choice. As we mentioned before, though, your particular life situation is, in the end, what determines your risk capacity.

Here's a quiz you can take to help you determine your risk capacity. Remember, the quiz just gives a snapshot of your risk capacity. Use it as a tool to help you decide, but not as an absolute answer to how much you should invest.

A. My age is:

___ 1. 35 or under

___ 2. 36 to 45

___ 3. 46 to 60

___ 4. Over 60

B. How many large expenditures do you expect in your future? Large expenditures might include paying college tuition, paying off a large credit card debt, living through a prolonged period of unemployment, supporting an elderly relative, medical expenses, or even taking a trip to Italy for your tenth anniversary.

___ 1. Maybe one or two times, but I'm still young

___ 2. Maybe one or two times, and it's most likely a problem

___ 3. More than twice, and I'm worried about it

___ 4. Expecting several large expenditures and it's a huge problem

C. What is the state of your health?

___ 1. I'm in excellent condition. I feel great!

___ 2. I'm in pretty good condition for my age.

___ 3. I feel fine at the moment, but there are serious medical conditions in my family history.

___ 4. I feel fine right now, but I do take a couple of medications for medical conditions every day.

___ 5. I take more than four medications for a variety of medical conditions.

___ 6. I take too many medications to list and I visit a physician frequently.

D. How knowledgeable are you about investing, borrowing money, and lending money?

___ 1. I'm an expert, and am frequently asked for advice about investments.

___ 2. I'm very knowledgeable about investing, borrowing, and lending. Other people sometimes ask me for investment advice.

___ 3. I know a lot about it and I've made a few good investment decisions.

___ 4. I can talk about the basics of personal finances in casual conversations.

___ 5. I'm not very knowledgeable about financial matters.

E. How many years before you retire?

___ 1. In more than 20 years from now

___ 2. In 11 to 20 years

___ 3. In 5 to 10 years

___ 4. In fewer than 5 years

___ 5. I'm already retired

F. How aggressively are you going to spend your retirement assets (such as cash and investments) once you retire?

___ 1. I'll stick to a budget and make my money last as long as possible.

___ 2. I plan to work part-time to supplement my income.

___ 3. I plan to spend a reasonable amount so I can enjoy life.

___ 4. I plan on spending all of it, because I can't take it with me.

G. On your current income, are you able to meet your financial goals for retirement?

___ 1. I'm exceeding my goals for retirement.

___ 2. I'm meeting my retirement goals.

___ 3. No, I'm not able to save for my retirement—I can barely pay my bills.

___ 4. I'm in debt and could use some financial counseling.

___ 5. I can't pay my bills and routinely bounce checks.

Add the numbers next to your choices. A low score means you have a limited risk capacity. The highest score is 33 and that means you appear to have a huge risk capacity. A score of 33 also means you're probably young, healthy, and rich!

Here's the key:

Score	Risk Capacity
7–12	Very little risk capacity
13–18	Little risk capacity
19–23	Some risk capacity
24–29	Pretty high level of risk capacity
30–33	High risk capacity

In the Red

Remember that these quizzes are designed to help you understand the concepts of risk tolerance and risk capacity. Under no circumstances should you rely on these quizzes as the sole determinant for your investment decisions.

Nothing replaces your own common sense. Risk capacity has an awful lot to do with your age. The closer you are to retirement, the less risk you should take.

But risk capacity also takes your current finances into consideration. If you're 75 years old and you've met your financial objectives for the next 30 years or so, your risk capacity is still likely to be high.

Diversifying Decreases Your Risk

Okay, you're now ready to talk about risk management. When it comes to managing risk, the mantra in P2P lending is "*diversify*, diversify, diversify."

If you've decided you're one of those "anything goes" thrill seekers, that's fine. But you still need to diversify. You're a risk taker, but you're not crazy, right?

Good Cents

Take real estate, for instance. What if you poured a ton of money into buying homes in a specific northeast neighborhood? You'd probably have lost your shirt by now. Diversifying means you take an approach where you're never heavily invested in one specific type of asset.

Here are some tips for keeping your loan portfolios diversified:

- Choose by credit profile. Even if you have high risk tolerance, spread out the risk by diversifying the credit profiles of borrowers you choose. Pick one or two who have low credit scores, a few who have average scores, and even more who are considered to have excellent credit.

- Choose by the type of loan. Have a portfolio that contains different types of loans (for instance, a mix of loans that are for business expansion, paying wedding expenses, or paying off credit card debt).

- Choose by the DTI ratio. If you take a chance on some who have a high ratio, balance those with loans to borrowers who have excellent DTI ratios.

- Choose by loan amount. Most P2P lending websites allow loans as low as $1,000. But there's a wide range of loan amounts on these sites, so have a range in your portfolio. If you're not comfortable lending money to someone who wants $15,000, stick with loan amounts ranging from $1,000 to $10,000.

Get the idea? You can go with portfolio plans set up with criteria determined by each site, or just set your own criteria based on your comfort level and on the amount of risk you feel you should take.

In the next chapter, we discuss the portfolio approach and managing your investments in more detail.

When Borrowers Are Delinquent or Default

In Chapter 3, you gained some insight into P2P etiquette. One of the rules for a lender was to never go after a delinquent borrower on his or her own. It's better for the borrower and much better for your blood pressure.

The P2P websites handle these things. There are serious legal issues involved, and you don't want to step into a legal quagmire. Leave it to the pros.

Hidden Treasure

Debt collectors have to take state and federal laws into consideration when dealing with delinquent borrowers. If you become your own debt collector, you run the risk of creating a legal liability for yourself.

So sit tight and let the P2P lending websites work with collection agencies. The website's personnel are trained to handle it.

That said, it's easy to get antsy. Know what the rules are for your site. On Prosper, there's a delinquency schedule. Lending Club, Fynanz, and Loanio have parameters, too. Go to your P2P lender's website and find out what the procedures are.

When a loan is really and truly defaulted, you may or may not receive any proceeds. On Prosper, 701 loans were sold to debt buyers in December 2007. Of these 701, 12.5 percent were homeowners; 9.6 percent had AA or A credit grades; 7.3 percent had E and HR credit grades; and 3.5 percent, interestingly enough, were from Texas.

Honestly, the P2P lending sites want to resolve these issues, too. It's not good for business to let any borrower default. Most of the P2P lending websites start taking some kind of action as soon as an account is late. So sit back, relax (at least try), and let the professionals do their jobs.

The Least You Need to Know

- Learn what your risk tolerance is before you make investments.
- Think about your current finances and your future expenses to understand your risk capacity.
- Strive for a diversified loan portfolio to spread out your risk.
- Accept that some P2P borrowers will default on their loans, and it's hard to predict who will.
- Never attempt to collect delinquent or defaulted loans from your borrowers.

20

Lending to Groups, Family, and Friends

In This Chapter

- ◆ The basics of being part of a lending group
- ◆ Lending to borrowers who belong to groups
- ◆ Issues with lending money to family members
- ◆ Things to consider when lending money to friends
- ◆ Why it's an extra good idea to document loans to family and friends

In Shakespeare's play *Hamlet*, Polonius may have said, "Neither a borrower nor a lender be," but he didn't know about P2P lending. Nowadays, he might add, "Unless, of course, you get legal documentation through a P2P lending site!"

Having it all legal and official helps, but it doesn't solve some bigger emotional issues that are bound to crop up when you lend money to family or friends. But having documentation goes a long way toward helping you stay calm.

In this chapter, we start out talking about lending groups and then move on and tackle a really fun topic: lending money to family members!

Being Part of a Lending Group

In Chapter 16, you got the scoop on borrowing as a member of a group. Again, we'll focus on Prosper because it's the P2P lending site that encourages group lending and borrowing. Just as we talked about groups for borrowers, there are also groups for lenders.

Interestingly, there are also groups that invite both borrowers and lenders to join. This isn't as odd as it may seem at first. A large number of borrowers become lenders (and vice versa). So it's actually not surprising that the two different camps would merge into one group.

For groups that share a special interest, such as sports car enthusiasts, they might set up a group that helps each other. The group might contain borrowers who want to buy the cars and lenders who want to help those who share a common interest.

Types of Groups

Just to give you an idea, here are some types of groups we've seen on Prosper:

- Small business owners
- Apple computer users
- Veterans who help other veterans
- Homeschoolers
- Brown University alumni
- Packer backers (yes, that football team in Wisconsin)

Different groups have different rules. Just browse the group listings until you find one that appeals to you (obviously, you don't want to approach the Packers group if your heart belongs to the Chicago Bears).

Before You Join a Lending Group

Most groups have a personal touch, and you may get a call or an e-mail from the group leader when you express interest. Take your time and get to know the leader.

You want to ask specific questions about the group. If you sense any hesitation when you ask questions (appropriate questions, of course), this might be a red flag. We're not saying that this is always the case, but most effective group leaders are ready and willing to tout the accomplishments of their groups.

Here are some sample questions for you to ask the prospective group leader:

- **What are the objectives of your group?** Some groups specialize in loans to purchase certain products (such as Apple computer products). Others have financial goals for the group. The answer to this question will tell you a lot about the group leader, too.

- **What's the membership criteria?** Find out what they're looking for. Do they welcome members who have only high credit ratings or from a certain geographic area? You'll find that some groups are not open to new members at all.

- **Do you welcome both borrowers and lenders?** This is important to know. If they do welcome both, are you free to loan money to borrowers who aren't in the group?

- **Do lenders pool money to fund loans?** Some lending groups pool all their funds together. But some groups are set up so that lenders choose their own loans. The group rating is based on the success of the group's loans, whether they were pooled or chosen by individual lenders. If you're an independent-minded soul, you may not fit in with a group that funds loans on a pooled basis.

- **Do lenders share the returns from loans as a group?** This is similar to the previous question. Some groups pool the interest and divide it, but some groups don't. Find out how the interest is divided among the group. Not all groups do it this way, but you need to ask the question.

- **How does the group communicate and how frequently?** Some groups talk a lot on the phone. Some meet in person once a month at a restaurant or coffee shop. Others communicate strictly by e-mail. If this is a group that likes frequent, in-person get-togethers but you have a busy family life, this may not be a good fit for you. But if you're dying to get out of your home office and see real people once in a while, then this might be the perfect fit.

- **Does the group fund loans where borrowers have below average credit?** This sounds like the membership criteria question, but it relates strictly to the financial aspect of membership criteria.

- **Is there a standard debt-to-income (DTI) ratio requirement when choosing loans to fund?** The answer to this question will give you a clue about the risk tolerance nature of the group. If they like to include loans where the borrower has a DTI ratio of 30 percent, be sure you're comfortable with risk.

◆ **What is the group's rating?** The ratings are on the group pages in Prosper, but some groups may not have one yet. If the group doesn't have a rating yet, ask the group leader to give you details on how the group is doing as a whole. Are default rates high?

◆ **What's the group's success rate, or estimated return on investment (ROI) with funding?** Ask what kind of returns the group's lenders have been getting. If it's a new group, these numbers may not be indicative of the future. But you'll at least get an idea of how the group is doing.

Use these sample questions to get you started. Talking to the group leader on the phone will naturally lead to questions you hadn't thought of before.

Lending Teams on Kiva

As we noted in Chapter 8, lending groups, or teams as they're called on Kiva, are fairly new to this website. Here are a few basics to give you an idea of how this works.

◆ Kiva team members lend as individuals, not as a team. But each member's total (how much they funded, for instance) is contributed to the team totals. So if 10 members individually funded a total of $2,500 in loans, then the team gets credit for the entire $2,500.

◆ You can create a lending team and even be the "captain" if you choose to.

◆ You can search for lending teams by going to Kiva.org and clicking on "Community."

◆ You can join more than one team.

◆ If you're on more than one team, you can decide which loans get credited to which lending team.

◆ You can quit teams whenever you choose.

◆ You can create lending teams for your company. For example, Microsoft has a lending team. But you don't have to be with a large company to start a lending team.

◆ You can create teams for a special event—for instance, a fundraiser or even a wedding.

From Kiva's community page, you can search for teams by category. For instance, you can search by: alumni groups, sports groups, businesses, events, youth groups, religious congregations, schools, friends, family, memorials, and more.

Lending to Borrowers Who Are Group Members

As you know, you can see a group's star rating on the "Group Listing" page. Sometimes a listing will say it's "not yet rated." This can mean that the group hasn't existed long enough or had enough loans to get a rating. Ask the group leader for an explanation.

If there isn't a group rating yet, ask the borrowing group's group leader to tell you what the delinquent and default rates are so far. Take a look at each listing individually, just as you would if they weren't part of a group.

It's true that group members have lower default rates, but don't let that guide your decision. Analyze the listing just as you would if there was no group connection.

All in the Family

Is a loan that you're considering giving to a family member for personal or business reasons? Personal reasons are usually easier to sift through. If it's for a student loan or for the down payment on a house, you probably have a good sense about your relative's motivation to pay you back. If you don't have a good sense about it, then it's time for a long talk before you agree to lend money.

If it's for a business loan, it can be tougher to decide. This situation calls for a lengthy discussion. You'll want to make sure your relative has done the proper amount of due diligence on the project. Ask to see a *business plan*. Review it carefully, and ask a lot of questions.

If you decide to proceed, go through a P2P lending website so you get proper documentation. The two of you should discuss the different sites that specialize in this type of loan. If it's a student loan, Fynanz, GreenNote, Virgin Money, or Loanio may work. On Fynanz, the student asks for the loan and often a family member bids and funds quite a bit of it. Or you can also help by just agreeing to be a cosigner.

def•i•ni•tion

A **business plan** is a written document that describes a proposed business. It includes a vision statement, marketing suggestions and statistics, and projections of profit and loss. It's like a road map for success.

On Virgin Money, you set up a loan for a student for the entire amount and get the right paperwork done in the process. If it's for a home mortgage or for a business loan, then Virgin Money also has a system that properly documents the loan.

> **Good Cents** _____
>
> If a family member wants money to start a new business, act like you're a bank officer. Ask to see a business plan complete with income projections. This is the very least that would be needed to get a bank loan. This also forces your relative to think through the business, and it increases the probability that the business will be successful.

Making It Official

Going through Fynanz, GreenNote, Virgin Money, or Loanio, you'll get the documentation to make the loan official. This is important for a few reasons.

It makes a case for a tax deduction. You want to be sure that you've covered the bases for any deductions to which you're entitled.

It keeps the deal structured. A loan that has a signed promissory note is more likely to be repaid. Without documentation, it's just too easy for the borrower to start thinking of the loan as a gift.

Having a payment schedule also removes some of the emotion from the situation. (Not all of it, of course, but at least you won't be making calls to remind your niece that her payment is due.)

Setting Up Payments

Going through an intermediary, such as Virgin Money, does more than just make it official. Sure, you get a signed promissory note—but you also get a payment schedule set up for you and the borrower.

Just like with a bank, there's a set amount that's due on a particular day of the month. If that date is missed, you have to deal with it as a late payment. Having legal and structured payments scheduled doesn't prevent all problems that arise when family and friends get involved in loans, but it at least might give someone pause before missing a payment.

After all, the date's right there in black and white. Of course, it's not as good as having a huge stone tablet to drag around like in the old days, but it's still pretty effective.

Look Before You Leap

You're smart and probably pretty savvy when it comes to finances. But when it comes to mingling family and finances, we can all be forgiven if it's difficult to avoid emotional decisions.

Here are some topics to think about before you make a decision to loan money to your granddaughter for graduate school. These are also things to think about before you loan your best friend money to start a consulting business. Whether family or a friend, set your emotions aside for a moment and answer these questions.

♦ **What's your *opportunity cost?***

For instance, you're considering lending $10,000 to your niece, Cassandra, for five years to help her with school expenses. You could earn 7.5 percent annually if you keep the money in its current investment vehicle.

Your opportunity cost is the interest income you forego to loan the money, which is $2,021.53. Assuming you're agreeing to give Cassandra the Applicable Federal Rate (AFR)—let's say it's 3.49 percent for a five-year loan—you'll receive $911.83 in interest.

def•i•ni•tion

The **opportunity cost** is the value that's given up when you choose one option over another.

So your opportunity cost is: $2,021.53 – $911.83 = $1,109.70.

You decide whether it's not a problem for you to give up that extra interest. If it's not, then consider giving the loan.

♦ **Will the borrower pay you back?**

This is a tough one. You'd like to think that your nephew would pay you back out of sheer gratitude that you came to the financial rescue. It's impossible to predict, but take a look at what you know about the person. Is he or she an individual who shows responsibility in his or her personal life?

♦ **Are siblings involved? How does the loan impact family members?**

If you loan money to Jared, your youngest son, will you need to be willing to lend it to Mark, your oldest son, too? It's hard to play favorites when it comes to money and families.

- ◆ **Can you spare it?**

  This would seem to be a no-brainer, but many relatives—especially parents—have a hard time saying no even if they can't afford it. Putting yourself at financial risk isn't going to solve someone else's financial issues. In fact, you could end up becoming *their* problem at some point.

- ◆ **Are you worried about the paperwork and whether this process will be time-consuming?**

  If that's your only concern, using a lending site will be a great help to you.

- ◆ **Can you keep yourself from speaking up if you don't approve of the borrower's spending habits?**

  It seems like one of the favorite formulas for TV comedies involves lending money to a family member. Then we get to watch the lender (usually the star of the show) go through a slow burn while watching the borrower spend the money on frivolous things, such as a vacation or a lobster dinner.

  But these episodes are usually funny because there's a bit of truth to them. If you can't lend the money and then bite your tongue when your nephew spends a weekend in the Bahamas, then don't become a lender to a family member.

- ◆ **Does the borrower have a problem with debt?**

  This is similar to the previous question, but this subject involves a pattern of mismanaging money. Anyone can have an occasional financial need—but if this is an ongoing drama, then steer clear. You'll also make things worse by becoming an enabler. Instead, offer to help your relative or friend get credit counseling.

- ◆ **Can you afford to lose the money?**

  In a perfect world, you'd be paid back with interest. But this isn't a perfect world. Just be sure that you can handle the loss of the money—both emotionally and financially.

If you've answered all these questions and don't feel great about moving forward as a lender, then give your regrets to the person who asked.

But if you feel like being a lender is something you can do, great! Next, take a look at some uncomfortable situations that might arise. But don't worry. You'll be able to handle them with aplomb.

Dealing with Dicey Situations

Even if you walk into a P2P lending situation with your family or friends with all of your legal ducks in a row, something's bound to happen.

In the Red

Never ever dip into your retirement account to give a relative a loan! When you loan money to a friend or family member, ask yourself whether you can afford to lose the money. It doesn't matter whether you have promissory notes if you can't get them to pay the money back. If your answer is no, then don't even go there.

Families carry around a lot of, um, emotional baggage. What you need are guidelines to get you through the dicey terrain ahead—and most importantly, to help you get through it with all your family relationships and friendships intact.

Family Issues

Let's take a look at some of the family issues (awkward situations!) first.

Good Cents

Try to defuse situations before they occur. Schedule a relaxing dinner and discuss the particulars of the loan. Go over the questions in this section and have a heart-to-heart talk while munching on some fine food. Oh, and resist the urge to make one of those cocktail napkin deals. You need the documentation!

What you should do if:

♦ **The borrower seems hurt that you want to go through a P2P lending site.**

Explain the situation in tax and in legal terms. If you need the documentation for taxes, use that for the excuse (not that you need an excuse, but this works when you're looking for tact).

Overall, stress how a promissory note and scheduled payments will help maintain the relationship and make repaying the loan easy and convenient for all involved. Be clear how legal documentation protects the borrower, too. This shows that you have his or her best interests at heart.

◆ **The payment is late.**

Have a conversation about how you're going to handle this situation before you lend the money. Agree on what the late fee will be and when it kicks in. Then, charge the late fee.

If you didn't have the conversation already, then tell the borrower what needs to happen based on what the loan documentation says. And ask for late fees if that's part of the agreement.

◆ **The loan is defaulted.**

Again, this possibility needs to be addressed before signing off on the loan. Be sure that the borrower understands the legal ramifications.

◆ **The P2P site is asking you for the money because you cosigned the loan.**

When you cosign a loan, you're making a promise that you will make the payments if the borrower defaults. Hopefully you thought this through before cosigning and decided you could forfeit the money if necessary.

The most important thing is to take your time with your decision. Family relationships and friendships are priceless.

Hidden Treasure

A PayPal UK study found the following:

◆ Forty-nine percent of those in the United Kingdom have loaned money to family or friends in the past year.

◆ Sixteen percent of lenders say a rift has developed between themselves and the borrower.

◆ Six million say they've loaned money to family or friends in the past 12 months.

Also, more people turn to Mom first when they need money.

Money does indeed create emotional issues, but with careful thought, tact, and use of a P2P lending site for the legal documentation, your chances of a successful experience improve greatly.

Issues with Friends

The advice you've read about dealing with family members can also work with friends. There are just a few differences to keep in mind, though.

It's much easier for a friend to walk away from an agreement that isn't legally documented. Your friend doesn't have to hide from you at the next office get-together or at your daughter's graduation party. So the issue of documentation is truly paramount when it comes to lending money to friends.

Because he or she is a friend and there's no issue of "keeping the money in the family," think carefully about your opportunity cost. You might consider charging more for interest than the AFR so you come out a little better financially.

Talk to your friend and come up with an interest rate that gets you a decent return yet saves your friend some interest expense. There's a middle ground where you can both be winners.

The Least You Need to Know

- If you'd like to join a lending group, have a long talk with the group's leader.
- If you're considering lending money to a borrower who's part of a group, it's also a good idea to talk to the group's leader.
- Check out the star ratings of lending groups you're considering joining.
- Check out the star ratings of borrower's groups to which you're considering lending money.
- Kiva offers lending teams that you can join, or you can create one of your own.
- It's important to document loans for tax purposes and to keep the relationship on an even keel.

Chapter 21

Meet Your Match

In This Chapter

- ◆ How to approach finding your perfect match
- ◆ Manually searching listings on Prosper
- ◆ Using Prosper's portfolio approach to find loans automatically
- ◆ Using Lending Club's LendingMatch to build portfolios
- ◆ Searching listings on other P2P lending websites
- ◆ How to find entrepreneurs on Kiva

You worked your way through college, so now you have a soft spot in your wallet for borrowers on Fynanz. Helping students realize their dreams is what it's all about for you. You also intend to check out borrowers on sites such as Prosper and Lending Club who want to go back to school while they continue raising their kids.

Or maybe you graduated from the University of Missouri and you want to loan money only to other alumni. Or you're from New Orleans and you want to loan money to borrowers who are still recovering from Hurricane Katrina. This is where P2P lending gets really personal. You can get a lot of satisfaction from lending money to others who you connect with on some level.

The way you search for loans has everything to do with the site you're using. Each website may have a unique platform for searching for loans that meet your criteria. Let's take a look at some.

Searching Loan Listings on Prosper

We talked about doing basic searches on Prosper back in Chapter 7, but now you're ready for some advanced searching. To do so, you must be signed in as a member. Once you've done that, you can get started on the search for your perfect match!

Using the Listing Categories

To give you an idea of how powerful Prosper's advanced search tool can be, we'll give you an overview of the different search criteria you can use.

You can search by:

♦ Credit grades. Here, you can limit your search to only those members who have A or AA credit grades. Or you can get a little risky and look for C-grade borrowers.

♦ Minimum interest rates. Here, you can limit the interest rate on which you're willing to bid.

♦ Loan category. For example, you can look only for borrowers who want to consolidate debt or those who are looking for business loans.

♦ Debt-to-income (DTI) ratio. You could limit your search to borrowers who have DTI ratios of less than 31 percent.

♦ The percent funded. Here, you could limit your search to loans that are less than 20 percent funded.

♦ Loan amount. For example, you can search for loans that are $2,000 or less.

♦ Homeowners only. Prosper loans are unsecured loans, but sometimes homeownership suggests stability. So this criterion might be a good one to choose if you are looking for more security.

♦ Automatic funding. If you select this criterion, you can choose only the loans where borrowers want automatic funding or only loans where that doesn't apply.

♦ Watched listings. Here, you can select loans to be watched.

♦ Listings you have bid on in the past.

♦ Current loans (loans you've successfully bid on and that are currently active).

Using Credit Information

You also can search using credit as the criteria. For instance, you can search for this information on a borrower:

- Currently delinquent loans

- Total past-due amounts

- Delinquencies in the last seven years

- Public records in the last 10 years

- Public records in the last 12 months

- Credit inquiries in the last six months

- When the first credit line was opened

- All current credit lines

- Credit lines reported on in the last six months

- Total number of credit lines on the credit report

- Outstanding balances on revolving credit lines within the last six months

- Ratio of account balance to the limits on each credit line (sum of balances/sum of limits)

Using Prosper Activity as a Search Tool

You can search by the activity of the borrower on Prosper. For example, you can find out the number of loans that have been issued to a borrower on Prosper. You can also see whether the loans are active and are still being billed.

In this category, you can also search using a number of different criteria:

- Principal amounts borrowed

- Current loan balance

- Number of payments made on time

- Number of payments made less than a month late

- Number of payments made more than a month late

- Total number of payments that have been billed to the borrower

- Changes in the borrower's credit grade while a member of Prosper

The preceding categories are very telling. You can get a sense of a borrower's payment history. It's also interesting to know whether the borrower's credit grade has slipped. This could indicate that he or she is having credit problems, and it showed up on his or her credit report when he or she asked for another loan.

Good Cents _____

You can choose three levels of searching, and you can specify the order in which you want the search conducted. So you can indicate the "primary, secondary, and tertiary" sorting criteria.

For example, you can choose to sort first by credit grade, next by occupation, and last by loan amount.

Using Social Criteria

Another way to search on Prosper is by using social criteria. This is a way to see whether there's a social network behind the borrower. Whether fair or not, lenders seem to trust borrowers more when they appear to have friends.

You can do searches based on the following:

- Show dollar bids from friends. Note that if a friend bids twice on the loan, it shows only one amount.

- Show number of bids from friends. Note that if a friend bids twice on the loan, it counts only one time. In other words, no double dipping when it comes to proving you have friends. If Catherine bids $50 five different times on Stacy's loan listing, it only shows up as one friend.

- The number of endorsements from friends. Endorsements are verified, so there's no fudging.

- The number of verified friends the borrower has.

As you can see, it's hard to commit "social fraud" here. The system is set up so that a borrower's social support system cannot be overstated.

Using Employment Information

Some lenders like to choose borrowers who have the same profession or occupation. Here's how you can search in this category:

- The employment status of the borrower. You can search for the following employment statuses: full-time, part-time, self-employed, unemployed, and retired.

- The amount of time that the borrower has been in his or her current employment status.

- The current profession or occupation of the borrower.

- The borrower's income range. This is according to the borrower, not necessarily according to documentation.

In the Red

Be aware that the borrower's income status isn't always verified. The borrower states his or her range in $25,000 increments up to $100,000. At that point, the income is just stated as more than $100,000. But in most cases, you're really taking the borrower's word for it.

So if you want to know whether there's a self-employed dry cleaner from Boston who makes $75,000 per year, you can do a search for just that.

Using Group Data

Groups are an important part of Prosper. If you think you'd prefer lending to borrowers who have been accepted as part of a group, you can search by using groups as a criterion.

Here's how:

- Search for members who are part of a Prosper group.

- Search by "star ratings" for groups. You'll get borrowers who are members of a group with your specified rating.

- Search by the number of loan payments that have been billed to group members. This indicates how long the group's history is.

- If you know the name of a group (or groups) you want to target, specify the name and you'll see the members with loan requests.

Groups, in general, do a good job of policing members. And there's always the peer pressure to keep borrowers on top of their payments. No borrower wants to be the one who made the group's star rating go down.

Saving Your Searches

Once you get into advanced searching, you can literally spend hours trying the combinations. Be sure you save the searches that brought results that interest you. You don't want to have to start all over.

At the top of the search page, you'll see a box. Enter the name of your search and click the "Save" button. You can edit saved searches, too. And if you decide you don't want to keep it after all, you can always delete saved searches.

Remember talking in Chapter 18 about what do if you come across a listing and you're not sure whether you want to save it? If you're one of those people who likes to mull things over for a while, you can put this listing on your "watch list." You can do this from any listing. Just click the "Watch" link. You'll be asked to sign in, and then this listing is added to your watch list. If you decide not to watch it any longer, it can be easily removed from your list.

Ouch! Handling Rejection

It's also a possibility that even if you have the borrower of your dreams (a Texan who works part-time as a carpenter with an A credit grade), your bid might be rejected. Remember, it's an auction system. It's not personal. Just move on to the next borrower who meets your criteria. Unlike some things in life, there are many more loans out there that you can consider funding.

Searching with LendingMatch on Lending Club

Lending Club refers to its LendingMatch technology as its "secret sauce."

LendingMatch uses an algorithm to find your borrower match. Now, don't fret over the fact that we're talking about algorithms. An algorithm is a sequence of instructions or a formula used to solve a problem. It's the algorithms that make this software so easy to use.

Hidden Treasure
The word "algorithm" comes from the name of the mathematician Mohammed ibn-Musa al-Khwarizmi. He was part of the royal court in Baghdad and lived during the ninth century.
Al-Khwarizmi's work is also probably where the word "algebra" got its name.

The algorithm helps you find borrowers with whom you feel comfortable. You're looking for someone who grew up in Indiana? It might be able to help you.

LendingMatch can find relationships based on:

◆ Geography

◆ Education

◆ Profession

◆ Connection to a social network

Lending Club's LendingMatch was designed with the portfolio approach in mind, but you can select the criteria for the search. That way, you'll end up with a portfolio of loans with which you have connections.

This whole idea of connections is in keeping with Lending Club's roots on Facebook. When you browse loans, you'll see the connections icons. Click them, and you'll view the borrower's connections to geography, education, employment, and associations or affinity groups.

You can also determine your criteria by risk tolerance. You'll decide your risk tolerance level, and Lending Club will select loans that match that level. If you completed the quizzes in Chapter 19, you already have a good idea of how much risk you can stomach. And don't forget to think about your capacity. Risk capacity isn't mentioned as frequently as risk tolerance, but it certainly is just as important.

For members, Lending Club offers a portfolio diagram that shows the composition of the portfolio for each risk level. You can set up more than one portfolio and have different risk levels for each.

In the Red

Risk levels are measured on a scale of one to five. Be careful to interpret the scale correctly. If you choose one, you're looking for low risk. If you choose five, you have a high tolerance for risk. Note that the risk level is tied to the loans currently available on the website when your portfolio is put together.

Here are some suggestions for choosing your risk tolerance level:

◆ Pick a risk level that reflects your risk tolerance level. If you haven't taken the quiz in Chapter 19, now's a good time to do so.

- Think about your risk capacity, too. Go back to Chapter 19 and take the quiz to determine your risk capacity if you didn't already do so.

- Determine how much of your Lending Club portfolio should reflect your total savings and investments.

- Consider having different risk levels in each portfolio so you can get a sense of the actual risk involved.

It's a good idea to browse the listings before you set up a portfolio. This will give you an idea of what kinds of loans and loan grades are currently listed.

Searching on Other P2P Sites

Let's take a look at how some of the other sites operate with portfolio systems. You learned in the last chapter how important diversity is. That's one of the reasons most of the sites have a portfolio approach available. They want to make it easy for you to get diversified.

Fynanz

Fynanz has a lot of lenders who loan money to friends and family. But even if you don't fit into that category, you can still loan money to borrowers.

Fynanz has a search system where you can choose the grade level of the borrower—either undergraduate or graduate student.

You can also choose the Fynanz Academic Credit Score (FACS) grade of borrowers. Here, you choose between the following:

- Platinum: Honors or Plus

- Gold: Honors or Plus

- Silver: Honors or Plus

You can also use Fynanz's "Smart Bid" software, which sets you up with a portfolio using your own set of predetermined criteria. In Chapter 22, we talk more about portfolio systems and how to use them to your advantage.

Loanio

Loanio's website is easy to navigate. There are loan listings on the home page, but you can also do your own searches based on the following criteria:

◆ Credit grade: Ranging from A+ all the way down to NC (no credit).

◆ Percent funded: Ranging from zero to 100; the ranges are in increments of 10, as in 10–20 percent funded and so on.

◆ Time left: Ranging from 1 day to 14 days before the loan listing expires.

◆ Advanced searches: This option is available once you register and become a member.

In Chapter 10, you learned about Loanio's Platinum Loan Listings. A quick refresher on this: borrowers prepay to have their loan listings considered for designation as Platinum Loans. This means that the borrower has taken the time to provide numerous sets of financial data to Loanio. If qualified, the borrower has the honor of a Platinum Loan listing.

If you're not comfortable with a lot of risk, be on the lookout for loans with the Platinum verification box in the listing.

Kiva

If you decide to put some of your lending dollars into Kiva, you have a lot of choices and can sort loans in a variety of ways. Because this is a loan that won't bring you a profit, you'll probably want to find an entrepreneur who you really want to help.

Hidden Treasure

Kiva has an "Impact This Week" heading at the top of the borrower listing where it flashes the impact that lenders have had during a given week. The numbers are impressive. One week in mid-August 2008, 1 loan was made every 37 seconds. Here's more from that week:

◆ New lenders: 2,207

◆ Loans completely repaid: 556

◆ Gift certificates purchased: 576

◆ Entrepreneurs funded: 1,398

◆ Number of lenders making loans: 7,776

◆ Amount lent: $580,225

When you're on Kiva's home page, click "Lend" and you'll go to the borrower listings. From here, you can do a search using the following criteria:

- The status of the loan. You can choose to ignore the status, or you can pick from the following:

    - Fundraising

    - Raised

    - Active

    - Paid back

    - Defaulted

- Select by gender.

- Choose by sector. This means the occupation or the industry in which the entrepreneur works. Here are a few of the choices:

    - Agriculture

    - Transportation

    - Clothing

    - Food

    - Housing

- Sort by region. You can ignore this or search by continent. For instance, you can search by:

    - North America

    - Central America

    - South America

    - Africa

    - Middle East

    - Asia

- Search by other criteria. For example, focus on entrepreneur listings that meet the following requirements:

    - Popularity

    - Loan amount

- Amount left
- Repayment term
- Oldest to newest loans
- Newest to oldest loans

Each time you select one of the preced-ing criteria, you'll see a list of entrepre-neurs who meet it. For example, when you choose "active" loans, you'll see all active loans. When you select "female," you'll see all active loans for females. Then, if you choose "retail" for the sector, you'll see females with active loans who work in retail.

Good Cents _____

When your Kiva entrepreneur pays back your loan, you can reinvest it in another entre-preneur. You can also donate the repaid loan back to Kiva to cover operational expenses.

Or you can use the money to buy a Kiva gift certificate for a friend or family member so some-one else can experience the joys of microfinance on Kiva.

You want to lend money to an entrepreneur in the Middle East? Select that criteria and you get a list of those who meet your criteria and who live in the Middle East. As you keep selecting criteria, your list gets narrowed down to what you're looking for.

You can put together a portfolio of loans this way. The entrepreneurs repay the loan over time. You'll get e-mails during the loan term so you can see how your chosen entrepreneur is getting along.

The Least You Need to Know

- You can use advanced search options on Prosper to find borrowers who meet a multitude of criteria.

- You can save searches you've made on Prosper's website and think about it for a while.

- Lending Club's LendingMatch software sets up a portfolio for you by using your set of criteria and desired connections.

- Fynanz lets you search by using academic criteria.

- Loanio has a Platinum Loan listing program that allows you to focus on borrow-ers that might be less risky.

- You can search on Kiva for entrepreneurs and narrow your search to the country, gender, and business sector in which you want to invest.

Managing Your Loan Portfolio

In This Chapter

- ◆ How you benefit from a portfolio approach
- ◆ Managing your Prosper portfolio
- ◆ Portfolio approaches on other P2P lending websites
- ◆ Using Smart Bids to diversify on Fynanz
- ◆ Diversifying your portfolio on Kiva
- ◆ Questions to ask yourself before you reinvest your returns

Does finding the loan listings that meet your criteria seem like a headache to you?

Some people enjoy the process. But if you're one of those people to whom the destination is more important than the journey, then you might consider trying the portfolio approach. Most of the P2P lending websites have this option. In fact, Prosper and Lending Club have quite a sophisticated way to establish your portfolio and keep tabs on it.

You want a self-employed female who's a high-tech consultant and lives in San Diego? Okay! Of course, your success depends on whether there is someone who meets your description who has a loan listing at the time of your search. At the very least, though, a portfolio brings you diversity.

Benefits of the Portfolio Approach

Prosper, Lending Club, and most other sites give you a chance to choose the *portfolio* approach. You can determine the criteria for loans based on each P2P lending site. The options vary by site, so the degree that you'll be able to narrow down your choice is dependent on the site.

Using a portfolio approach has several benefits:

def•i•ni•tion

A **portfolio** is a collection of investments held by an individual or an organization. In the case of P2P lending, it's the collection of loans that a lender has funded.

- It saves you a ton of time.

- It makes the process easy for you.

- It's more efficient if you know what you want.

- You can have several different portfolios.

- It's a good way to get *diversified* in a short amount of time.

def•i•ni•tion

Diversification involves investing in loans that include borrowers with high credit scores as well as some lower credit scores.

The lower credit scores bring a higher return on investment (ROI), but a corresponding higher risk of default. You can minimize potential losses by including loans from borrowers who are excellent credit risks.

Using Portfolios on Prosper

You already know that in Prosper's world, a portfolio plan is a tool you can use to automatically bid on listings that contain your predetermined criteria.

For example, you can set up your criteria so that you don't bid on anyone with a credit grade of less than A or with a debt-to-income (DTI) ratio greater than 35 percent. Or you can set it up so you go as low as C-grade borrowers but only those who have DTI ratios of less than 30 percent. Pretty cool, huh?

There are more benefits of using the portfolio approach:

- Obviously, it saves you time.

- You have control over the criteria.

- You can build a portfolio of loans quickly.

- You can diversify with smaller loans.

Prosper has templates you can use that range from conservative to aggressive. Here's how the estimated returns work out with portfolio plans on Prosper:

- Conservative (very low risk): 5.4 percent

- Balanced (low risk): 7.82 percent

- Moderate (medium risk): 8.78 percent

- Aggressive (high risk): 9.69 percent

- Start from scratch (unknown risk): you can devise your own criteria. Your estimated return is unpredictable.

Notice that the higher the risk, the greater the return. But the higher the risk, the greater the chance of default. You know how this works from the chapter on interest rates, so this isn't a surprise. It's just another time when you have to decide what's best for you.

Nothing is written in stone, either. You have control over your portfolio and you can make changes whenever you want. You can even override your portfolio plan and make a manual bid on a loan that didn't meet your specified criteria.

But remember, once a bid on a loan is made, you can't take back the bid. You have to wait and see whether you're one of the winners before you can use that money anywhere else.

Helping a Borrower on Prosper Make a Payment

You know that delinquency is a possibility, so it shouldn't be a surprise if it happens. Banks deal with this situation all the time, and that's why the cost of borrowing money at a bank is so high.

With P2P lending, there's an unusual option (at least on Prosper, there is). It's called a *community payment*. Any Prosper lender can decide to make a payment on a borrower's behalf.

def•i•ni•tion

A **community payment** is when a Prosper member makes a payment for a borrower who's more than a month late with a loan payment.

Can you imagine a bank executive giving you a call and saying, "Don't worry, Mr. Smith. We'll cover your payment this month!"

No, of course you can't. But a community payment has happened in the movies, though. Remember in *It's a Wonderful Life* when George Bailey was about to go to jail because his Uncle Billy lost $8,000? The community rallied and raised the money to save George.

Well, think of a community payment as a mini version of that scene. The sentiment behind it is the same. These community payments occur when a lender believes the late payment is an aberration and the borrower needs a helping hand to make it through a tough time. There's no expectation that the borrower will repay the lender for the community payment, so be prepared for that.

You can also decide to help the borrower with a minimum of $25. Sometimes just a little bit helps the borrower over a hump. At the very least, you've shown some goodwill in the community by helping out.

In the Red

If you make a community payment and the loan is never repaid, your payment may be considered a gift for tax purposes. This would make it taxable income to the recipient. This would also have tax implications for the lender.

It's a good idea to seek tax advice on this issue if your community payment is not repaid.

The money from community payments is applied (in order) as follows:

- Non-sufficient funds (NSF) fees to Prosper
- Late fees to lenders
- Bank draft fees (if applicable)
- Interest expense
- Principal amount

Basically, the amount of funds from community payments is treated the same way as a regular loan payment coming from a borrower.

Portfolios on Lending Club

You learned in Chapter 21 that Lending Club's LendingMatch system uses a portfolio approach, and we discussed how diversity decreases your risk in Chapter 19.

With LendingMatch, you can set up a portfolio with the "connections" that are most important to you personally. And it's easy to set it up with varying credit grades to spread out your risk. It's about diversification, after all.

Take a look at a snapshot of the national averages of interest rates that were effective in early 2008:

Investment Vehicle	Interest Rate
Checking account	1.00 percent
Money market account (MMA)	2.75 percent
1-year CDs	3.09 percent
Online savings accounts	3.54 percent
Lending Club average portfolio performance	11.28 percent

Note that the interest rates provided were effective in October 2008 per Bankrate. com. The average annual portfolio performance includes all lenders from 5/24/07 through 2/22/08.

You can see from the preceding chart that the portfolio approach on Lending Club has worked well for its lenders. Again, this is just a snapshot of a specific day, so only use it as a guideline for decision making. With the up-and-down economy, these rates will change weekly, so go to Bankrate.com to get the most current rates.

Building Portfolios on Kiva

Remember talking about microfinance—lending small amounts to borrowers? This is a unique P2P lending situation, so let's take a look at how you can stay diversified with your portfolio.

On Kiva, you're involved in lending small amounts, so it's pretty easy to spread your dollars around and build a portfolio. You can lend $25 to a grocer in Malaysia and also lend $25 to a clothing store owner in Tajikistan.

You can see your portfolio by logging on to your Kiva account. Click the "My Portfolio" button, and then click the "Loans" button.

> **In the Red**
>
> Please take note that on Kiva, loans are not in default until they are still unpaid at six months past the due date. With microfinance, the borrower is given every reasonable opportunity to repay the loan.
>
> You just need to remember that this is different from lending on a site such as Prosper, Lending Club, or Loanio, where the delinquent and default dates are reached sooner.

Here are a few more things to keep in mind with your Kiva portfolio:

- If one of your borrowers makes a partial payment, you cannot withdraw the funds. So, for example, if you lend $25 and the borrower repays $15, you must wait until the entire $25 is repaid before you have access to the money.

- If one of your borrowers defaults on the loan, you'll receive a proportionate amount. For example, if you loaned $25 on a loan amount of $1,000, you'll receive 2.5 percent of the amount that was collected (25 ÷ 1,000 = .025, or 2.5 percent).

- A loan is considered to be in default when it's six months after the due date of the loan.

- Kiva doesn't take action against defaulted loans. You can't forgive a loan on your own. All the lenders involved in the total amount of the loan must agree to let it go. You are not the only lender that funded the loan, so you can't forgive the loan all by yourself. But given the mission of this website, the other lenders are likely to be inclined to forgive the loan. Just assume that as a lender, you won't receive any money on a defaulted loan.

- When you put your portfolio together, you can spread the risk by choosing a variety of field partners with whom your borrowers work.

- Check the list of field partners and note the star ratings. As you put together your portfolio, think about diversity regarding the field partners to spread out your risk.

Consider the following statistics for Kiva as of mid-October 2008.

	All Partners
Total Loans	$48,821,285
Completed Loans	$15,412,135
Default Rate on Completed Loans	1.35 percent

The total loan amount in the preceding table represents all loans on Kiva at that point in time. The "Completed Loans" amount represents the loans that are either completely paid or the term for the loan has ended—whether the loans were defaulted or paid in full. The overall default rate on completed loans was only 1.35 percent, not bad considering the environments these borrowers must succeed in.

Consider the delinquency and default rates of Kiva field partners based on their star ratings.

Field Partner Ratings	1 Star	2 Star	3 Star	4 Star	5 Star
Delinquency Rate	26.4 percent	32.2 percent	28.5 percent	12.4 percent	6.1 percent
Default Rate	3.5 percent	0 percent	9.1 percent	0 percent	0 percent
Amount Repaid Versus Expected Rate	72.7 percent	86.3 percent	84.5 percent	94.2 percent	100 percent

A couple of things in the preceding chart merit mentioning. Let's take a look at the delinquency rates first.

- Note that the highest delinquency rate is with two-star partners.

- The one-star partners have a better track record with on-time payments than the three-star partners.

- Field partners with five stars are superior, but the four-star partners are not too far behind.

A look at the default rates is somewhat surprising, too. Notice the following:

- Partners with two-, four-, and five-star ratings have perfect records.

- The two-star partners have the highest delinquency rate, but at least their entrepreneurs haven't defaulted.

- Three-star partners have the highest default rates.

The "Amount Repaid Versus Expected Rate" is the difference between what Kiva has received in loan payments versus what they expected to receive. So if Kiva expected $100 in repayments by a certain date but received only $90, then the rate is 90 percent (90 ÷ 100 = .90, or 90 percent).

This data reveals some interesting points as well. Consider the following:

◆ Five-star partners are doing great. Their rating is perfect!

◆ Four-star partners aren't far behind.

◆ Two-star partners have the highest delinquency rates, yet are doing pretty well at the end of the day with an 88.7 percent repayment rate.

When you're putting together a portfolio, you have to look at the entire picture. Consider that although some partners have lower delinquency rates, they may have higher total default rates.

Hidden Treasure

Kiva receives quarterly loan payments from their field partners. These funds aren't distributed to lenders. The funds are deposited in a U.S. bank account, where they draw interest until the loan is completely repaid.

The interest earned is used to cover Kiva's operating expenses. When the loan is completely repaid, the lenders are then repaid for the loan.

Kiva states that as its staff grows, it may reconsider this policy. But at the moment, it isn't feasible for Kiva to process partial repayments to lenders.

There's not a magic formula here, but just remember to think about all the facts. If you're leaning toward including some one-star partners, note that their "amount repaid versus expectancy rate" is only 72.8 percent.

Using Portfolios on Fynanz

On Fynanz, you can use "Smart Bids" to set up your portfolio. This is Fynanz's name for its portfolio matching system. For the sake of diversity, it's a good idea to mix up your portfolio with loans that include different age groups and different Fynanz Academic Credit Score (FACS) grades.

You can choose a predetermined set of criteria, such as the following:

- FACS grade

- School (college, university, and so on)

- Year of study (freshman, sophomore, and so on)

You can also bid equal dollar amounts (but different rates) on different listings. You know the diversify mantra by now. There are several different ways to stay diversified on Fynanz.

> **Good Cents**
>
> It's a good idea to read the FAQs on every P2P lending site you're considering. On some sites, you have to dig around to find them.
>
> On Fynanz, click the "Help" button and you'll get a list of categories: general overview, Fynanz basics, borrowing, lending, and privacy and security issues.

Reinvesting Your Returns in New Loans

We've discussed the different sites and how reinvestments are approached. Read the FAQs on every site and you'll find this topic is usually covered.

Take stock before you *reinvest* your returns in the same site. Consider the following questions before you move forward with another loan:

- What kind of ROI did you receive? If you were disappointed in the result, review the kinds of loans that you chose. Did you take a risky approach and choose borrowers who had lower credit grades?

- Was the P2P lending site you used responsive to your questions?

- Were you able to view your statements as needed?

- Overall, was it a satisfying personal experience for you?

If you're not happy with any part of your experience, consider how to make it better next time. Perhaps you just need to adjust your criteria for your portfolio. Or if you had a hard time keeping up with multiple loans, maybe you're better off choosing your loans one at a time instead of using a portfolio approach to P2P lending.

> **def•i•ni•tion**
>
> To **reinvest** in P2P lending means to take your profits (interest income) and put them right back into other P2P loans.

If you decide to forego the portfolio approach, though, be sure you maintain diversity even if you choose only a couple of loans.

The Least You Need to Know

- ◆ Benefits of the portfolio approach include saving you time and helping you get diversified in a short amount of time.

- ◆ You can set up a portfolio on Prosper using several different templates they provide or even determine your own set of criteria.

- ◆ Most sites allow the portfolio approach, so read the FAQs on every site to understand their approaches.

- ◆ Fynanz has a Smart Bid portfolio approach.

- ◆ Lending Club uses the LendingMatch technology to facilitate a portfolio.

- ◆ Before you reinvest your money, evaluate your experience with your current site.

Chapter 23

Receiving Statements

In This Chapter

- ◆ Receiving statements from P2P lending sites
- ◆ What to expect from Prosper's monthly and year-end statements
- ◆ Receiving statements from some of the other P2P lending websites
- ◆ Avoiding gift taxes when your loan is processed through Virgin Money

In most cases, you'll be able to view your P2P lending statements online. In this chapter, you get an idea of what's in those statements—and, perhaps more importantly, why you need to keep physical copies in a safe place.

Just as we were winding up this book, Prosper made an announcement that it had filed a registration statement with the SEC and had entered a quiet period. The quiet period should be over by the time you're reading this book. Be sure to check Prosper's website to see if there are any changes to the procedures for monthly and year-end statements.

Receiving Statements from Prosper

You'll receive a monthly statement from Prosper that gives you the current details on your account. The statement reflects activity up until 11:59 P.M. on the last day of the month. For example, your statement for May 2009 reflects all activity through 11:59 P.M. on April 30, 2009.

The Monthly Statement

You can view your "Monthly Lender Statement" online through your Prosper account. Be sure to print a copy to keep for your own records. As of this writing, Prosper wasn't keeping copies from previous months online, so print out your monthly statement to keep a copy for your files.

The first section of this statement shows your account summary. It includes the details of how your money was distributed during the month. The second section covers loans and payments. The third section details account activity.

Here's what you'll find in the account summary:

- Your cash balance. This doesn't include funds that are active winning bids. The funds in your account are set aside when you have a winning bid even though the loan isn't yet formally funded.

- The active loan value. This is an accrued value of your outstanding loans, so it changes every day.

- Borrower payments that are in transit. These payments have been made, but the funds haven't been placed in your account yet.

- Your winning bids. This is the amount of your funds that are held in active bids. Some of these may be partially winning bids. If the loan doesn't go through, the money is returned to your account.

- Your winning bids that are pending review. If you have a winning bid on a listing that Prosper is reviewing, your funds will not be transferred until the review is complete. If the loan doesn't pass the review process, your money goes back to your account.

- Your account total. This is the sum of all of the items we listed here. The account total represents the value of your current lending account.

Look at this section of your statement and make sure everything appears to be correct. You need to keep track of your investments and the financial details related to the borrowers you're funding.

In the next section of the monthly statement, you'll get a detailed summary of all of your accounts that had some activity during the month. This includes items such as defaulted accounts and new loans you've funded.

Here's what to expect when you view the "Active Loan Value" table in this section:

> **Good Cents** _____
>
> Prosper doesn't keep records from prior months online. You must print your own copy, because you'll lose access to the data when the next month's statement is generated.

- The starting loan value. This is the value of your loans on the very first day of the statement period. The ending loan value on your previous statement becomes your starting loan value for the current month.

- The new loans you've funded. This number is the principal amounts of any new loans you've funded during this period.

- Accruals on your loan portfolio. This is the total of all interest and fee accruals on the loans in your portfolio.

- The amount of payments from borrowers. This total includes late fees, interest, and principal paid during the statement period.

- The amount of defaulted loans. This doesn't include any actual recoveries from loan sales. If applicable, that amount would appear in the account activity section of your statement.

Here's what you'll find in the "Loans Held" table in this section.

Regarding the loans:

- Loan ID information. Each loan has a unique identification number. You can match this ID number to the loan on the website.

- The status of your loans. This is the status as of the last day of the statement period. You'll see where payments were made.

- The current value of the loans. This is the value as of the last day of the statement period.

- The principal balance of the loans. This is the principal balance as of the last day of the statement period.

Regarding the payments:

- The payment ID of each loan. Each loan has a unique ID, and so do the payments.

- The payment status of each loan. This is the status as of the last day of the payment.

- The date of the post.

Other highlights in this statement:

- The amount you received.

- The total interest accrued. The total of the interest accrued on each loan during the statement period. Remember that interest is accrued daily, so the totals depend on factors such as the principal amount and the interest rate.

- Amount of fees accrued. This refers to the total accrued amount of borrowers' late fees during the statement period.

- The amount of interest paid.

- The amount of fees paid.

- The principal amount paid. This is the principal amount paid by the borrower during the statement period.

- The amount of service fees. This refers to the total amount of fees that you, the lender, paid.

- The amount of collection fees. If it applies to your situation, this is the total amount of fees that you paid to collection agencies.

Next in the statement is a section you'll enjoy perusing. This contains all of your account activity. Here's a sample of what you'll find:

- Transaction ID. This is the original ID for the transaction.

- The date of the transaction. This includes the date and the time. They're all listed in Pacific time (Prosper is based in California).

- The type of transaction. This describes the transaction. It's identified as either a deposit (a positive) or a withdrawal (a negative) from your cash balance.

- ◆ The purpose of the transaction. This section has a lot of "mini" sections within it, including:

  - ◆ Your manual bids

  - ◆ A community payment on a late loan

  - ◆ Late fees from borrowers

  - ◆ Principal payments you've received

  - ◆ Interest payments

  - ◆ Lender service fees

  - ◆ Funds you transferred to your Prosper account

  - ◆ Resolution of any disputes

  - ◆ Adjustments due to resolution of disputes

- ◆ The related loan ID. This identifies loans related to the transactions.

- ◆ The transaction amount. This is the total amount of the transaction.

Your monthly statements are valuable, so it bears repeating: keep copies!

The Year-End Statement

Prosper will send you a statement at the end of the year that details all of your loan activity. In a moment, we'll discuss why you need this for taxes. First, let's review what's on the year-end statement.

Good Cents _____

Prosper has a referral program that encourages members to bring their families and friends on board. Here's how it works:

Refer a borrower and you'll receive $50 as soon as your friend makes the first monthly payment on his or her loan. Refer a lender and you'll receive $25 as soon as your friend funds his or her first loan.

In the tax reporting section, you'll find:

- ◆ Account name. This is important because it's the name under which taxes will be reported.

◆ Account type. If you're not an individual, the entity's name will appear here.

◆ Tax reporting number. This is typically your Social Security number. Check this number carefully, because it's used to report tax information.

In the lending summary section, you'll find:

◆ Principal balance at the start of the year. This is the principal balance of your loans on the first day of the calendar year.

◆ Principal balance at the end of the year. This includes the total principal balances of all of your loans on the last day of the year.

◆ Receipt of principal payments. This doesn't include principal payments that are still in transit on the last day of the year.

◆ Receipt of interest payments. As with principal payments, this doesn't include interest payments that are still in transit on the last day of the year.

◆ Receipt of late fee payments. The amount of late fees that borrowers paid for late payments. Again, this doesn't include late fees that are still in transit on the last day of the year.

◆ Service fees you paid. This shows the amount of servicing fees you paid as a lender.

◆ Collection fees you paid. This is the amount of collection agency fees you paid during the calendar year.

◆ Referral rewards you've received. If you received any rewards, the amount will appear here.

Hidden Treasure

If your principal balance at the start of the year (January 1st) doesn't match the ending balance of the previous year, it may be due to unusual payments that were applied to the previous year.

For instance, collection agency fees or manual checks related to the prior year's loan may have been in transit and not applied to the last year's statement. In this case, there would be a discrepancy.

In the "Loans Held" section, you'll find the following:

- ◆ Loan ID. This is the unique ID associated with your loan.

- ◆ Origination date. This is the start date of the loan.

- ◆ Payment status. This shows the payment status of each loan as of the last day of the calendar year.

- ◆ Principal loaned. This is the original principal amount that was loaned to the borrower.

- ◆ Start of year principal balance. If the loan has an origination date in the current year, this field will be empty.

- ◆ Start of year principal payments in transit. This includes principal payments that were not yet received by you at the start of the calendar year.

- ◆ End-of-year principal balance. The principal balance on the last day of the calendar year.

- ◆ End-of-year principal payments in transit. This is the total amount of principal payments that have not yet been received by the lender on the last day of the calendar year.

- ◆ Principal payments received. This is the total amount of principal payments received from the borrower during the calendar year.

- ◆ Interest payments received. This shows interest payments received from borrowers during the calendar year.

- ◆ Late fee payments received. These are the late fee payments received from borrowers during the calendar year.

- ◆ Service fees you paid. These are service fees you paid during the calendar year.

- ◆ Collection fees you paid. These are the fees you paid to collection agencies during the calendar year.

Next, the loan sale summary section shows the impact of your lending activity. If you didn't have any loans default or resold, this section won't appear in your statement. If this section applies to you, you'll find:

- ◆ The pre-sale principal balance. This is the total principal of all your loans sold because of default or repurchased before they were sold.

- ◆ Net proceeds from sale. This is the amount that was recovered from loan sales.

If you do have loans repurchased by Prosper, you'll see a section with these headings:

- Loan ID.

- Purchase date.

- Purchase price.

- Repurchase date.

- Pre-repurchase principal balance. This is the principal balance of the loan at the point before it was repurchased.

- Net proceeds from repurchase. This is the amount received from Prosper.com in the repurchase.

Next in the year-end statement is the section that deals with "Loans sold to *debt buyer.*" Again, if this didn't happen to one of your loans, this information won't be on your statement. For your sake, we hope this doesn't apply to you!

def•i•ni•tion

A **debt buyer** is a company that buys debt. Usually, the debt is loans that are written off or otherwise considered uncollectible. On Prosper, for instance, loans that are more than 120 days past due are offered to debt buyers. The loans are sold to the debt buyer that makes the best bid on the delinquent loans.

If this section applies to you, you'll find the following:

- Loan ID.

- Purchase date.

- Purchase price. This is the principal balance of the loan on the purchase date.

- Sale date. This is the date the loan was sold to a debt buyer.

- Pre-sale principal balance. This is the total principal balance of the loan right before it was sold to a debt buyer.

- Proceeds from sale to debt buyer. This is the amount that's recovered from the sale of the loan to a debt buyer.

- Proceeds from forfeited group rewards. If the borrower is a member of a group that took group leader rewards, this shows the lender's share of the forfeited group rewards upon sale.

◆ Net proceeds from sale. This is the total amount received from the debt buyer and forfeited group leader rewards. In other words, what you have left!

The year-end statements are especially important because you'll need this information for your taxes.

Receiving Statements from Other P2P Lending Sites

Many sites don't advertise their statements and what to expect. And at the time this book was written, Lending Club was just coming out of a quiet period with the U.S. Securities and Exchange Commission (SEC). To get details on statements you'll receive from Lending Club, check its website.

Good Cents

Some sites may offer phone numbers, but on most P2P lending websites, communication (at least initially) is conducted via e-mail. On most websites, you can find e-mail addresses (and possibly phone numbers) by clicking on "Contact Us" or "About Us."

But if you have questions that haven't been satisfactorily answered, don't hesitate to get in touch the old-fashioned way. Pick up the telephone!

But be assured that websites will give you what you need for tax purposes. If you want to be clear about the documentation that sites provide, you can e-mail the sites before or after you join and get more details.

Receiving Statements from Virgin Money

There are several reasons why you need to pay close attention to statements (and keep them) when you're lending money to family members.

We talk more about the tax implications in the next chapter, but for now you should be aware that there's a thing called the "gift tax regulation" that's important to the IRS.

You want to hang on to your Virgin Money statements in case you need to prove to the IRS that the money you received was a loan and not a gift. Following is what you need to know for now.

- If you chose an interest rate that at least matches the Applicable Federal Rate (AFR), you're in good shape. Your statement will prove that this is the case.

- If you chose an interest rate that's lower than the AFR but the loan is less than $12,000, you may still be okay.

- Maintain a physical file for the loan documentation that includes the promissory note and other important papers that prove it was a loan.

In the Red

If you charged an interest rate lower than the AFR or didn't charge interest at all, the IRS may view your loan as a gift. If the amount of the loan is less than $12,000, this may not be an issue. If the loan is greater than $12,000, though, you may owe taxes on the amount of foregone interest that the borrower didn't have to pay. It's a good idea to consult with an attorney if you think this is an issue for you.

See why it's important to have documentation? Keep those statements just in case you need backup for anything that's tax related. As long as you have proper documentation, you're prepared if the IRS comes calling.

The Least You Need to Know

- It's vital that you keep copies of monthly statements, even if you're viewing them online. Remember that some sites don't keep prior months' records online.

- You must keep physical copies of all year-end statements for tax purposes.

- If you have questions about the statements you'll receive, contact the site via e-mail either before or after you join.

- If you loaned money through Virgin Money, keep your year-end statements in case you need to prove that the loan wasn't a gift.

- Keep all loan documentation, including the promissory notes, in a safe place.

Chapter 24

Taxing Matters for Lenders

In This Chapter

- ◆ How the IRS classifies P2P lending websites
- ◆ What you need to know about federal income tax on interest income
- ◆ Understanding Form 1099
- ◆ State tax issues
- ◆ Why gift tax issues are tricky when it comes to taxes

Comedian Jay Leno once said about taxes, "Worried about an IRS audit? Avoid what's called a red flag. That's something the IRS always looks for. For example, say you have some money left in your bank account after paying taxes. That's a red flag."

That's one of those so-funny-it's-sad things, isn't it?

Let's begin by taking a look at how the IRS views P2P lending websites—in a way that's similar to brokerage houses.

IRS Classification

Under Internal Revenue Service section 6049, P2P lending sites such as Prosper and Lending Club are known as intermediaries, or *nominee recipients*. Nominee recipients must report income sent to recipients via the Consolidated Form 1099.

def•i•ni•tion

A **nominee recipient** receives funds that belong to someone else. In the case of P2P lending, sites receive the interest income as the intermediary and then disburse it to the lenders. The sites must report this on their tax returns.

This nominee recipient concept makes sense if you think about it. The P2P lending sites have become the intermediaries in place of banks. The P2P lending sites are collecting the loan payments and distributing them to you, the lender.

Stock brokerage firms also operate in a similar fashion, and they fall into this nominee recipient category. A brokerage firm (or any other entity) that receives funds on behalf of others is a nominee recipient in the eyes of the IRS.

Federal Income Tax

The bottom line is that your interest income is taxable income.

If you earn more than $600 in interest income in a calendar year, you'll receive a Consolidated Form 1099 from your P2P lending site. Your 1099 summarizes your taxable interest income. The sites then report your income to the IRS.

Note that there are exceptions to the $600 rule in some states, which we review later in the chapter.

Interest Income

You'll receive your 1099-INT statement and then report your income on your own personal income tax return on Form 1040, the U.S. Individual Income Tax Return. The interest income is reported on line 8a.

If your interest income is more than $1,500, you may need to report that on Schedule B, "Interest and Ordinary Dividends." It's best to consult with your tax accountant if you need to fill out this form. You can get the forms at IRS.gov.

The Consolidated Form 1099

If you're a lender on Prosper, you'll receive Consolidated Form 1099. The consolidated form reports on these areas: the recipient and payer information, the full amount of interest received, miscellaneous income, and proceeds from the sale of defaulted loans to debt buyers. If you're lending money through another P2P lender, check its website for information on the forms you can expect to receive. If you can't locate the information on the site, find the contact button and send an e-mail requesting tax-related details.

> **Good Cents**
>
> Entities send out 1099 forms at the end of January. Contact your P2P lending site if you don't receive one.
>
> If you receive your Form 1099 and any of the information is incorrect, contact your P2P lending site and ask it to issue you a new, corrected 1099. If you don't get mistakes corrected, it can cause a terrible headache later on (including penalties). Even if you're not at fault, it will take time and energy to resolve.

Your year-end lender statement and your 1099 will help you complete your income tax return. Let's take a look at each section of your 1099.

Recipient and Payer Information

This section includes the following:

♦ The date and period of the statement

♦ Your name

♦ Your Social Security number

♦ The P2P site's tax information

Check all this information carefully and make sure the basics are correct.

Form 1099-INT

You'll receive this form in tax years when you've received at least $600 in interest income. This section includes the following items.

- Your name and address

- The full amount of interest you received during the calendar year

- The recipient's name (your name)

- The recipient's ID number

- The recipient's address

- The recipient's account number

- Any other income, such as U.S. Savings Bonds

Form 1099-MISC

This form reports on your miscellaneous income and may include the following:

- Late fees

- Referral fees

- Any group leader rewards

- Other miscellaneous income, such as medical and health-care payments or crop proceeds (no kidding on that last one)

Form 1099-B

Hopefully you won't get too much experience with this form!

This document is used when defaulted loans are sold to debt buyers during a calendar year. The official name of the form is "Proceeds from Broker and Barter Exchange Transactions."

On this form, you'll find some of the following:

- Your name and address

- The recipient's name (that's you, again)

- The recipient's address

- The date of sale or exchange

- A description of the transaction

- ◆ Gross proceeds
- ◆ Profit or (loss) realized
- ◆ Aggregate profit or (loss)
- ◆ Federal income tax withheld

You need the information from this section to calculate your net losses on defaulted loans. This information, used in conjunction with the pre-sale amortized principal balances from your year-end lender statement, will give you the numbers you need to calculate your loss. We discuss net losses in the next section.

Losses on Defaulted Loans

Are you still awake? This tax talk can get a little dry, can't it? Get a strong cup of coffee (or a quick nap, if you must) and forge ahead. You'll get just enough information to give you a working knowledge of this issue.

Losses on defaulted loans can generally be written off as investment losses. Your proceeds will appear on Form 1099-B as discussed in the previous section.

When you record *capital losses*, you'll determine the amount after you've offset the losses against any *capital gains tax*.

def•i•ni•tion

You have a **capital loss** when an asset, such as an investment, decreases in value. The loss is realized when the asset is sold for a price that is lower than the original cost.

The **capital gains tax** is levied on capital gains incurred by individuals (and by corporations). Capital gains are the profits that an investor realizes. For example, let's assume you bought stock in ABC Company. When you sell your ABC Company stock, your capital gain is the difference between what you paid for your stock and what you sold it for.

On Form 1040, "U.S. Individual Income Tax Return," you'll report this item as an investment loss on line 13, "Capital gain or (loss)." You may need to include Schedule D, "Capital Gains and Losses," where you record the details of your losses.

There's a $3,000 cap on investment losses that you can deduct in a calendar year. You can carry over the excess amount to the next year. This is another tricky tax situation, though, so it's a good idea to consult with a tax advisor.

> **In the Red** _____
>
> Watch out! Be sure that if you're reporting a capital gains loss, you've netted your losses against any gains. This amount is your net capital gain (or loss). Your tax return will be incorrect if you look only at the loss figure and ignore any gains you've had.

Understanding the Gift Tax

This is a situation that comes up when you loan money to a relative at a very low interest rate. If you loan money to a family member—or even to a friend—at a rate lower than the current AFR, the IRS may view this loan as a gift.

A few things to note:

◆ The annual gift tax exemption is $12,000. This can be a gray area, though, so get tax advice if you're in this territory.

◆ There's a lifetime maximum on the gift tax exemption of $1 million. This means that once you've made gifts that total $1 million during your lifetime, you can't use the gift exemption again. If you've got millions to worry about, you definitely need professional tax advice!

◆ If the loan is greater than $12,000 and you gave the borrower a low interest rate, then the IRS may view this loan as a gift.

You learned in the last chapter that if a loan is viewed as a gift, then you may owe taxes on the *imputed interest* to the IRS. It would be a shame to do a favor for a relative and then have to deal with a dicey tax issue that can cost you.

def•i•ni•tion _____

If you loan money to a relative (or a friend) at a rate lower than the AFR, the IRS views the "lost interest" as **imputed interest.**

For example, if the AFR is 3 percent and you loan $12,000 at 2 percent, then the borrower pays less interest expense. But the IRS sees this as lost interest. The imputed interest is the difference between what the borrower paid (2 percent) and what he or she should have paid (3 percent).

You want to hang on to your statements in case you need to prove to the IRS that the money was a loan and not a gift. But hopefully, if you understand the rules ahead of time, you can avoid problems with the IRS.

Here's what you need to keep in mind to steer clear of tax problems:

♦ Choose an interest rate that at least matches the AFR. Your statement will prove that this is the case.

♦ If the loan is for less than $12,000, you're probably okay even if you agreed to an interest rate that's lower than the AFR. But this bears repeating: if you're in this area of the tax code, get professional tax advice.

♦ We know you're tired of hearing this, but it bears repeating again: keep paper copies of everything related to this loan. This includes everything from the promissory note to all the other important papers involved, such as the payment schedule or collateral agreements.

Hidden Treasure

According to the IRS, you may give a gift up to $12,000 per person, per year without any tax consequences. As the receiver of gifts, you can receive up to $24,000 (gifts from two individuals) each year from your parents.

For the receiver, it gets even better if there's a spouse. Borrowers can receive gifts up to $48,000. This is a gift from each parent to the borrower and to the spouse.

The P2P lending websites are pretty quick to tell you that if you find yourself in a predicament over the gift tax, consult with a tax advisor. Don't get yourself in hot water trying to figure out an unusual tax situation.

On the other hand, if you do decide to make it a gift, write a letter stating that you don't expect any repayment of the loan. Why? Because if you passed away, the letter tells your other relatives that the loan was a gift.

Otherwise, the borrower may take heat from relatives who think the loan represents proceeds to them. Yes, it seems morbid to bring this up, but this is exactly why having everything legal is so important. The documentation protects you and the borrower.

State Income Taxes

Remember when we talked about states that are exceptions to the $600 interest income rule?

Here's a list of those states. Be sure you check this out carefully, because tax rules do change. A quick visit to your state's website will probably let you know whether there are any changes. And do check, because taxes change frequently.

As of this writing, here's the chart with exceptions to the $600 interest income rule.

State	1099-INT	1099-MISC
Arkansas	$100 or more in interest	—
California	$10 or more in interest	—
Colorado	More than $0 in interest	—
Connecticut	More than $0 in interest	More than $0 in interest
District of Columbia	More than $0 in interest	—
Delaware	More than $0 in interest	More than $0 in interest
Hawaii	More than $0 in interest	—
Iowa	More than $0 in interest	—
Idaho	More than $0 in interest	—
Kansas	More than $0 in interest	—
Kentucky	More than $0 in interest	More than $0 in interest
Massachusetts	More than $0 in interest	—
Michigan	More than $0 in interest	—
Minnesota	More than $0 in interest	More than $0 in interest
Montana	More than $0 in interest	More than $0 in interest
North Carolina	More than $0 in interest	—
North Dakota	—	More than $0 in interest
Oklahoma	$500 or more in interest	$500 or more in interest
Oregon	More than $0 in interest	More than $0 in interest
Puerto Rico	$500 or more in interest	$500 or more in interest
South Carolina	More than $0 in interest	—
Virginia	More than $0 in interest	More than $0 in interest
Vermont	More than $100 in interest	More than $100 in interest

Some states don't have income taxes at all. Interest income is usually considered taxable by the state where you have your permanent residence.

Ever notice that a lot people migrate south to Florida when they retire? Yes, the warm weather has a lot to do with it. But so does the state's approach to personal income tax. Florida does tax certain business assets, but in general there's no tax on personal income. When you retire and start drawing income from your IRA, the savings on taxes can really add up.

Good Cents

Make no mistake: every P2P lending website will suggest that you speak with a tax advisor. But getting an overview and educating yourself about the topic is a good idea.

Here's a list of the states that give you a free pass on state income tax:

- Alaska
- Nevada
- South Dakota
- Texas
- Washington State
- Wyoming
- Florida (no personal income tax, but there may be tax on the value of certain business assets because there's a corporate income tax on businesses; check with your tax accountant to determine if business-related property falls into that category)

Tennessee and New Hampshire don't tax individual wage income, but they do tax interest income (as well as dividend income). But after you start factoring in federal taxes, breaking states into "low tax" and "high tax" groups isn't so easy anymore.

Some of these interest income issues will be evident when you read the instructions in your state's income tax returns. If it's not clear, seek tax advice. This can certainly get complicated if you've lived in more than one state and the states have different tax rates.

You know how the media loves to tell us where the best places to live are? Sometimes these lists are based on low taxes or low real estate prices. Don't rely on articles in magazines, on the Internet, or in newspapers (or blogs, Tweets, and so on) that tout the best places to live for low taxes. It's rarely that simple.

Hidden Treasure

A good place to start your research is at Bankrate.com's "State tax roundup" section. There's an interactive map, and you can click on a state and get a brief summary of the state income tax laws. You get an excellent—and quick—overview. Go to www.bankrate.com/brm/itax/state/state_tax_home.asp.

If you're considering moving to a new state, do your own research (and maybe get professional tax advice) so you can make your own informed decision.

In the Red

There are some situations, such as moving to a new state, that require finesse. States have varying regulations on how to apportion your interest income between the states. Take care that you report your income properly so you're not hit with penalties later.

We started this chapter with a quote, so we'll end with one, too.

Albert Einstein once said, "The hardest thing in the world to understand is the income tax."

And that's coming from a pretty smart guy. So don't feel bad if you're having problems wrapping your mind around some of these tax matters. We all feel the same way (yes, even Albert Einstein).

The Least You Need to Know

- The IRS classifies P2P lending sites as "recipient nominees."

- As a P2P lender, you must pay taxes on interest income.

- You'll receive Form 1099 from the P2P lending website through which you've funded loans.

- You can deduct net losses on your tax returns if you've experienced defaulted loans.

- You must know your state's requirements for personal income.

- If you've lived in different states during the tax year, you need to educate yourself regarding apportioned interest income.

Appendix A

Glossary

adjusted gross income (AGI) Gross income minus allowable deductions. *See* net income.

annual percentage rate (APR) A measure of the total cost of borrowing over the term of the loan, including any additional fees associated with the loan.

annual percentage yield (APY) The effective annual rate of return when considering the effect of compound interest.

annual servicing fee The amount lenders pay to reimburse a P2P lending site, such as Prosper.com, for servicing loan payments from borrowers.

Applicable Federal Rate (AFR) The minimum interest rate set by the U.S. Treasury to calculate interest charges. Lenders must charge an interest that meets the minimum rate required by the federal government or the foregone interest will be considered a gift to the borrower.

balloon payment After a period of equal monthly payments, the borrower makes a large payment to repay all the principal and any charged interest.

blog feed A data format used for publishing frequently changing content; also sometimes called a "syndicated feed."

business plan A written document that describes a proposed business. Depending on the business, it may include a vision statement, marketing suggestions and statistics, and profit and loss projections.

capital gains tax   A tax levied on capital gains incurred by individuals (and by corporations). A capital gain is the profit that an investor realizes.

capital loss   When an asset, such as an investment, decreases in value. The loss is realized when the asset is sold for a price that is lower than the original cost.

charge card   A card that doesn't charge interest. However, you must pay the full amount due when the bill arrives each month.

closing fee   A fee that borrowers pay to obtain a loan.

community payment   A payment made by a Prosper member on behalf of a borrower who is more than a month late with a loan payment.

cosigner   An individual who accepts responsibility for paying off a loan if the primary debtor doesn't pay. The cosigner basically guarantees that the lender will get his or her money back.

credit bureau   An agency that functions like a clearinghouse for credit information. These organizations collect and rate consumers' credit information. The three largest credit bureaus in the United States are Equifax, Experian, and TransUnion.

credit card   A card issued by a financial company that gives the card holder the ability to borrow funds while paying interest.

credit inquiry   An item on a credit report that shows a business requested a copy of the credit report. Only the inquiries that are related to credit applications (a "hard" inquiry) have the potential to reduce the credit score.

credit union   An independent financial cooperative that is "owned" by members of the credit union. Profits are shared among the members. Credit unions may be set up to serve a specific group, such as those serving in the military.

cuneiform   A type of wedge-shaped writing created by the Sumerians, an ancient society that recorded "loans" on stone tablets. The word is also Latin for "writing."

debt buyer   A company that buys debt, such as loans that are in default or otherwise uncollectible.

default risk   The probability that an individual will fail to repay a loan.

discount rate   The interest rate that banks pay when borrowing money from the Federal Reserve.

disintermediation   This situation occurs when the typical middleman in a financial transaction, such as a bank, is replaced by another entity.

diversification   An approach to an investment portfolio that includes different types of investments with the objective of spreading out risk.

due diligence   A term used to describe the process an individual uses to determine whether an entity or an investment is legitimate.

e-commerce   The buying and selling of goods or services over the Internet; also sometimes referred to as "e-business."

endorsement   A written recommendation by someone who knows the borrower very well.

federal funds rate   The interest rate at which banks lend money to other banks.

Federal Reserve   The central bank of the United States that sets monetary policy by controlling the money supply and interest rates.

fixed interest rate   The interest rate on a loan that remains the same throughout the term of the loan. Mortgages often have fixed interest rates.

fully amortized   A loan where there are scheduled, regular payments that include both interest and principal.

Google Alerts   E-mail updates of news, such as articles and blogs, that contain search terms the user requested. You can also set up e-mail alerts for when someone clicks on your website or links to your page.

historical default rates   This information is provided by credit bureaus and is based on the past behavior of consumers. Those who have higher credit scores tend to have historically lower default rates on loans.

home equity loan   A type of loan that allows the borrower to use the equity in his or her home as collateral. The borrower's equity is the difference between what he or she owes on his or her home and his or her home's market value. It's also called a second mortgage.

identity verification   A process where P2P lending sites compare the information the borrower or lender gives them to the data from the credit agencies. This process is designed to verify a person's identity.

imputed interest   The interest that the IRS considers lost when someone loans money to a relative (or a friend) at a rate lower than the Applicable Federal Rate (AFR).

installment loans   Payments made at regular intervals over a predetermined period of time. Examples are mortgages and car loans.

interest rate   The amount of interest charged per year on a loan.

intermediary   An entity or institution that acts as the middleman between borrowers and lenders. In P2P lending, the P2P website plays this role.

judgment rate   The interest rates that judgments bear in a case regarding usury law limits.

legal rate   The highest interest rate that most states allow to cover contractual obligations without a specific term.

lump sum payment   A single payment that pays off an entire loan as opposed to periodic payments.

microcredit   A small amount of money that is loaned to an individual or to a group.

microfinance   The supply of loans to poor and low-income individuals or groups in developing countries.

microfinance institution   An organization that provides microfinance services targeted to the poor.

money management   The process of budgeting, spending, saving, and investing.

net income   The amount of income left after required or voluntary deductions, such as federal and state taxes and Social Security.

nominee recipient   An entity that receives funds belonging to someone else. In the case of P2P lending, sites receive the interest income as the intermediary and then disburse it to the lenders.

opportunity cost   The value that is given up when you choose one option over another. For example, if you have choices A and B and you choose A, you've given up the value you could have received with B.

origination date   The date when a borrower literally has access to the borrowed funds. This is also the date that the borrower's interest starts accruing.

portfolio   A collection of investments held by an individual or an organization. In the case of P2P lending, it's the collection of loans that a lender has funded.

prime rate   The interest rate that banks give to creditworthy customers.

principal   The original loan amount.

principal balance   The total amount of the principal that still must be repaid.

principal paid   The total amount of the loan principal that has already been paid on a loan.

promissory note   A legal document representing a promise by a borrower to repay a loan to a lender. The document is signed by both the borrower and the lender.

quiet period   The extent of time between when a company files a registration statement with the Securities and Exchange Commission (SEC) and when the SEC declares that the registration statement is effective.

recurring debt   A debt that occurs on a continuing basis until the debt is repaid. Examples are child support, mortgage payments, and installment loans.

regrade   The process of receiving a new credit grade when a borrower requests a second loan on a P2P lending site.

reinvest   A strategy of taking profits (interest income) and putting the money back into other P2P loans.

requester   The P2P lender on the W-9S form. For example, if a borrower received a loan from Fynanz, then Fynanz is the requester.

risk capacity   The amount of risk that an individual *should* accept.

risk tolerance   The amount of uncertainty that an individual can emotionally handle when it comes to negative changes in the value of his or her investments.

secured loan   A loan that requires pledging property to cover the debt. This type of loan gives the lender security in case the borrower defaults on the loan.

social finance   A term coined by Zopa, an online P2P lender, to describe financial transactions between individuals.

social lending   A process in which borrowers and lenders make a financial agreement without the involvement of an intermediary, such as a bank or other financial institution.

tangible asset   A valuable asset that has a physical form, such as equipment.

transparency   The extent that information about the services and financial data of a company are readily available. In the case of P2P lending, this concept contributes to trust among lenders and borrowers.

Truth in Savings Act   A federal law that was enacted to allow consumers to make informed decisions about accounts at financial institutions. The act requires disclosure of interest rates and associated fees so consumers can make comparisons between potential accounts.

Twitter A free social networking tool. Users send text-based updates, or tweets, via cell phones to people who have signed up for them. People who "follow" you get updates on their phones, on your Twitter webpage, or on your Facebook page.

unsecured loan A loan that is not secured by collateral, such as a house or stocks.

usury laws State laws that cap interest rates at certain levels.

usury limit The maximum interest rate that state usury laws allow.

Helpful Resources for P2P Borrowers and Lenders

Whether you need to find a P2P lending site to help you consolidate debt or to help you get a student loan, this resource appendix is here to help you find what you need.

You'll find information on all the major P2P lending websites, information about the credit reporting agencies, and free articles to help you manage your money.

P2P Lending Websites

The major players in P2P lending:

www.prosper.com
Prosper (general P2P lender)

www.lendingclub.com
Lending Club (general P2P lender)

www.virginmoneyus.com
Virgin Money (loans between family and friends)

www.fynanz.com
Fynanz (student loans)

www.greennote.com
GreenNote (student loans)

www.kiva.org
Kiva (microcredit loans to entrepreneurs)

www.loanio.com
Loanio (general P2P lender, but accepts co-borrowers)

www.loanback.com
LoanBack (focuses on P2P lending between family and friends)

Other sites related to P2P lending:

www.globefunder.com
Globefunder (direct-to-consumer lending)

www.nolo.com
Nolo (source for legal documents)

www.microplace.com
MicroPlace (microfinance site using an investment platform)

www.microfinancegateway.org
Microfinance Gateway (resource site for microfinance)

New P2P Lending Websites to Watch

www.communitylend.com
Community Lend (based in Toronto and launching in 2008 or 2009)

www.pertuitydirect.com
Pertuity Direct (appears to be general P2P lending)

Credit Bureaus

To obtain personal credit histories, contact:

Experian
P.O. Box 2002
Allen, TX 75013
1-888-397-3742
www.experian.com

Equifax Credit Information Services, Inc.
P.O. Box 740241
Atlanta, GA 30374
1-800-525-6285
www.equifax.com

TransUnion
P.O. Box 2000
Chester, PA 19022-2000
1-800-680-7289
www.transunion.com

To obtain free personal credit histories from all three credit bureaus, contact:

www.annualcreditreport.com

To obtain free credit score offers, contact:

www.cardratings.com

Websites with Free Articles About Credit and Personal Finance

www.cardratings.com

www.myfico.com

www.bankrate.com

www.creditcards.com

www.crediteducationbureau.com

www.experian.com

www.credit.com

www.creditbloggers.com

Government Websites

www.irs.gov
Internal Revenue Service

www.federalreserve.gov
Federal Reserve Board

www.usurylaw.com
www.lectlaw.com/files/ban02.htm
Usury laws for your state

Federal Regulations

www.dol.gov/compliance/laws/comp-ccpa.htm
The Consumer Credit Protection Act

www.fdic.gov/regulations/laws/rules/6500-200.html
Truth in Lending Act

http://www.ftc.gov/bcp/edu/pubs/consumer/credit/cre15.shtm
Equal Credit Opportunity Act

www.ftc.gov/os/statutes/fcradoc.pdf
The Fair Credit Reporting Act

www.ftc.gov/bcp/edu/pubs/consumer/credit/cre16.shtm
The Fair Credit Billing Act

www.fdic.gov/regulations/laws/rules/6500-1350.html
Electronic Fund Transfer Act

www.ftc.gov/bcp/edu/pubs/consumer/credit/cre27.pdf
Fair Debt Collection Practices Act

www.ftc.gov/os/2001/06/esign7.htm
Federal Electronic Signatures in Global and National Commerce Act

www.ftc.gov/bcp/menus/consumer/credit/loans.shm
Federal Trade Commission (FTC)

www.federalreserveconsumerhelp.gov/?District=0
Federal Reserve's Consumer Help

www.ftc.gov/bcp/edu/pubs/consumer/tech/tec01.shtm
FTC's Consumer Guide to E-Payments

Starting a Business

Check out this advice before getting a P2P loan:

www.sba.gov/smallbusinessplanner/index.html
U.S. Small Business Administration

The Complete Idiot's Guide to Business Plans (Alpha Books, 2005)
By Gwen Moran and Sue Johnson

www.irs.gov/businesses/index.html
Internal Revenue Service

www.irs.gov/businesses/small/article/0,,id=98810,00.html
IRS: Checklist for Starting a Business

www.entrepreneur.com/bizstartups/
Entrepreneur magazine

www.inc.com/guides/start_biz/
Inc. magazine

Money Management Software

www.Mint.com
Mint

www.quicken.intuit.com
Quicken Deluxe

www.mvelopes.com
Mvelopes

www.microsoft.com
Microsoft Money Plus

www.moneydance.com/other
Moneydance

www.mechcad.net/products/acemoney/
AceMoney

www.financialplan.about.com/cs/budgeting/l/blbudget.htm
www.office.microsoft.com/en-us/templates/CT101172321033.aspx
Free spreadsheets/templates for budgeting

Index